The Plays
of Benn Levy

Benn Levy. (Courtesy of Constance Cummings.)

The Plays
of Benn Levy

Between Shaw and Coward

Susan Rusinko

Rutherford ● Madison ● Teaneck
Fairleigh Dickinson University Press
London and Toronto: Associated University Presses

Associated University Presses
440 Forsgate Drive
Cranbury, NJ 08512

Associated University Presses
25 Sicilian Avenue
London WC1A 2QH, England

Associated University Presses
P.O. Box 338, Port Credit
Mississauga, Ontario
Canada L5G 4L8

The paper used in this publication meets the requirements
of the American National Standard for Permanence of Paper
for Printed Library Materials Z39.48-1984.

Library of Congress Cataloging-in-Publication Data

Rusinko, Susan.
  The plays of Benn Levy : between Shaw and Coward / Susan Rusinko.
    p.   cm.
  includes bibliographical references and index.
  ISBN 0-8386-3556-3 (alk. paper)
    1. Levy, Benn W. (Benn Wolfe), 1900–1973—Criticism and
  interpretation.   I. Title.
  PR6023.E92Z87   1994
  822'.912—dc20   94-10592
                                                                       CIP

PRINTED IN THE UNITED STATES OF AMERICA

For Constance Cummings Levy

Contents

Chronology

Unless otherwise indicated, theaters are in London.

1900   Born 7 March 1900 in London to Octave and Nannie Joseph Levy; grandson of the Honorable J. Levy of Sydney, Australia.

1918   Served in the Royal Air Force.

1919–22   Attended University College, Oxford; earlier, Repton School, Derbyshire.

1923   Began publishing career, rising to the managing editorship of Jarrold's Publishers.

1925   October 18, *This Woman Business*, Royalty Theater.

1926   April 15, *This Woman Business* moved to the Haymarket Theater; December 7, *This Woman Business*, Ritz Theater, New York.

1928   February 27, *A Man with Red Hair,* adapted from Hugh Walpole's novel, Little Theater; May 9, *Mud and Treacle,* Globe Theater; November 8, *A Man with Red Hair,* Garrick Theater, New York; December 5, *Mrs. Moonlight,* Kingsway Theater.

1929   November 12, *Art and Mrs. Bottle,* Criterion Theater; film, *Blackmail,* with Charles Bennett for RKO, reputed to be the first English talkie.

1930   January 12, *The Devil,* Arts Theater; September 29, *Mrs. Moonlight,* Charles Hopkins Theater, New York; February 12, *Topaze,* Music Box Theater, New York; October 8, *Topaze,* adapted from Marcel Pagnol's play, New Theater; December 3, *Ever Green,* a musical, book by Levy, music and lyrics by Richard Rodgers and Lorenz Hart, Adelphi Theater.

1931   April 16, *The Church Mouse,* adapted from Siegfried Geyer's and Ladislaus Fodor's play, Playhouse Theater; October 15, *Hollywood Holiday,* with John Van Druten, New Theater; film, *The Gay Diplomat* (for RKO); December 9, *Springtime for Henry,* New York, Bijou Theater; *Anniversary,* or *The Rebirth of Venus,* BBC Radio.

1932   January 4, *The Devil,* as *The Devil Passes,* New York, Selwyn Theater; November 8, *Springtime for Henry,* Apollo Theater; films: *Lord Camber's Ladies* (for RKO), *The Old Dark House* (with R. C. Sheriff for Universal), and *The Devil and the Deep* (for Paramount).

1933   Married Constance Cummings Halverstadt, American-born actress.

1934   Directed Clemence Dane's *Wild Decembers* and Vincent Lawrence's *Sour Grapes* in London and Samson Raphaelson's *Accent on Youth* in New York.

1935   Film, *Loves of a Dictator,* Ludovico Toeplitz.

1936   November 19, *Young Madame Conti,* adapted with Hugh Griffith from Bruno Frank's play, Savoy Theater; first appearance of Constance Cummings in a play by her husband.

1937   March 31, *Young Madame Conti,* New York; November 16, *Madame Bovary* (with Constance Cummings as Emma), adaptation of Gaston Baty's play from Flaubert, New York, Broadhurst Theater.

1938   January 24, *If I Were You,* with Paul Hervey Fox, New York, Mansfield Theater.

1939   March 1, *The Jealous God,* Lyric Theater.

1941–42   Served in World War II, Royal Navy; wounded in the Adriatic and decorated with MBE in 1944.

1942   Directed in London Samson Raphaelson's *Skylark.*

1945–50   Labour Member of Parliament for Eton and Slough, Buckinghamshire.

1946   August 14, *Clutterbuck,* Wyndham's Theater; chairman, executive committee, League of Dramatists.

1947   Continued above position in League of Dramatists, and again from 1949–1952.

1949   December 3, *Clutterbuck,* Biltmore Theater, New York. Directed in London Rodney Ackland's *Before the Party.*

1950   November 29, *Return to Tyassi* (with Constance Cummings as Martha Cotton), Duke of York's Theater.

1950   Directed in New York James Gow's and Arnaud D'Asseau's *Legend.*

1952   March 31, *Cupid and Psyche,* King's Theater, Edinburgh; September 14, *Triple Bill: The Great Healer, The*

	Island of Cipango, and *The Truth about the Truth,* BBC television.
1956	November 18, participation in symposium on British playwriting, Royal Court Theater (with Wolf Mankowitz, Arthur Miller, John Whiting and Colin Wilson).
1957	December 12, *The Rape of the Belt* (with Constance Cummings as Antiope), Piccadilly Theater.
1959	March 20, Levy addresses an antiwar and antinuclear rally in Trafalgar Square.
1960	February 24, *The Tumbler,* New York, Helen Hayes Theater. November 5, *The Rape of the Belt,* Martin Beck Theater, New York.
1966	August 17, *Public and Confidential* (with Constance Cummings as Liza), August 17, Duke of York's Theater.
1969	June 24, *The Poet's Heart,* Bristol University, featuring two actors—Tim Pigott-Smith and Jeremy Irons—before their rise to prominence among the new generation of English actors.
1973	December 7, died in Oxford and is survived by his wife, two children, Jemima and Jonathan, and six grandchildren.

Preface

In a career intermittently and unevenly divided three ways—playwriting for stage, screen, radio, and television; activism in liberal moral causes (e.g., nuclear protest and stage censorship at home and aid to South Africa abroad); and varied participation in organizations for the encouragement of the arts—Benn Levy took time out to serve five years as Labour M.P. for the normally Conservative constituency of Eton-Slough. Also, he served in both World Wars, and he was involved in the publishing business at the beginning and near the end of his life.

Similar to his contemporaries, Noel Coward (1899–1973) and Terence Rattigan (1911–77), in their reputations as writers of middle-class plays for a middle-class West End audience, he was unlike them in his shifting career allegiances, particularly in the 1940s and 1950s when he was active in political issues and movements of the time.

Calling attention to his being "loved by everyone who knew him · to an unusual degree because . . . of his friendliness and geniality to all people regardless of race, colour or creed," his immediate successor, Slough's M.P. Fenner, now Lord Brockway, wrote on the death of Levy:

> The only pity was that he was a man in a dilemma. He wanted to write, but didn't feel he had the mind to write while still in politics. But even when he left Parliament he remained so interested in politics that I'm not sure he was able to write as he intended. That was a great loss to all of us.[1]

Another colleague spoke of Levy's "surgeries" in the House of Commons that

> used to go on from morning until late evening, and no case or cause was too trivial for him to champion. On one occasion he spent hours persuading a Naval deserter to give himself up, and after he had done so represented him at the court martial.[2]

Unflinchingly his own man and despite being Jewish, Levy "refused to join the 'bandwagon' for vengeance on the Germans"[3] after World War II, and he even pleaded for increasing their 1,000-calorie diet allotment, which contrasted sharply with the 3,000-calorie allotment of the British. In the face of disapproval of fraternization with the enemy, he supported the British soldiers' right to marry German girls. He renounced terrorism, including Jewish terrorism in Palestine. He opposed the death penalty, arguing that "capital punishment brutalizes all of us."[4] His causes included opposition to "the obscenities of McCarthyism in America and the secret police peril on . . . [the British] side of the Atlantic."[5] C. H. Rolf described Levy's life as "a salutary lesson in the strength that can sometimes flow from gentleness."[6]

On the political front, Levy was, according to Michael Foot, his contemporary, "the best polemicist of the post-1945 period. When he turned his practised playwright's hand to political controversy, he wrote devastatingly argumentative pieces, worthy of his master and mentor, Bernard Shaw himself. It was hard to know which to admire most—the wit, the eloquence, the pungency, the glistening clarity. Time and time again he spoke the last word in some controversy of the time."[7] Foot writes of Levy's magnetic power as a writer to present the whole argument, a qualification that entitled him to be the unquestioned appointee to write the Arts Council Working Party report on the obscenity laws. "No one could replace his particular combination of gifts."[8]

> But he loved the theater. He loved politics, too. He loved the liberties which people in this country enjoyed and which he so often saw to be in jeopardy and which he would fight so fiercely to protect. He loved the socialism which he still described in that last contribution quoted earlier. In his hands, socialism and freedom were intertwined together and could never be wrenched apart without injuring each fatally. Bernard Shaw had never grasped that truth, but Benn Levy had, and it gave a nobility to his politics and the gentle enlightenment which he bestowed on us all.[9]

But in the end, even as he continued his political interests, Levy returned to the theater. In the subject of his final play, *Public and Confidential*, Levy's divided career allegiances became one as in no other of his writings in the political or theatrical arenas.

One division in Levy's life with which he had lived comfortably involves his American connections. As a dramatist who at times seemed, at least to Americans, as much American as English, Levy enjoyed unusually close ties with the American stage, *Springtime for Henry* having provided an eighteen-year acting career across the United States for Edward Everett Horton. In addition, some of his plays premiered in New York. His American-born wife, Constance Cummings, after her marriage to Levy in 1933, acted in many of his plays, receiving high praise whether in plays by her husband or in those of other dramatists, such as O'Neill's *Long Day's Journey into Night* at The Old Vic (with Sir Laurence Olivier).

Critics and reviewers generally agree on the comedy and farce as Levy's dramatic forte, the most successful of these realized in *Clutterbuck* (in the manner of Coward's *Private Lives*) and *Springtime for Henry* (a middle-class farce about two rakish businessmen). Alan Strachan refers to Levy as a dramatist who "shows that within the framework and demands of the Broadway and West End commercial theatre system it is possible to create comedy of genuine style" and whose "best work has a symmetry and sense of form (seen at its happiest in his favourite quartet-relationship comedies) allied to an elegance and wit not usually found in combination on the English Stage."[10]

In addition to comedies and farces, Levy wrote a body of literate, witty, civilized comic-fantasies and morality plays that incorporate prevailing themes and modes of midcentury English drama. Yet his plays have a strikingly contemporary resonance, for example, *Young Madame Conti* (1936), which reverberates with echoes of the Clarence Thomas–Anita Hill hearings of 1991 in which a female defendant confronts an all-male court. Although the feminist concerns of his literary predecessors and contemporaries are his inherited tradition and a part of the context in all his dramas, they constitute the central text of some plays in the form of Shavian debates and Barrielike escapist plays in which fantasy and reality eventually collide.

Levy's debates and fantasies are conducted within a moral framework of good and evil, these terms defined variously as mind and body, sometimes, god and the devil. Whether in the personal, societal, or moral arena, the conflicts generated by these warring forces dominate Levy's subjects. In his last stage play, *Public and Confidential* (1966), retitled in publication *The Member for Gaza,* all three converge in this dramatization of a politician whose reformist energies are thwarted by personal problems as perceived in the hypocrisy of a puritanical society and its press. Thus, both *Young Madame Conti* and *The Member for Gaza* retain a startling immediacy for the last decade of the twentieth century.

Beyond their topical nature, however, the polemics of Levy's plays are deeply rooted in the Faustian notion of becoming rather than of being, evil serving to activate the good in man. Whether in the style of the comedy or farce, a psychological thriller about a psychopath, the comic-fantasy, the problem play, or mythic reenactments or adaptations, Levy's dramas pit evil (or disruptive forces) against good, not as absolutes, but as a means of one, the devil, inciting the other, god, to awaken in man a Faustian awareness of a moral sense.

Eclecticism, not innovation, characterizes the styles and themes of Levy's dramas, which can be seen as an interesting barometer of the stage trends of his time. Spanning the middle half of the twentieth century, his plays form a collective chronicle of that time. They hold a place in twentieth-century stage history possible only to a writer in the mainstream of a time influenced by the strong voices of Ibsen, Strindberg, Chekhov, Shaw, O'Casey, and others such as Priestley, Fry, Barrie, Coward, and Rattigan. Yet, there is a sense of dis-ease with the trends of his time, as seen in Levy's attempts to de-emphasize plot and to emphasize rational discourse, very often in the form of morality debates. The dis-ease of the so-called 'twilight era' between the Edwardian years and the stage revolution that broke loose with John Osborne's Jimmy Porter in *Look Back in Anger* (1956) haunts the moods of his plays, and solutions to their personal and sociomoral conflicts elude the characters in his plays. That dis-ease breaks out, no-holds-barred, in the huge variety of new playwrights who began their invasion of the London stage, even as Levy's polite, Shavian high comedy of ideas, *The Rape of the Belt,* opened in 1957.

Acknowledgments

I am most grateful to Constance Cummings Levy whose generosity in granting me access to her husband's published and unpublished plays and papers has made this book possible. My appreciation includes her permission to quote from Levy's plays, her providing of photographs, her hospitality in allowing me to spend time in her late husband's study, and her reading of the manuscript for factual errors that I would have had no other way of correcting.

I wish also to thank the Manuscripts Section of the Library of the University of Sussex at Brighton, where Levy's non-Parliamentary papers are deposited, for permission to include material in the appendices. Acknowledgment is made of permission to publish photographs of Levy's American productions from the Billy Rose Theater Collection at The New York Public Library for the Performing Arts at Lincoln Center.

To Virginia Duck and Gerald Strauss, I am indebted for invaluable aid in proofreading the manuscript at various stages of preparation and for a ready ear during the course of my writing. I thank the following members of the Harvey A. Andruss Library at Bloomsburg University, who, as with my previous books, have provided necessary library services: Acquisitions Librarian Aaron Polonsky and, in Access Services, Josephine Crossley, Alice Getty, Monica Howell, and Alex Shiner.

In the preparation of photographs, I wish especially to acknowledge the help of the following members of the faculty and staff of Bloomsburg University: Dana Ulloth, Chair of the Mass Communications Department, and Joan Lentczner and Joan Helfer of the University Relations Office. For providing long-standing secretarial help and advice, I thank Melanie Dworsak of the English Department and Marlyse Heaps, Staff Assistant to the Provost. As recipient of a number of summer research grants over the years, I am grateful to Bloomsburg University for encouragement in the writing of books, articles, and reviews.

The Plays
of Benn Levy

1

Introduction: Chronicler of an Age

In 1973, the year of Benn Levy's death, Alan Strachan commented on Levy's last stage play—*Public and Confidential.* Retitled in publication *The Member for Gaza,* the play is about the personal and professional struggles of a politician. Strachan attributes its cool reception in 1966 partly to the story's closeness to the Profumo scandal and partly to its appearance at a time "when the 'well-made' play was in something of disrepute. Should it be revived, its virtues of solid craftsmanship as well as its understanding of political realities may be more recognized on their intrinsic merits."[1] As well as *Public and Confidential,* other of Levy's plays merit a hearing, now that the English stage experiments of the second half of the twentieth century have settled into the stage mainstream and the pejorative nuances of the term *well-made* have receded.

The Profumo scandal as well, has settled into its time frame. Since that time, public attitudes toward private morality have been undergoing a slow change. In the 1990s, openly-dealt-with sexual scandals in the lives of politicians such as Paddy Ashdown in England and Gary Hart and Bill Clinton in the United States have caused the beginning of a public willingness to separate issues of public morality from those of private behavior. Thus Strachan's comment about the merits of *Public and Confidential* is an especially timely one even many years later.

Similarly, the critical derision experienced by Levy and others for writing the old-fashioned, formulaic, well-made play during the heady revolution that began in 1956 with John Osborne's *Look Back in Anger* has subsided. Brechtian and Beckettian innovations, influential in the plays of dramatists such as John Arden, Harold Pinter, and Tom Stoppard, are now a matter of theater history. Yet even during the two decades of stage experiments, pejoratively labeled dramatists of well-crafted drawing-room comedies or the middle-class problem plays (e.g., Noel Coward and Terence Ratti-gan) were enjoying the lion's share of popularity. Levy wrote about the same middle-class English life as did J. B. Priestley, Coward, and Rattigan. His drawing rooms, characters, liberal social atti-tudes, and domestic problems were similar to those of his more famous contemporaries.

Levy's life was one of middle-class privilege. The grandson of the Honorable J. Levy of New South Wales, he was born in London on 7 March 1900 to Octave and Nannie Joseph Levy and given the advantages of education at a public school, Repton. Following service in the Royal Air Force in 1918, three years at Oxford, and a brief career in publishing, where he rose to the managing direc-torship at Jarrolds Publishers, he found his interest steadily turning to the stage.

At the age of twenty-five, he enjoyed a first-play success with *This Woman Business*. He followed this comedy with at least one play every year for the next decade. His writing for the stage was occasionally interrupted for the next four or five years by his involvement in scripts for motion pictures. With Charles Bennett, he wrote *Blackmail* for Alfred Hitchcock, a film regarded as the first British talkie. Other film credits include *The Gay Diplomat* (1931), *Lord Camber's Ladies* (1932), *The Old Dark House* (1932, in collaboration with R. C. Sheriff), *The Devil and the Deep* (1932), and *Loves of a Dictator* (1935).

The vintage years were 1930–31, during which six plays (*The Devil, Topaze, Ever Green, Hollywood Holiday, Springtime for Henry,* and *The Church Mouse*) were produced in London and two (*The Devil* and *Springtime for Henry*) in New York.

In 1933, he married American-born actress, Constance Cum-mings Halverstadt. In 1936 and 1937, respectively, she appeared in two of Levy's adaptations, one (written with Hubert Griffith) from the German of Bruno Frank's *Young Madame Conti,* and the other, *Madame Bovary* from the French of Gaston Baty's dramati-zation of Flaubert's novel. The performances of Ms. Cummings received critical plaudits, plaudits that continued throughout her long and illustrious acting career.

His life again interrupted by world events, Levy served in the Royal Navy for three years during World War II, first as a seaman, then with the rank of lieutenant. Wounded in the Adriatic, he was honored with the order of MBE in 1944. Prior to his Navy years, he was, with other theatrical personalities such as Noel Coward, based in a Manhattan hotel, to persuade Americans that Hitler could be defeated and that the United States should enter the war.

Turning to politics after demobilization, he was elected Labourite M. P. for the Eton-Slough constituency. His five-year term in Parliament was characterized by his strong championing of liberal causes. Also, he increasingly devoted time to activities in the arts such as chairmanship of the executive committee of the League of Dramatists (1946–47 and 1949–52) and membership on the executive council of the Arts Council (1953–61).

Among the many causes for which he fought and for which he vigorously debated are the abolition of the censorship law in effect since Fielding's time in the eighteenth century, nuclear disarmament, the injustices of British criminal law, and aid to South Africa. The extent of his activism in and out of government is seen in a cursory glance at the catalog of some of his papers deposited at Sussex University. The list is a litany of liberal causes during the middle of the twentieth century, causes which even in the final years of the century remain as problems demanding solutions. Their categories include The Arts Council of Great Britain: Theatre Censorship Reform Committee and Working Party on Obscenity Laws; Campaign for Nuclear Disarmament; Campaign for the Limitation of Secret Police Powers; Censorship of Plays (Repeal) Bill 1949; Common Market; Fabian Society; Movement for Colonial National Council for Civil Liberties; UNESCO International` Conference on Artists 1952.

His activism took the form of newspaper articles, reviews, lectures and speeches, reports, pamphlets and leaflets, and voluminous correspondence with famous figures—Bertrand Russell, Hugh Gaitskill, Michael Foot, Richard Findlater, Wolf Mankowitz, Sir Kenneth Clark, Aneurin Bevan, and fellow playwrights Noel Coward, Robert Bolt, James Bridie, and John Mortimer. In 1949, the bill he introduced to repeal stage censorship was detained en route to passage. Shortly thereafter, Levy left Parliament (1950) for personal reasons, and the bill, shunted aside because of more pressing Parliamentary issues, died for lack of action.

Not until nearly twenty years later was the long-detested stage censorship law repealed when the bill was brought forward by his friend, the M. P. George Russell Strauss. Five years before his death, Levy lived not only to witness that repeal, but also to participate once more in the proceedings. When he joined John Mortimer and John Osborne as witensses in the 1966–67 hearings on a bill similar to the original "Benn Levy Bill," he had lost little of his ardor for the cause. He was quoted by Lord Goodman, whose proposal for a voluntary system of censorship Levy had strongly denounced, as going so far as to convey "the firm impression that all my [Lord Goodman's] ancestors had been illegitimate."[2] With the influence of the League of Dramatists, whose position Mortimer represented, and, after the requisite three Readings in Parliament and the "Royal Assent," the Theatres Act of 1968 abolished the Lord Chamberlain's influence on the stage. This time no urgent business plagued the passage of the new version of the 1949 Benn Levy Bill. The secret for its sucess may well be due to the composition of the Committee that, in addition to the eight members from the House of Lords, consisted of eight Commoners, among whom were seven Labourites, two Liberals, two Independents, and only five Conservatives.

A playwright whose life was divided between the theater and active participation in the issues and events of his time, Levy imbued his writing with some of that dividedness, and he remains an incisive reflector of the uncertainties of the times. His style of lively debate and socio-moral partisanship was reflected in his postgovernmental activism and in the lively debates and witty repartee of characters in his plays. Yet, aware of the need to rein in his debating self, he referred to himself as a rational humanist who too often allowed his head to rule his heart.

Levy died in Oxford on 7 December 1973, and is survivied by his wife, Constance Cummings, who resides in their Chelsea home, designed for them by Walter Gropius in 1936. It is the only house in England designed by the father of the Bauhaus School of Architecture during his two years as a refugee from Hitler's Germany. Levy is also survived by their two children, Jonathan and Jemima, and six grandchildren: Augustus, Emily, Olivia, Francesca, Tessa, and Alessandro.

Concerned with women's issues throughout his plays, Levy first dealt with the subject in his first stage play, which was also his first success. The play appeared in 1925 (the year of Coward's *Hay Fever*) and is a comic spoof of a group of temporary misogynists retired to the country for a time away from feminine distractions. Feminist concerns intensify in two succeeding plays about marital problems, one a Barrie-like comedy-fantasy and the other a satirical comedy, *Mrs. Moonlight* and *Art and Mrs. Bottle*, respectively. In a progressive shift to Ibsen-like dramas such as *The Jealous*

God, Levy dramatized women's problems in the context of social attitudes of the times, frequently mixing morality with sentiment and comedy. Feminist issues intact, Levy, however, kept returning to the comic genre that brought him his largest measure of both critical and popular success.

Feminism, mixed with the theme of judicial injustice, is the exclusive focus in an early play, a realistic courtroom drama, *Young Madame Conti* (1936), an adaptation of a central European play about the trial of a prostitute who kills her lover. In *The Jealous God* (1939), Levy dramatizes with Ibsenite realism the story of a woman, Kate Settle, who takes control of her life, barely surviving both World War I and the strictures of a male-dominated society. Its context the bleakness of the early World War II era, *The Jealous God* is about the collision of liberal attitudes with harsh wartime realities, issues dealt with in a Rattigan play, *After the Dance,* which appeared the same year.

Cupid and Psyche, a postwar comedy, carries the feminist battle to the societal front, with its Pankhurstlike, liberated, middle-aged woman who romps through a group of youthful artists and intellectuals with lessons for all. Having thus far raised feminist concerns on the personal, social, and moral levels, Levy aspires to mythic stature in a dramatization of the Theseus-Hippolyte–Heracles-Antiope legend in *The Rape of the Belt,* his antiwar high comedy of ideas.

His feminist sympathies, however, exist in a broader context than the socially topical one. They are part of the Faustian restlessness in characters who are challenged by a "devil" to exercise the good in themselves. References to the devil or god abound in his morality plays, two of these even titled *The Devil* and *The Jealous God.* In the former the devil is a necessary means in man's quest for truth, a quest spurred on seriously by a Mephisthophelean curate and comically by a self-educated, working-class Labourite championing social change. Serious and comic debates dominate, leading to tragic consequences whose touches of the psychologically grotesque are a carryover from earlier plays about psychopaths—*A Man with Red Hair* and *Mud and Treacle.*

In addition to his twenty-three produced stage plays, Levy's credits include six screenplays, a radio play, and a triple bill for television. Among his twelve unproduced and unpublished plays are some that bear the influence of Samuel Beckett, including one that he had been asked by Kenneth Tynan to write as a sketch for the erotic *Oh, Calcutta!* His contribution, *A Tap on The Door,* developed, however, into a twenty-five-minute play and was considered to be out of "key with the twenty odd other sketches he [Tynan] showed me."[3]

Levy's comic plays run the gamut of English comedy from the well-honed, Restoration-style farce, *Springtime for Henry* (featuring that stock-in-trade of the farce genre, the rake), to the high comedy of ideas, *The Rape of the Belt* (in the style of Shaw and Giraudoux). With near unanimity, critics called attention to his talent for witty dialogue and for his "turning of the farcical kaleidoscope."[4] His most popularly received farce in the United States, *Springtime for Henry,* created a near-career for the American actor, Edward Everett Horton, who took the farce on an eighteen-year tour of the United States before returning it to Broadway in 1951. In London, the play ran for only 104 performances, whereas in New York the run was 198. However, the farcical *Clutterbuck,* with its variation on the geometric design of Coward's *Private Lives,* enjoyed a London run of 366 performances, surpassing the English popularity of any other Levy play, a contrast with the 218 run in New York. This divergent appeal to two very different audiences is one reason that Levy has at times been mistaken for an American.

His writing in the post–World War II years diminished noticeably in contrast with that of the prewar era. Levy wrote only six more stage plays, all of which were produced before his death. Three are myth-based. *Cupid and Psyche* (1952) is a farcical view of the contemporary bohemian generation. *The Rape Of the Belt* (1957), a high comedy of ideas that Kenneth Tynan "placed squarely in the tradition of Shaw and Giraudoux,"[5] seamlessly blends the Heracles-Antiope story with contemporary attitudes. About a contemporary Electra, *The Tumbler,* written in a mixture of turgid poetic diction and stichomythic verse, premiered in New York to mixed or negative reviews. Levy's last stage play, *Public and Confidential* seemed lost in an eventful year (1966), the highlight of which, in retrospect, was Tom Stoppard's *Rosencrantz and Guildenstern Are Dead,* produced at the Edinburgh Festival. Appearing at the peak of the experimental era, *Public and Confidential* was both a stylistic and topical victim of a time regarded by some as the start of the second wave of the English stage revolution.

During the pre–World War II so-called twilight era of English drama, just before 1956, the stylistic influence of Ibsen, Strindberg,

Wilde, Shaw, and of lesser dramatists—Henry Arthur Jones, Arthur Wing Pinero, James Barrie, John Galsworthy—lingered in the popular and polite plays of Levy and his contemporaries.

His first play, *This Woman Business*, reflects Levy's kinship with them. More important, the play called attention to his talent and skill in writing dialogue, described by a *Times* reviewer as exhibiting "plenty of wit (not exactly Congrevean, yet excellent 'back-chat') . . . abundant humour and good humour,"[6] a reputation he maintained throughout his more than forty years of intermittent writing for the stage.

The drawing-room play (with its formulaic French windows for convenient exits and entrances) from which the title "well-made" derives consists of a good story, carefully plotted, with recognizably mannered characters, witty dialogue, and varying degrees of social commentary. It is a play designed primarily to entertain, but also to comment on contemporary mores. In one of the many touches of irony of the new drama, Osborne's *Look Back In Anger*, the opening salvo in the English stage revolution, is stylistically as traditional as any play by Coward, Rattigan, or Levy. In another ironic note, the new era saw the emergence of some other young dramatists who wrote in traditional style or variations thereof: Alan Ayckbourn, Robert Bolt, Michael Frayn, John Mortimer, James Saunders, Anthony Shaffer, and Peter Shaffer. All enjoyed popular success even in a time in which critical attention focused on the innovators.

With his structural plot variations, his skill in dialogue, and his realistic concerns, Levy found himself frequently defending his practice of traditional techniques in the theater. He rejected the narrow definition of the well-made play (one, in his opinion, based on the dramatist's use of conventions of the past) as necessarily an ill-made play. "Once a play is fighting to be born, it is futile to call upon its forefathers. . . . Derivations may have an honourable place in all the arts but just as it is vain (in both senses of the word) to deny them, so it is disastrous to rely upon them."[7]

Feeling, as did Rattigan and Ayckbourn, the injustice of criticism for writing in traditional, well-made style, Levy became defensive:

Waiting for Godot is a superbly well-made play. So are the plays of Pinter. *St. Joan* could not carry the weight of its discursiveness nor *The Three Sisters* its burden of inertia nor *Lear* its narrative puerilities

nor *Hamlet* its exploratory diffuseness, if their authors had not been
by inalienable instinct master-mechanics of the theatre.[8]

Now that the stylistic experiments of the heady new drama have
themselves become tradition, the sharp divisions between the conventional and experimental have clearly eased. In fact, one traditionalist, Alan Ayckbourn, has not only survived the revolution,
but also continues to succeed, writing at the rate of one new play
a year, with tryouts at his theater in Scarborough and productions
in both the commercial and subsidized theaters in London. Ironically, the London stage of the early 1990s, with the exception of
an occasional new play by David Hare, Stephen Poliakoff, or Simon Gray, has been noticeably inhabited by time-honored dramas
of Shakespeare, Shaw, and Chekhov or by the popular, well-made
modern comedies and farces that English audiences love so well.

In his play introductions and prefaces, Levy frequently invokes
the names of Shakespeare, Shaw, and Chekhov. Of the two major
dramatists who influenced the new drama—Bertolt Brecht and
Samuel Beckett—Levy's sympathies lie with the latter. About his
own short, Beckett-like play, *Shan't Be Long,* Levy writes that he
"had no thought of Becket[t] in mind once I had started work . . .
and had no sense of debt to that ancient, and, to me, always conge-
nial genre, lately relabelled the Theatre of the Absurd."[9]

Contrasting Brecht with Shaw, Levy holds that the latter never
committed the double betrayal of allowing social concerns to "in-
vade and warp" his plays, nor permitting "reason to lead, under the
delusion that it could strengthen illumination instead of dimming
it. Brecht nearly always did."[10] One major exception, however, is
Brecht's character Mother Courage, who, like Shakespeare's Fals-
taff, is an "outsize figure with independent life and the scars and
flaws of humanity so recognizably our own that neither we nor
Brecht could cast a censorious stone."[11]

Levy extends this criticism to himself, a political animal who
considered neutrality to be a double betrayal and sometimes allowed reason to lead. However, he adds, "Perhaps the true compassion is neutrality."[12] Levy's self-criticism is borne out by the fact
that he is remembered for his witty, literate, civilized comedies,
rather than for plays like *The Devil,* with its sometimes distract-
ingly polemic pleas for a rational humanism. In some morality
plays, such as *The Jealous God* and *Public and Confidential,* however, Levy does succeed in achieving more than a measure of artis-

tic neutrality in his portrayals of idealists trapped in the web of their principles, as he had in his earlier (and more popular) Barrie-like *Mrs. Moonlight.*

In their constrasting representations of Levy's divided stage universe—the ideal and the real—two of his last three plays are an appropriate summary of this division. The ideal antiwar, matriarchal society in *The Rape of the Belt* is the antipodal version of the politically realistic world in *Public and Confidential.*

Participating in an epistolary battle of the theaters in *The New Statesman* in 1950 (a debate launched by Rattigan against Shaw and the play of ideas), Levy defines a great play as one whose "first essential . . . is a heated intellectual or poetic imagination, and preferably both."[13] In supporting one of Rattigan's statements on the present state of the theater in England, Levy applies Shaw's own life force theory to the current malaise on the English stage. He sees the force as about "to start shaking us. He [Rattigan] is probably right, for fifty years in the Ibsen-Shaw idiom is a fair spell."[14] Attempts to revitalize the stage by poets such as Christopher Fry and T. S. Eliot had not brought about the needed change. Neither Rattigan nor Levy, however, had any way of knowing how prophetically imminent or forceful that shaking up was to be after 1950, with a bifurcation occurring on the world stage with the plays of Brecht and Beckett and on the London stage with the appearance in 1956 of Jimmy Porter and again with Rosencrantz and Guildenstern in 1967. The death in midcentury of Shaw (1950) seems a natural confirmation of the end of the so-called twilight era and of the approach of the English stage revolution.

Straddling both old and new eras, Levy wrote two of his most popular plays, *Springtime for Henry* and *Clutterbuck,* in the first half of the century and what may be seen as his two most sophisticated plays, *The Rape of the Belt* and *Public and Confidential,* in the second half. In a retrospective of twentieth-century English drama, Levy's eclecticism provides an interesting overview of the stage currents of his time, more so, perhaps, than do the plays of more famous contemporaries such as Shaw, Barrie, Fry, Priestley, Coward, and Rattigan—all of whom have earned stronger reputations than has Levy. Part of the reason lies with their having established and sophisticated their unique forms throughout their careers. Shaw's brilliantly philosophical plays of ideas, Barrie's fantasy plays, Fry's and Eliot's verse drama, the popularly poignant problem dramas and sophisticated comedies of Priestley,

Coward, and Rattigan in a so-called twilight era—all these are part of the sharp self-definitions provided by their writing.

Levy set his plays in the same middle-class English life as did Coward, Rattigan, and Priestley, with roots in the same socially liberal attitudes that characterized his more popular contemporaries. His forte—a talent for writing dialogue—was blunted by the lack of a consistently strong focus of either style or content. The many morality plays, for example, seem divided in their purpose and loose in plot construction. Moral themes sometimes seem repeated rather than developed. Perhaps the reason is a sense of an ambivalence between issues (not necessarily ideas) and the ability to make those issues convincing. The plays at times seem a forum for topical matters diffusing the artistic unity. Levy is thus at his best in comedy and farce, where issues do not distract, but rather, where they do exist, contribute to the unity of the play.

Levy's place in British theater history is, at least, that of a mirror of the dramatic themes and forms of his times. Nearly fifty years later, the issues have lost little of their relevance on the personal, professional, societal, and moral levels. This is why *The Rape of the Belt* and *Public and Confidential* do not seem dated. In the tradition of Ibsen and Shaw, his women test the limits of social behavior and take charge of their lives, rather than, as in Barrie's plays, merely being the power behind the male or, as in Pinero's or Rattigan's plays, the suicidal victim of societal restrictions. Levy's women, even as they remain in the drawing room, insist on equal footing with the men.

As eclectic chronicler of the dramatic styles and themes of the first half of the twentieth century, he tempers his English traditions with continental influences, evidenced mostly in his adaptations, but present in his original plays in the form of the macabre or the touch of cynicism. *A Man with Red Hair* (although English) begins Levy's treatments of psychologically grotesque behavior. The effects on others of a totally corrupted mind is a chillingly fascinating study of Crispin, whose inflicting pain on others for his own pleasure is not only his raison d'être, but also is raised to an art form and, according to Hubert Griffith, "the best grand guignol I have ever seen."[15] Evil in the form of pure sadism brooks no effective opposition. Crispin's mental torture of others eventually involves him in a physical fight in which both he and his opponent are hurled to their deaths. The metamorphosis from simpleminded innocence to total moral corruption is dramatized in *Topaze,* an adaptation from the French. And in an absorbingly morbid study of the mind of a prostitute who murders her lover in *Young Madame Conti* (Austrian), Levy treats a personal tragedy exposed to the glare of a public court. Evil, personal or institutional, feeds on good in Levy's choice of adaptations, with elements of the same pathological psychology that supply grotesque touches in his original plays, such as as *Mud and Treacle, Mrs. Moonlight, The Devil,* and *The Tumbler.*

Levy's good consists of the necessity of self-examination and of making choices, choices that run counter to prevailing and socially approved customs, institutions, and attitudes. These choices are rooted in the struggles of a divided self—mind versus body, the rational versus the instinctive, inner truth as opposed to outer appearances, and, ultimately, the ideal versus the real. Dualities are dramatized empirically in the experiences of his characters and intellectually in the form of the debate. When the experience and intellect collide, the consequences are costly, often indeterminate, sometimes grotesque.

What has been criticized by some as the diffuseness of a Levy play, in theme or plot, may be seen as a parallel to the divided nature of his own varied career: publishing, politics, artistic and political activism, writing, and directing. His directorial work involved many of his own plays—*Art and Mrs. Bottle, The Devil, Hollywood Holiday, Springtime for Henry, Young Madame Conti, Madame Bovary, The Jealous God, Clutterbuck, Return To Tyassi,* and *Cupid and Psyche.* He directed other playwrights' work as well: Clemence Dane's *Wild Decembers,* London, 1934; Vincent Lawrence's *Sour Grapes,* London, 1934; Samson Raphaelson's *Accent on Youth,* London, 1934, and *Skylark,* London, 1942; Rodney Ackland's *Before the Party,* London, 1949; and James Gow's and Arnaud D'Asseau's *Legend,* London, 1950.

Levy's stage world was inhabited by talented actors on the London scene. Beginning with Fay Compton and Leon Quartermaine in *This Woman Business* in 1925, continuing through 1957 (when the English stage revolution was in its infancy) with Constance Cummings, Kay Hammond, John Clements, and Richard Attenborough (who was also the director) in *The Rape of the Belt,* Levy's plays attracted outstanding actors. The powerfully chilling performance of Charles Laughton as Crispin in *A Man with Red Hair* in 1928 comes to mind immediately in the memory of at least one person interviewed for this book. Tallulah Bankhead as Polly Andrews in *Mud and Treacle* in 1928; Joan Barry and Leon Quartermaine in *Mrs. Moonlight* in 1928; Irene Vanbrugh in her tempestuously welcomed return to the stage in *Art and Mrs. Bottle* in 1930; a stage full of reknowned actors—Diana Wynyard, Sybil Thorndike, Jean Cadell, Lewis Casson, and Ernest Thesiger in *The Devil* in 1930; Raymond Massey and Donald Wolfit in *Topaze* in 1930; Kay Hammond and Jean Cadell in *Hollywood Holiday* in 1931; and the much applauded quartet of Leslie Barnes, Nigel Bruce, Helen Smith, and Frieda Inescort in *Springtime for Henry* in 1931 are only some of the many actors whose roles in Levy's plays received accolades, even in those plays whose critical reception may have been mixed.

Then, beginning in 1936, one year after her marriage to Levy, Constance Cummings first appeared in an adaptation *(Young Madame Conti)* by her husband, receiving acclaim for her performance. She played Emma in *Madame Bovary* in 1937, with Harold Vermilyea as Charles Bovary, Ernest Thesiger as L'heureux and Eric Portman as Rodolphe Boulanger, and in 1939, Cummings and Vanbrugh appeared together in *The Jealous God.* About Cummings's performance in *Clutterback* in 1946, *The Times* reviewer (15 August 1946) wrote that, although condemned "for long periods to sit and bicker, . . . Miss Cummings . . . takes with splendid assurance the one chance she has to throw some weight about, and her faint in the third act is superbly sudden and complete."[16] As Martha Cotton in *Return to Tyassi* in 1950, as Antiope in *The Rape of the Belt* in 1957, and as Liza Foote in *Public and Confidential (Member for Gaza)* in 1956, she turned in extraordinarily fine performances.

In plays by other dramatists, Cummings's distinguished acting career includes a 1939 stage performance at the Old Vic as Shaw's St. Joan (having consulted with the author himself about the role), two performances of that role on BBC radio in 1941 and 1947, and yet another on BBC television in 1951. She also appeared with Rex Harrison in the 1945 movie version of Coward's *Blithe Spirit,* and as Mary Tyrone opposite Laurence Olivier in the Old Vic's 1973 production of *Long Day's Journey into Night.* On Broadway, more recently, she played the title role in Arthur Kopit's *Wings,* about a stroke victim, and repeated the role in a televised version. Off-Broadway she appeared with Irene Worth in Enid Bagnold's *The Chalk Garden* in 1982.

In one of the final productions of a Levy play before his death, two young actors who have since gone on to make their mark on stage and in film—Jeremy Irons and Tim Pigott-Smith—appeared in 1969 in Bristol University's production of *The Poet's Heart,* previously unproduced, although published in 1937.

In the United States, Edward Everett Horton entertained audiences across the country for eighteen years in a touring company of *Springtime for Henry.* On the other hand, an interesting failure of a Levy play in the United States featured Rosemary Harris and Charlton Heston in *The Tumbler,* directed by Laurence Olivier.

One last note remains about the use of the terms *comedy* and *farce.* Although *Springtime for Henry* is clearly a Restoration-style comedy of manners, *Clutterbuck* is an Edwardian farce, and *The Rape of the Belt* is a high comedy of ideas, the two terms are generally used interchangeably. Farce is a term applied to the play in which theme and realistic characters are subordinated to plot, the plot seems impossibly complicated, and characters are caricatures. Comedy, subtler in its attack on the vices and manners of an age, relies more on ideas, on realism of characterization rather than on stereotypes or caricatures, on correction of societal vices rather than on laughter-creating behavior, and on shrewd insights into human frailties balanced with societal vices. Both genres depend on wit, the wit in farce strongly one of physical action, that of comedy verbal and intellectual.

Levy's comedies, *This Woman Business* and *The Rape of the Belt,* are idea-based. His clearly farcical plays, *Springtime for Henry, Hollywood Holiday,* and *Cupid and Psyche,* depend on plot. Yet in the latter group, ideas are discussed, and in the former, farcical actions occur. Sometimes the distinction between the two genres blurs, and thus both terms are loosely applied to the play as a whole and specifically used about a particular action. In the morality plays the humor takes the form of verbal or situational irony.

The justification for a book about Levy's plays resides in his thematic and stylistic eclecticism that provides an overview of his time, particularly in its dis-ease with itself. This overview may be denied major dramatists whose names, like Shaw's, have given adjectival status to their unique ideas and styles. It is their uniqueness that separates each from other writers of his time. By contrast, Levy, in drawing on the traditional forms of both predecessors and contemporaries, is a chronicler of the trends of his age, perhaps even the elegist. His last play produced in London,

Public and Confidential (1966), completes that chronicling which begins with the comic dis-ease of the male community in the 1925 production of *This Woman Business.*

Finally, the choice of a chronological organization of the discussion of Levy's plays is mostly arbitrary, but, partly at least, one that is amenable to the traditional nature of his plays. Organization by genres—comedies/farces, fantasy/sentimental dramas, morality plays, adaptations of other writers' works—would have presented difficulties in that in some plays the genres are mixed. Organization by theme would have had its own problems, as a theme such as feminism, which permeates most of his work, is dramatized in a variety of situations rather than in a progression of change. Only in the discussion of the last six plays does chronology give way slightly to the grouping by genres: comedies and straight dramas.

Benn Levy, circa 1905. (Courtesy of Constance Cummings.)

Benn Levy. Bust of Levy by Jacob Epstein, 1933. (Courtesy of Constance Cummings.)

Georgie, Constance, and Benn Levy, in front of their Gropius-designed home in London's Chelsea section, circa 1950. (Photograph by George Konig, courtesy of Constance Cummings.)

Benn Levy, Lieutenant in the Royal Navy in World War II. (Photograph by John Vickers, courtesy of Constance Cummings.)

Benn and Constance Levy, with their children, Jemima and Jonathan, at Dinard on the north coast of France, circa 1954. (Courtesy of Constance Cummings.)

Benn Levy and Charlie. (Photograph by David Whitney, courtesy of Constance Cummings.)

2

1925–1928: Contemporary Attitudes

This Woman Business
(1925)

About five pseudo-misogynists of varying ages who retire to a country house to escape the company of women, *This Woman Business* employs for its structural framework a centuries-old dramatic idea, most notably dramatized in Shakespeare's *Love's Labour's Lost*. The common bond among the males is proclaimed in the name of their club, The Worshipful Association of Confirmed Misogynists. As in the sixteenth-century play, the complications begin with the intrusion of a female (in Levy's comedy, of course, through the French windows). She then becomes the catalyst for events in the play and for the puncturing of male pomposities and self-deceptions, eventually dissolving the antifemale railings. In the course of events, each male is given opportunity for a lengthy disquisition on his particular reason for assailing the female sex.

In the manner of contemporary drawing-room comedy, Levy employs the traditional plot artifices of comedy—secrets withheld from the audience, letters that lead to the disclosure of those secrets, *quid pro quo* misunderstandings and their necessary corrections, witty dialogue, confused identities and resolution of the confusions—to construct a plot so entertaining that the opening night audience at the Haymarket Theater "would not depart until it had had a glimpse of the bashful author."[1] A first play for its author, *This Woman Business* enjoyed a run of 187 performances.

Comic stereotypes, the male quintet consists of the young and impudent poet Honey; the late-thirtyish Hodges, host of the gathering and apparently the strongest woman-hater of the group; the anthropologically inclined Crofts, fifty-four; the retired Judge Bingham, eighty-one; and the only married male, Brown, forty-eight (and the father of seven girls). A libertine named Addleshaw, who makes an appearance as a visitor, serves as antagonist to the play's misogynists and, also, the means of revelation of the formulaic secret on which the plot turns.

Their occupations during this retreat consist of Honey's writing poetry, Croft's writing about his travels, Hodge's writing a mock-serious essay on women, and Bingham's reading. Brown seems to have none.

The play opens with the poet as the first in the lineup to show his colors as he superciliously reprimands Hodges for enticing him with promises of a Cornwall hideaway where he would enjoy the company of "men, men's men, woman-haters like yourself,"[2] but then within two hours of arrival finds himself having been kissed by the maid, Nettlebank. In reality, although the maid attempted to resist his advances with only the requisite protestations, she was most unimpressed by his flowery comparisons of her with Helen, Cleopatra, Dido, and by his equally showy attempt at punning as in "I know a bank where the nettles grow" (10). Pretending distaste at having been approached by Nettlebank, Honey insists that she be fired, whereupon Hodges admits that the maid has already been given notice but provocatively omits the reason for the notice.

Even as Honey is molesting Nettlebank or Crawford, he is accusing them as his molesters and continuing his diatribes on women. A variation on Marchbanks of Shavian fame, he blames them even for having made a poet of him. "How can a man live a clean, vigorous, creative life when he has women for breakfast, women for luncheon, women for dinner, and women for tea?" (14). He dreams of sitting for Parliament and of the possibility of a prohibition involving antifeminist legislation.

In a formal setting up of the arguments for their hatred of women, Honey proposes Hodges as chairman, and, as such he speaks first. Hodges bases his hostility to females on their inferiority mentally, physically, and psychologically. Like Professor Higgins of *Pygmalion,* he holds that education would only "produce a woman who *seems* more capable of grasping wider issues, who *seems* more rational, less petty, who *seems,* in short, more like a man . . . but for all that I believe, myself, that at bottom, deep down beneath the surface, you will not have touched the Eternal Feminine, the woman as we know her now, a servant of every kind of pettiness." (17).

As a judge in the divorce courts, Bingham asserts he is here because his many years on the bench have only made him more ignorant of women. "At any time of life Man is an open book to me and Woman a sealed one. Among men I feel a god; among women I feel—a man! And that wounds my vanity" (19). He is here merely to pass on his ignorance.

The core of Honey's argument is, as he invokes the support of famous figures like Samson, Roger Bacon, and Schopenhauer, that "Woman is in every way the enemy of Art" (24).

Crofts can only compare English treatment of women with that of an East African tribe, the Rongas, who in their wisdom managed women as child bearers, domestic servants, and industrial or agricultural workers. He concludes with the observation that there is no more monstrous abortion than a graduate of Girton College, his remark offending Brown, one of whose seven daughters attends Girton.

The final disquisition is Brown's. His grounds for membership in the misogynist conclave are purely familial: he joined the group on his doctor's recommendation that he take a holiday from the pressures of domestic disputes. He is the "victim of a difference of opinion in which one of my seven girls, not excepting our youngest-born, Olivia, has seen fit to give me wrong" (27). His entire domestic upheaval "is due if we trace it back far enough, to no bigger object, to no more important an article, than a coffee-bean. Not a bag of beans, mark you, but . . . one single, solitary, isolated, malevolent coffee bean" (27). His purpose is only to be "freshened and steadied to return with a lighter heart . . . to domestic life" (10).

The male Eden, thus established, is suddenly interrupted by two disheveled figures struggling with each other—Trent, the butler, and a young woman, Crawford, with a wad of money in her hands, claiming to be a thief. Torn between their chivalric solicitude for the plight of the well-spoken woman and their just-vocalized positions on women, the men agree to let her stay on as a substitute for the recently departed Nettlebank.

As life settles into a boring routine, the presence of Crawford affects all the men in some way. She only reinforces Bingham's self-proclaimed ignorance of women as he, feigning sleep, watches her eventual rejection of Honey's romantic overtures in favor of pursuing Hodges, Shavian style. She reminds Brown of his wife and seven daughters, particularly the one at Girton College. As a result, he writes to his wife, mentioning Crofts. Much to his surprise, Crofts receives a letter from Mrs. Brown that explains why she had run away from him (Crofts) many years earlier. Only Addleshaw, the self-declared rake, remains unchanged, giving the lie to the pretensions of his fellow misogynists. He confesses to being a complete libertine. "I'm human; I'm animal; I'm sensual. I admit it. I glory in it. It's my creed" (77).

With the appearance of a second intruder, Addleshaw, the tables are temporarily turned on Crawford, who confesses, as Addleshaw's employee, to having stolen the money from him, and, consequently, from Hodges who is Addleshaw's partner. Like the conventional comic character who has been forced to assume a disguise, she is someone other than she appears to be, with the eventual revelation of her family connections to Bingham.

The comic interest of the play thus lies in the reversals of identities and, more important, in the Chekhovian progression of the disparity between the male arguments and the reality beneath their words. It is only poetic justice that Hodges, the strongest misogynist, is pursued and eventually snared by Crawford.

Brown's desire to forget his domestic problems weakens its hold on him, as his wife and seven daughters now seem irresistibly preferable to his present company. He finds sympathy with Crofts in the latter's comic reminiscence of the beauty of young Mrs. Brown. Bingham, pretending to the end to doze off while in actuality he is observing the foibles of his companions, is presumably decreasing his claimed ignorance of women.

Levy's use of autocharacterization, a technique by which instant audience recognition is achieved, is the cause of much instinctive laughter, as each male establishes himself by his habits of speech. The most obvious of these is Honey's habit of quoting authorities and the repetitive beginning of his speeches with lines like "I think it was Samson who said . . ." (24). During the play he evokes the names of Granville-Barker, Roger Bacon, Richard Sheridan, Schopenhauer, the Dean of St. Paul's, and even Sir Arthur Bingham. He misquotes frequently, providing others with opportunity to give him a taste of his own medicine. Crofts also is characterized by his habitual references to Ronga tribal rites as preferable to those in England.

Crawford has her delightfully frank moments, contrasting sharply with the male posturings. After agreeing with Bingham's conjecture that the swine into which women turn men (as charged by Hodges) may be all for the good, she turns to Hodges:

It's time you had some material for your essay. And I'll give you some. You say I've flaunted my sex. That's right. I have, unconsciously. You say I lied. I did, once, about my father. And I've cajoled you, too, all of you. I didn't think I had. I didn't know it at the time. But I know it now. Those are the three weapons of my sex. Oh, men use them too, when they can, just as women use force when they can. But force is not supposed to be as immoral as fraud. That's because men make morality. If you were on the point of going to prison, I suppose you'd run or fight. I hadn't the strength to run any more. I had to whimper and fawn. Well, I'm not ashamed of it. (116)

In some places Shavian wit pervades the play directly as in Bingham's reference to the law as legalized malevolence (like Shaw's definition of marriage as legalized prostitution). Earlier, Bingham, in responding to Brown's irritation on finding himself defending Bingham's profession, replies: "You do it so much better than I could. I could only say that if people WILL have laws, they can only expect to suffer for it. The same applies to any other dangerous eccentricity" (35). As the men at one point are reminded of their having been made fools of by Crawford, Bingham reinforces Addleshaw's view, listing the ways in which she has been all things to all men: "A mother to Brown, a sister to Honey, a daughter to Crofts, a siren to Addleshaw and . . . something else to Hodges. She makes few mistakes. At one time she thought I needed a great-granddaughter, but the mistake was soon remedied" (81–82). A Shotover-like figure, Bingham loses himself in the memory of someone he knew fifty years ago as he observes Crawford's "tilt of the nose, or that long thin eyebrow" (39).

A very funny scene is a comic convention made famous in its use by Shakespeare and Gogol: Crawford's devilish reading aloud to the male assembly of Mrs. Brown's apologetic letter to Crofts about her sudden rejection of him (Crofts) many years ago. She admits to deceiving Brown to whom she was secretly engaged during the time of her liaison with Crofts and feels she owes him an explanation. She admits to Brown as a darling who is "not handsome, rich, nor clever, but he has a heart of gold. He has always been an angel to me" (106). Brown, simpleminded and increasingly uncomfortable with the hostilities of his more artisitic or intellectual comrades, can only wipe away a tear.

As catalyst for the revelations necessary to the unwinding of the plot and to the puncturing of male egos, Crawford succeeds in attracting the most unromantic and misogynistic of the lot. In her reply to Hodge's jealous accusation of her as a Circean adventuress with Honey, she fires off her own Shavian argument as her contribution to his essay on women: "You think Woman's inferior to Man because she can't waste time on his morality and art and laws and the rest of his toys. It's quite true, she can't. She'll smash them to pieces when they interfere with her own ends; but her own ends are the human race!" (116). She is the first of a long line of Levy's females to deflate male egos and to win the grudging admiration of even the most cynical of her antagonists.

Within its conventional framework and familiar male debates, the play evoked critical praise for dialogue, one reviewer commenting on its "polish and finish all out of proportion to the phlegmatic drama."[3] The same reviewer, Brooks Atkinson, goes on to explain this phlegmatic quality as "a lack of movement [that] often seems a Chekhovian design to pack the story between the lines."[4] The *Times* critic called attention to the "plentitude of wit (not exactly Congrevean, yet excellent back-chat)," and still another referred to the play as "vitriolically clever in the telling."[5] To the *Punch* reviewer, the "playing was faultless," and the play "a piece that plays itself."[6]

Levy's concern with strong female characters, his talent for witty dialogue, and his exploration of contemporary attitudes on a variety of topics have become hallmarks of his work. *This Woman Business* introduces Levy as an entertaining dramatist, whose wit seldom failed when employed in his comedies, although not as successful in the serious dramas. Also, Crawford's listing of male interests—morality, art, laws, and the rest of the toys of males—is a general introduction to the topics of the intellectual debates and personal conflicts whose core is Levy's pervasive theme: the battle of the sexes.

In subsequent plays, the character of Crawford progresses in complexity from Polly Andrews in *Mud and Treacle* to Liza Foote in *The Member for Gaza,* with her emotional strength, moral integrity, intellectual conviction, and a wit that at times can be searing. Levy's male characters, as well, have origins in *This Woman Business.* The poet is a full-fledged character in *The Poet's Heart.* The M. P. Honey dreams of becoming is the protagonist in *The Member for Gaza.* The anthropologist reappears as the archeologist in *Return to Tyassi.*

Yet, although *This Woman Business* contains the seeds of later plays, it stands its own ground as a successful comedy whose gently satirized attitudes have the ring of authenticity and universality and whose witty repartee entertains still.

Written when Levy was eighteen years old and produced when he was twenty-five, *This Woman Business* caused the *Observer* critic to note that "to have written this play at all was a feat, but to have written it at Mr. Levy's age is a marvel." Questioning some unconvincing plot details, such as Crawford's theft, the reviewer goes on: "But Mr. Levy can write dramatic dialogue; he has an universally keen eye for people, and he has an almost inexhaustible flow of wit and humour."[7]

An interesting footnote to this first success of a twenty-five-year-old playwright is that a decade later, Terence Rattigan's successful *French without Tears,* also his first professionally produced play, is about similar concerns, only his male gathering consists of students at a summer foreign language crammer school in France. Both plays introduced their authors as writers of entertaining comedies.

A Man with Red Hair
(1928)

It is difficult to imagine two more wildly different plays than *This Woman Business* and *A Man with Red Hair,* Levy's adaptation of Hugh Walpole's chilling horror novel. Gothic in its setting, main character, plot, and theme, its style, like that of Levy's first play, consists of long dialogues and intellectual disquisitions, the latter, however, carried on almost exclusively by the main character, Crispin. Plot and characterization proceed in a relentlessly singleminded progression of a human monster, whose absolute power over others in all its horror is seen in the very physical appearance of the man:

> The most remarkable feature of this remarkable-looking man is undoubtedly his hair—the reddest of red crests, dressed *enbosse,* crowning a high, white, round, shiny dome of a forehead. His face is chalk-white, his mouth a thin but startlingly bright vermilion line. His eyes are large, dark, melancholy, but their effect is disconcerting for the eyebrows are hairless. For the rest, he is a fat man, short, pot-bellied, fleshy of neck and jowl, with short, stumpy legs, and diminutive feet. He carries himself, none the less, with a dignity rare among persons of his shape."[8]

The grotesqueness of Crispin's deformity is only accentuated by the meticulousness of his dress, his taste for the best brandies, the curious dignity of his bearing, his urbane and suave manner, and his intellectual, if sophistical, arguments.

Thus the character, Mr. Crispin, Senior, is introduced in this story of unrelieved gothic horror. With his quiet, stealthily moving Japanese servants (at least one of whom has lost his tongue in an incident whose telling is too horrible for Harkness to listen to), and his son Herrick—a hollow shell of a man—he lives in an old house high atop a steep cliff in Treliss, Cornwall, which, the villagers tell visitors, overhangs the cliff dangerously.

Of the many stories circulating in the village about Crispin's strangeness, one concerns an old woman whom he half-dazed, half-fascinated with his soft beautiful voice. "Suddenly he took hold of her old wrinkled neck and began stroking it, putting his face close to hers, talking, talking, talking all the time" (43). His Japanese servant was about to pull her head when he was stopped from further action by the appearance of Herrick.

The action of the play consists of the arrival of some visitors: David Dunbar, Charles Harkness, Hesther Tobin, and Dr. Tobin, Hesther's father, who has already become victim to Crispin's simultaneous financial benevolence and intellectual tyranny. The underplot consists of Dunbar's pursuit of Hesther, whom he has known all his life and whom he is bent on wresting from the control of Crispin. Crispin reaches Hesther through her father, an alcoholic to whom Crispin serves the finest brandy, forcing Dr. Tobin to listen to his theories on pain and power. When accused by Dunbar of taking advantage of Tobin's weakness, Crispin merely replies that as a doctor Tobin has the right to prescribe his own medicine. Crispin's experimentation with humans progresses from Tobin to Hesther, to Dunbar, and, eventually, in an unintentional way, to Harkness, who finally is made to feel sensations but not of the sort he had in mind.

Adding to the gothic strangeness of location, story, and character is the village's annual holiday, during which a bacchic dance occupies the villagers all day and night. This ritual is the one that has attracted the shy American to this corner of Cornwall. On the recommendation of a "slight acquaintance," Sir James Maradick (to whom something had happened there), Harkness visits the town to witness the revels. Describing himself to Dunbar as one who "somehow never know[s] anybody intimately" (7), the well-traveled Harkness is comic in his repetitive tale of his world, which consists of his sisters Hetty and Jane back in Baker, Oregon, and of his own roaming the world with his three friends (in place of a wife). Those friends are copies of Rembrandt's "Flight into Egypt," Muirhead Bone's "Orvieto," and Whistler's "Drury Lane," pictures for which he claims more fondness than for any living persons.

Having spied Harkness on a walk in the village and taken a fancy to him, Crispin lures him to his home on the pretext of showing him his paintings. To this most recent of visitors, he explains his philosophy of life, which he labels the philosophy of sensation. Of all the sensations, the greatest is pain. God, the supreme sensationalist, asks only of man that he "develop, refine and exploit them [senses] to the last degree. Only the wicked and cowards avoid sensation" (28). Crispin's game is one of power gained by inflicting pain on others.

He engages his victims in long monologues about bonds between people, bonds realized by equal power achieved through pain, pain that one takes, twists in one's hand, and then throws away. A missionary in the cause of his gospel, he speculates on a new acquaintance as a further experiment in the exercise of his power. Before he inflicts physical pain, he subjects his victim to long sermons. "One of the ugliest things that men have ever laughed at" (61), he now has power over the beautiful things that are now his and his to destroy.

Gothic grotesquerie and medieval morality unite in this tale of pure evil versus a very weak good. The embodiment of evil at its purest, Crispin is joined by his son Herrick (who is evil simply because of his acquiescence) and by the Japanese servants who are forced accomplices. A stark contrast to Crispin, Harkness, a symbol of total innocence, cannot imagine himself as a competitor with Dunbar for the hand of Hesther, to say nothing of his inability to sense the evil in Crispin, as can Dunbar. So it is only when Crispin and Dunbar in their final struggle are hurled out the window onto the cliffs below that Harkness cuddles with Hesther, who has earlier indicated an interest in him.

Another type of good, not so innocent as that of Harkness, is Hesther, the mainstay of the Tobins, a family that includes small children and her alcoholic father. Early in the play, she defends Crispin to Dunbar, acknowledging his eccentricity but emphasizing his kindness to her family. Out of obligation to her familial duties, she marries Herrick, thereby giving Crispin the hope of complete power of the ugly over the beautiful. She marries Herrick despite her attraction to Harkness and her lifelong friendship with Dunbar,

toward whom she feels no romantic attraction but merely friendship with which both have grown up.

The appearance of Harkness in this strange menage becomes a
means of halting Crispin's control over the Tobin family, Dunbar's
efforts having proved futile until now. The subplot, involving
Hesther, Dunbar, and Herrick, supplies a dimension of normalcy
in the story, but its powerlessness in the face of Crispin's power
only gives horror added vitality.

"A revoltingly brilliant study of an obsession," Crispin was played
with equal brilliance by Charles Laughton who "by face, by voice,
above all by imaginative bodily movement, compels suspension of
disbelief. You see before you a fanatic who has raised a lust for the
infliction and the endurance of pain to the level of a faith."[9]
Laughton's performance brought "shouts of 'Bravo' and every sign
of universal satisfaction brought down the curtain"[10]—all this from
an audience in which sat Miss Marie Tempest, Miss Gertrude Lawrence, Miss Isobel Jeans, Miss Ethel Levey, and Miss Dorothy Dick-
son, a veritable actor's hall of fame. In New York, Edward G.
Robinson's performance, although not "the high spot of his career,
. . . ranks well at the top"[11] in bringing out all "the insane, demoniacal
qualities in this cruelest of stage portraits."[12]

Chillingly absorbing, this gothic tale of evil, played out in dramatic black-and-white colors, is a romantic symbol of the themes
argued and dramatized in some of Levy's subsequent plays. On
a decidedly less gothic and more discursively rational level, the
Reverend Mr. Messiter in *The Devil* at one point wishes to "reveal
God to be the mad, malignant bully that he is"[6]. The Faustian
struggle between mind and body is not there in Crispin, for in
him the two have joined. Like the medieval belief in the correspondence between the spiritual and physical, the deformity of
Crispin's moral and intellectual self corresponds to his physical
grotesqueness.

The good-evil forces in characters of Levy's morality plays are
not so joined. They exist in conflict within characters and also
between a character and societal attitudes of his time. They are
frequently played out on the verbal level by debates. In fact, in
Mud and Treacle, the physical grotesquerie is dispensed with in
the prologue so that its moral nature is emphasized in the verbal
exchanges during the play. In *Mrs. Moonlight* and *Art and Mrs.
Bottle*, the grotesque gives way to fantasy and sentimentality, and
in *Topaze* to savagely satirized financial greed and political corruption. Touches of the grotesque are in evidence even in *The Tumbler*,

Levy's penultimate play, but nowhere in its total form as in *A Man with Red Hair.*

The intellectual disquisitions, although one-sided in this play, continue the technique of discourse that characterizes the style of *This Woman Business.* The discursiveness in *A Man with Red Hair* works well for, almost solely, it creates the chilling suspense of the story. Both plays also are set in Cornwall, a place of retreat for one group and a haven for evil in the other.

The subplot of *A Man with Red Hair,* complete in itself in a minor way, suffers from the inability of its characters to counter Crispin's intellectual arguments and his financial largesse, both of which weaknesses victimize them throughout. Only Harkness—whose shyness has been progressively diminished by his attraction to Hesther, and, finally, by the giantism of Crispin's evil—emerges changed. As his mentor of sorts, Sir James Maradick, had predicted, that change does little to diminish the impact of Crispin's horror in the play. His immorality is the energizing force in the play, right to the end in the final catastrophe. In other of Levy's plays, the diabolic serves as catalyst for change rather than, as in this gothic tale, an energetic, living embodiment of evil for its own sake.

The ending in a strange way is reminiscent of the ending of John Osborne's *Look Back in Anger,* in whose concluding scene Alison and Jimmy (the bear and the squirrel) are huddled as Jimmy comments: "There are cruel steel traps lying about everywhere, just waiting for rather mad, slightly satanic, and very timid little animals."[13] Hesther and Harkness are huddled like Alison and Jimmy, victims of a madness of sorts, madness exorcised at a cost of pain to all involved.

In the medieval sense of the conflict between good and evil, Walpole's *A Man with Red Hair,* with its gothic setting and intellectual and moral ramifications, is an interestingly proper vehicle for adaptation for a writer whose serious dramas take on the form of modern morality plays.

Mud and Treacle or The Course of True Love
(1928)

Mud and Treacle is Levy's first try at conducting a serious debate on moral issues, personal and societal. The subject of the main debate is love, but other topics are introduced, providing diversion from this main course. Carried on largely in the witty manner of Shaw, the dialogue is a mixture of comic wit and serious argument. The resolution of the main debate, although its physical consequences are clear, is one of indeterminacy.

On a personal level the moral debate is conducted primarily between Polly Andrews (polyandrous by nature) and Solomon Jack, a visitor who, in the time since his youthful affair with Polly, has become a socialist. Their discussion is of sex, love, and male-female rivalry as rationality is pitted against instinct. On the societal level, the debate on economics and politics is a one-sided comic affair conducted by one Alfred Turner, nicknamed Doggie, whose talking nobody apparently can stop. His understanding of the literature of the left is to quote snippets such as "Sydney Webb says, in his *History of Trade Unionism,* that—By the way, if you want facts, try a little Sydney Webb."[14] His mission is to convert the butler to the equality and dignity of all work. On both personal and societal levels, class snobbery is debated and, as well, demonstrated in the marital problems of Pearl and Archie Pretty.

Like that of *This Woman Business,* the setting is a social gathering in a conventional country house, owned by Roland Pretty, a vapidly political liberal and the host to a party consisting of audaciously spoken Daisy Andrews (also serving as hostess for Roland); her liberated daughter, Polly; Hector Wilson, a conservative aspirant for political office; Archie Pretty, son of Roland, and Archie's wife, Pearl, socially beneath her husband; Lafayette, the butler who insists on the protocol of his position even as he pseudonymously writes liberal newspaper columns; Solomon Jack, a cousin of Daisy, former clergyman, now a socialist whose mission is to educate workers in the pottery towns; and, finally, Solomon's surprise guest, a miner, turned political evangelist, Alfred Turner (Doggie), a product of Solomon's educational endeavors.

Daisy, related by marriage to Roland, manages the guest list, anticipating that the presence of the cynical and predictably discordant Solomon would create an entertaining diversion from the usual country idyll. Later in the play, Daisy admits to Polly that she hadn't invited Solomon with any motive other than to help him recover from a recent breakdown, but that, as always, she had "envisioned all possibilities" (109).

The diverting conversations in the play take the form of disputations. In one, early in the play between Polly and her mother on the sexual freedom of women, a good deal of male nose-tweaking makes for lively repartee. In putting her views into practice, Polly keeps turning down Hector's marriage offer even as she engages in an occasional amorous rendezvous with Archie and finally falls in love with Solomon for a second time. Daisy, on the other hand, although proclaiming that she is as sexy as ever, confines her views to the verbal level and enjoys shocking others with them. Her wit is mainly in the form of epigrams that she draws on regularly for effect. Polly, well taught by her mother, has indeed become her mother's own daughter. When she expresses her wish to be as clever as her mother, Daisy replies:

> *Daisy:* No girl ever is.
> *Polly:* Is the same true of fathers and sons?
> *Daisy:* No, the reverse is true. . . .
> *Polly:* I wonder why?
> *Daisy:* Because experience helps women and hamstrings men. They're apt to let it supplant imagination. (52)

Solomon accuses Daisy of being the Old Woman and Polly the New Woman, the only difference being that "Polly puts her cards on the table, and the Old Woman here *(Daisy winces)* puts them up her sleeve" (44). In an ensuing discussion on the roles of females in the romantic chase, Daisy picks up a Shavian turn of phrase as she proudly points to Polly's conquests to date:

> At the age of six she kissed the under-gardener's small son. At the age of eight, her social ambitions soaring, she kissed the gardener's son. At the age of ten she kissed the head gardener. At fourteen she used to kiss Hector here quite a lot—oh, and Archie, alternately. (47)

Daisy and Polly, a free-wheeling variation of the mother-daughter team in Shaw's *Mrs. Warren's Profession,* air their views on sex and love with abandon. Polly, according to her mother's boast, "was known as the Blarney Stone or Gentleman's Relish: quite locally, you know—just in the country." Forcing the lock on Polly's diary, Daisy "was filled with pride to think what a busy, friendly little daughter I had. So kind to everybody." Solomon takes issue with the idea of Polly's friendliness, noting that "at the age of seventeen she bit me; in the wrist" (48).

The change from the flirtatious to the serious Polly is the point at which the play as comedy takes its unexpected lurch to the serious and grotesque. Love to Polly Andrews, until now had meant conquests—a pro forma liaison with Hector and a brief fling with Archie, who is married. With the rekindling of her youthful attraction to Solomon, she admits to boredom with both Hector and Archie. Of her own selfish drift into her liaisons, she confesses: "If it had been someone else, I should have known the right name for myself before now. . . . I'm a damned little bitch, Mother" (111).

To her assertion that passion without love is gross and disgusting, Solomon insists that 'passion without love is something simple and clean and real and decent. Love is simply the elaborate, tawdry trappings that cowardly people set up between themselves and the frighteningly elemental passions—people who dare only to play at life" (91). His words evoke those of Shaw's definition of the seekers of happiness (in *Man and Superman*). Going further, Solomon asserts that man and woman can meet usefully only in bed. Polly taunts him with being only an observer of the stream of life who dares not jump in but who will once again be pulled in by someone. To her challenge, he describes that stream, not as "cold and sparkling and invigorating" water, but as a repulsive mixture of "mud and treacle—lust and sentimentality" (93). If someone pulls him into that stream, Solomon contends, he will hate her with all his soul. Their debate is an accurate prediction of subsequent events. As the attraction between them grows, tensions tighten to a breaking point. Sensing Solomon's growing rigidity of mind, Polly, at the end quietly suggests that only a kiss may give him back his sanity. Physically attracted and intellectually repelled, he gazes at her silently and strangely, his love-hate turning into madness. In a bizarre scene, he strangles her, leaving her body in the room in which the butler discovers it in the prologue.

In their debates on the roles of the sexes, Solomon discounts Polly's Shavian idea on the life force in a dialogue that evokes suggestions of the argument between John Tanner and Ann Whitefield in *Man and Superman*.

Polly: . . . Proper love is unselfish.

Solomon: No one really thinks that. It's egotism and vanity. A lover's joy and desire is to see himself as he isn't in his lover's eyes. The world revolves around him, instead of his being a tiny serving part of it. There is no world but himself, his lover, and his love. Obligations vanish. A man loves when he hasn't the strength to live; and a woman too.

Polly: (thrown back on a line of defence she herself cannot even trust,
a little wildly): The race must go on. Love is nature's device—
Solomon: That specious plea, my dear? Nature doesn't need such a
device. The race of fishes continues! (92)

The feminine life force in Levy's plays does not unite in a marriage with the male intellect as in Shaw's plays. Instead, the consequence is madness, suggesting Levy's continued interest in
psychopathy, as in his earlier character, Crispin. More like a
Strindbergian or Zolaesque ending than that of Shaw, the strangling
of Polly evokes the psychological grotesquerie of Browning's
poem, "My Last Duchess," or more literally of the strangling in
"Soliloquy in a Spanish Cloister."

In their final argument, Polly calls Solomon's argument against
that "divine attribute, that heavenly emotion, love" mere "mad-
house logic" (126). Solomon envisions a jury, perhaps like that jury
that Levy later dramatized in his adaptation of *Madame Conti,* a
jury bewildered as they "burrow hopelessly for a motive":

He killed his love because he hated her; he hated her because he loved
her. Poor, puzzled jury! He killed her because he lost his temper—
coldly, deliberately lost his temper. He killed her to perplex a jury!
(Then suddenly his tone changes to one almost of exaltation.) He killed
her in a fit of spiritual revulsion. (126)

Polly's quiet request for one kiss that may give them back their
sanity is ignored as Solomon's revulsion at the mud (sex) and treacle (sentimentality) is taken to its logical conclusion. He can no
longer live with the divided self. Like Crispin, who can remain in
the stream of life only on his own terms, Solomon, in the grip of
his rational self, will not allow himself to be pulled into that stream.
His resistance to being "stuck fast in that cloying, sluggish stream,
just like a mere human being" (95) wins out.

About Levy's self-styled tractarian nature of the play, Labourite
arguments provide comic relief to the serious events more than as
part of a convincing lead up to those events. Vehemently pro-
pounded by Doggie, the satire is aimed comically at Lafayette (who
turns out to be the pseudonymous Hawk's Eye, author of a liberal
newspaper column in the *Herald*) and seriously at Pearl who has
moved up the social ladder because of her marriage to Archie. By
Doggie's standards, both are traitors to their class origins. The
comic tractarianism argued by Doggie offsets the tightening ten-

sions betwen Solomon and Polly. Like the ever-quoting Honey in *This Woman Business,* Doggie indulges in a litany of references to authorities: Josiah Stamp's *Wealth and Taxable Capacity,* Sydney Webb's *History of Trade Unionism* and other contemporary sources in his attempts to convert Lafayette and Pearl to the Marxian theory of surplus value.

Solomon is also part of the political debate, but without Doggie's heated evangelism. He sees socialism as a matter for the experts and commissions, for how should Polly, Archie, Doggie, or Roland know "which industry is suitable and which isn't?" His insistence on logic and rational pursuits as male territority spills over into his personal attraction to Polly, as seen in his annoyance with her for drawing him into speaking about political issues in mixed company. It is also her drawing him into the sticky treacle of love at the end that pushes him to his final insane act. Neither Solomon with his history of mental instability nor Polly with her history of romantic conquests is remotely a figure of tragic stature. Solomon is a study in psychology and Polly a study in the social mores of the time. The combination of the two lacks the moral dimensions necessary for comedy or tragedy.

A foreshadowing of the weakness attendant on some of Levy's later "serious" dramas, the additional ideas and subplots, diverting in and of themselves, seem only loosely to progress the main action. Focus is lost and then regained in a series of situations such as the battle of the sexes as practiced by mother and daughter, the class conflicts engaged in by Doggie and Lafayette, the marital problems of Archie and Pearl, and the revelation of the double life of Lafayette, a variation of the standard secret revealed at the end, like that in *The Importance of Being Earnest,* but without the necessary connection to the central idea.

On the cover of his book, Levy describes the play as "a comedy or perhaps rather, a tragedy, a murder mystery, and a shameless tract in three acts and a post-dated prologue." The comedy is due in no small measure to a self-taught Labourite worker by the name of Doggie, whose habits of mind and speech in his propagation of Labourite politics suggest Snobby Price in Shaw's *Major Barbara.* There is little of tragic substance and even less of mystery to the murder silently discovered by the butler in the prologue.

There are perhaps too many debates on too many topics, and these remain inconclusive except as targets for gentle satire. Some seem only loosely linked with the plot. The blend of the comic battle of the sexes of *This Woman Business* with the sadism of *A Man with Red Hair* disperses the focus of the main plot rather than leading to the inevitability of the ending. Similarly, the issues debated—politics, economics, sex, love, and social inequalities—lack a unifying theme. The *Times* review concludes that the disclosure of the murder in the prologue was necessary as a trick to carry off the ending. "If he had been able to dispense with it [the trick], he would, we think, have disposed with a good many other stage 'props.'"[15] The role of Polly was played by Tallulah Bankhead "on about half her acting power."[16]

The weakness of *Mud and Treacle* is that it partakes of too many genres—partly drawing-room comedy of manners, comedy of ideas, romantic comedy, shameless tract (Levy's own words). Most important, however, in the context of his entire work, *Mud and Treacle* is a morality play in its dramatization of the conflict between body and mind, conflict that does continue as central to all or most of Levy's subsequent plays. More directly and perhaps more important, the roles of women that increase with every succeeding play are put squarely on center stage, in equal competition with those of the males.

Mrs. Moonlight: A Piece of Pastiche in Three Acts (1928)

Levy's fourth stylistic experiment in as many plays and his third play produced in 1928, *Mrs. Moonlight* is a romantic comedy whose plot is based on the artifice of the supernatural, a device that provides the structure for a fantasy plot and the means for realistic characterizations. The device takes the form of a wish granted to the owner of a turquoise necklace, with the attendant irrevocability of choice or consequences. Comparisons with James Barrie's *Peter Pan* inevitably followed the production of *Mrs. Moonlight,* one critic invoking even Swift's Laputan journey.

The theme is a variation of the many Greek myths concerned with obsessional desire for immortality to stave off the ravages of time on physical beauty. Within this fairy-tale device, Levy has woven an adult story that, however castigated by some critics as sentimental, syrupy, and saccharine, has caused others and sometimes the same critics to describe it as a "remarkably good play," a play "not for the cynical, even though those persons be the real sentimentalists at heart";[17] and a play that "may seem intolerable even in the theatre to some who can preserve their judgment undisturbed. But they will need to be hard of heart. The piece has a way with it."[18] British and American critics alike wrote of the charm of the writing and acting, at the same time criticizing the play for its substitution of sentiment for the tragic potential of its premise. One critic noted that Joan Barry's performance was of "genuine distraction and . . . exquisite grace, almost persuading us that tragedy is where tragedy is not. So let the critical sleeve yield its reserve. Let us weep and be thankful for having been so delightfully undone."[19]

A major quality of the play is its seamlessness of theme and characterization, even as the plot moves through fifty years and three generations. The smooth progression is due in large part to the dialogue that moves from line to line with a wit and grace that are uninterrupted by moral discourse or, for that matter, lengthy disquisitions of any kind. Also, Sarah, the leading character, at the age of twenty-eight, understands her private conflict between the ideal and the real. As a rational person, once her wish has been granted, she remains a stable character throughout the changes in her family, and she is thus able to act as catalyst for those changes at great cost to herself. The critic who faults Levy for treating sentimentally what should have been handled tragically ignores the premise of the play—Sarah's sensitivity to the truth throughout and her need to act out that truth. No need exists, then, for the requisite growth in moral stature as in traditional tragedy.

Although Sarah functions in part as a Wendy character, there is an underlying sadness from the very start that keeps her escapist action realistic rather than romantic. The situation may be fantastic, but the characterizations are realistic in a blend that muted even the comments of the most cynical critics. The two are consistently in balance, creating a willing suspension of disbelief throughout. Add to these some of Levy's best dialogue, his realistic use of the changes that accompany long time spans, the touches of irony that grow noticeably, and one comes away with a sense of substantive and stylistic satisfaction.

Its events spanning nearly fifty years and three generations, the play focuses on Sarah Moonlight who, when she is twenty-eight (and looks nineteen) in 1881, suddenly and mysteriously leaves home. She vists her family seventeen years later in the guise of her niece Joy and then again, in a bedraggled state, in 1928 (the year the play opened in London). Her final appearance involves a reunion with her now-senile ex-husband, who recognizes her as she was when she left him, and he dies in her arms. Her own death follows shortly.

Given the necklace in her youth by her lifelong Scottish maid, Minnie, Sarah, acting on the legend in order to keep Tom's love, was given her wish of eternal beauty. By her twenty-eighth birthday she had begun to have nightmares stemming from fears that she will become a freak. Minnie's efforts to calm her prove futile, and Tom's joking comments about freaks and witches only intensify her anguish. So, having carefully made her plans and written suicide notes, Sarah suddenly disappears one Sunday shortly after Tom and Edith (Sarah's adopted sister who has been in love with Tom) have left for church.

When she returns seventeen years later in the guise of a niece, Joy (an illegitimate child of a sister now living in Italy), it is in time to head off what she sees as an unwise marriage of her daughter Jane to a romantic wastrel, Willie Ragg. Sarah thus succeeds in bringing about the marriage of Jane to Percy Middling, who provides her with a sensible and happy life. To achieve her aim, Sarah must use her own wiles to attract Willie into following her to Paris.

Within this artificial device, Levy weaves a Jane Austen–like sensibility theme in which Jane marries the right man, Percy. Unlike Austen's heroines, however, she marries him hastily in a tiff and is educated into the wisdom of that marriage only after her marriage. Her education consists of a gradual accommodation to the comfort and properness of marriage to an unromantic husband. Although Levy does not give the details of that experience, as does Austen in her novels, the practical advantages of Jane's marriage to Percy are clear. Only Sarah, however, by her deceptions can prevent the potentially disastrous marriage of Jane and Willie.

The three generations of Moonlights gather for a final time, along with Willie who hasn't changed, but who in his way has become, like Sarah, a caricature with his combination of youth and age, for even with the ravages of aging, he maintains his youthful activities and his youthful self in general.

For her final visit, Sarah is unexpectedly introduced at a family gathering by her grandson, Peter, who has come down from Oxford. He has found her dirty and bedraggled outside the house, and against protestations from the family he has befriended her. Minnie, her faithful and acerbic self, recognizes her charge immediately, and, with her Scottish wit, wisdom, and loyalty to Sarah and the family, she causes the three-generational tale to come to a satisfying conclusion, just as she has been the instrument of the effortless movement of that tale throughout.

If the play's plot is supernatural and its premise unabashedly sentimental, the dialogue serves as a realistic counterpoint to the former and an ironic undercutting to the latter, although not in either case diminishing what most reviewers called the charm of the play. There are, for example, the grotesque and frightening consequences of the granting of her wish, contrary to surface appearances. As she becomes aware of the grotesque combination of old age and youthful beauty, she experiences nightmares, waking from those nightmares screaming. Unable to communicate her secret to anyone, she handles its terrors indirectly as when she asks the unsuspecting Tom what would happen if someone were born who would never grow old. Tom's response is that she'd probably make a fortune in a freak show. He treats her as Torvald does Nora in Ibsen's *A Doll's House:*

Sarah: Please be serious, Tom.
Tom: How can I be serious about such nonsense?[20]

Tom goes so far as to suggest that in "olden times she'd probably have been burnt as a witch" (149). Nowadays, however, she would be just a freak and could not be loved as such. With each comment by her husband, her worst fears rise to the surface until the very reason for her foolish invocation of the necklace's power—to keep Tom's love—has been replaced by the terror of the grotesque possibilities, a terror worse than that of loss of her youthful beauty. The desperation of her condition drives her to what can be seen as a rational action, one that, even in its preternatural framework, suggests that of Nora. In both cases, the women's leaving home is rooted in the husbands' unwillingness to take the wife seriously.

Levy's leading female character again illustrates his sympathy for the woman in her socially prescribed roles and the inability of males—Tom, Percy, or Willie—to understand them. However, there is Peter, of the third generation, who does represent some change in attitudes, illustrated in his compassion for the bedraggled Sarah, whom he had noticed hovering outside the house for a few days.

Sarah's obsession with youth and her even stronger obsession with the fear of freakishness in old age suggest a touch of madness as in the opening scene in which she works herself up to a fever pitch, confiding to the understanding Minnie her fear of going mad. A variation of the element of the strange, grotesque, or the mad—total in Crispin *(A Man with Red Hair)* and progressive in Solomon *(Mud and Treacle)*—Sarah becomes an excessively rational planner in her deception of others. Rather than the power-mad Crispin or the murder-mad Solomon, however, she becomes the freak her husband had predicted.

Her careful planning includes a convincing suicide note, a crucial action that allowed her stepsister, Edith, to marry Tom. Her first reappearance to insure the right type of marriage for her daughter ironically reflects the suitability of marriage between the proper Edith and Sarah's stodgy, unromantic husband, Tom. In her second and final return, the tale sentimentally concludes the lives of both Sarah and Tom. The blend of fairy tale with psychological realism (in Sarah's case) and with social realism (in the marriage of Jane and Percy) is smooth. Fantasy and reality are one in the final scene in which Sarah (old) dons the very same dress that Tom had bought her for her twenty-eighth birthday. For them time has frozen on that date. Their reunion is a reenactment of the first scene of the play as Sarah accompanies herself on the piano in her rendition of "Oh for the Wings of a Dove."

An added note of psychological realism is Tom's senility, which enables him to revive distant memories clearly even as he fails to recognize immediate realities. In an ironic version of the traditional recognition scene, Tom acknowledges Sarah, but not Peter, in response to the latter's question about who his wife is.

> *Tom:* Eh? She's called Sarah. Sarah Jones before she met me. . . . I'll tell you something if you want to know. She used to say that's why she married me. See? Couldn't stand Sarah Jones at any price.
> *Jane: (Softly)* He—he thinks it's his first wife. (220)

Gently ironic undercutting of the romantic by the realistic permeates the dialogue between the pragmatic Minnie and Tom, particularly in the open scenes. Having been accused of being a most disagreeable old woman by Tom, Minnie saucily reminds him that she is thirty-nine and he forty-four.

> *Tom:* But *my* forty-fourth year only contains twelve months.
> *Minnie:* Your collar's turned up at the back.

Tom: (a beaten man) I know. I like it like that. . . . By the way, Minnie,
I've been thinking quite seriously of giving you notice.
Minnie: If it weren't for your sweet wife I'd let you. Do you suppose
I'd be here if she went? (130)

Minnie continues her good-naturedly ironic barbs in her dealings
with the next adult generation. To middle-aged Jane, who has been
sentimentally requesting a promise from balding Percy to "continue to be your own sweet, slow-witted, idiotic, adorable self,"
Minnie rejoins: "He'll do that all right" (203). And to the end,
Minnie is her unchanging salty self as she disagrees with Tom on
the number of blue bows on the birthday dress that Sarah (old)
dons at (old) Tom's request.

The use of telling names adds to the thematic aspects of the tale.
First is Tom Moonlight, whom Sarah teasingly says she married
to change her unromantic name of Jones. Yet he has none of her
romanticism. Percy, with his rocklike stability a variation of Hector
in *Mud and Treacle,* lives up to his surname, Middling, in sharp
contrast with the name, Willie Ragg, a wastrel who even in old age
engages in financial speculation that will, like all his others, fail.

Hardly a reviewer on both sides of the Atlantic seemed able
to resist an apologetic tone for being drawn into the "smiles and
tears" of *Mrs. Moonlight.* Ironically, the review in the *Times* (London) was devoted largely to overexplaining this "embarrassing"
experience:

There have been occasions in the past—and the best of men have
confessed it—when the most discerning of critical eyes, forsaking dis-
cernment, have savagely insisted upon handkerchiefs paying no regard
whatever to Reason's harsh suggestion that the place for handkerchiefs
was up the critical sleeve. It is one of the tricks of the theatre, one
of the most embarrassing weaknesses of the flesh, and the man who
experiences it has no consolation but the thought that he is being weak
in good company. But stay—he has another consolation: that he enjoys
himself, and we will confess that in spite of Reason's frown, we enjoyed
the company of Mrs. Moonlight.[21]

And so the reviewer continues, interrupting the confession to
allow Reason a few lines of critical comment, only to resume the
confessional in the last third of the review. The seductiveness of
Mrs. Moonlight, attributed partly at least to the exquisite performances of actors Joan Barry and Leon Quartermaine, was experi-

enced by audiences and critics alike, the production having run up 321 performances in London and a successful run in New York in 1930 with Guy Standing and Edith Barrett in the lead roles.

Mrs. Moonlight, despite Levy's intentions of writing it as a parody of James Barrie (possibly of Barrie's *Mary Rose*) resonates movingly, its combination of fantasy and reality a universal experience unfettered by time and place. One critic, describing the play as a "frank burlesque on Barrie," goes on to say that "if Levy set out with satirical intentions, he was mastered by his theme before he had done with it."[22] One may add also that if Levy described his play as pastiche, the pieces of that pastiche are woven into a seamless cloth of fantasy commingled with grotesque reality.

3

1929–1931: Games of Truth

Art and Mrs. Bottle: or The Return of the Puritan (1929)

In this second of Levy's romantic comedies about a wife who suddenly abandons husband and children to reappear twenty years later, Levy again writes a problem play about marriage but without benefit of fantasy or the supernatural. The difference between the two plays is aptly contained in the names of the women, Mrs. Moonlight and Mrs. Bottle. In the former, the fantasy carries its own emotional truth, moving even the cynics with its sentiments. The other begins as a comedy of manners and then sinks into a heavy sentimentality, in a prolonged morality debate about the respective merits of art and business.

Without benefit of charmed necklace, Celia Bottle simply and directly deserts husband and two very young children to live with an artist, who shortly thereafter deserts her for a life of philandering with other women. She then lives what turns out to be a comfortable but sordid life with a much older man, Prince Rhostov. Meantime, George Bottle, a sanitary engineer specializing in lavatories, has lived a properly conventional family life, having told his children that their mother had died. Unlike Mrs. Moonlight, Mrs. Bottle returns to resume her place as wife and mother in the Bottle household. Her manner of reestablishing herself as the legitimate head of her family leaves her husband no choice but to make way for her and to inform his business friends of the new arrangement.

George Bottle—plain in ideas, deportment, and language and straight man to the antics of his wife and children—tries to hide his shyness at the prospect of confronting any kind of intimacy. He finds himself in the awkward position of arriving home early to explain to his two grown children, Judy, twenty-one, and Michael, twenty, that their mother, Celia, is not dead, as he had led them to believe, but rather that she had deserted the family after three years of marriage and is about to reenter their lives on this day. Unlike their proper father and very much like their unconventional mother, Judy and Michael are artists, and romantics as well, occupied on this eventful day in painting (Michael) and sketching (Judy) a model in the basement studio of their home. Before George's arrival, a telegram, addressed "To the Bottles" and signed Celia Bottle, had caused some excitement in the two. They conjecture all kinds of possible blood ties to a Bottle about whom they had never heard. Their questions are quickly answered on Celia's arrival.

The aplomb with which Celia re-enters the family institution and, even more, assumes control of that same institution entertains in its reversal of customary traditions. With the self-assurance of her witty lines, she explains to her children her erring ways of the past twenty years. On the basis of that experience, she proceeds to avoid any possibility of similar errors in her children's lives, were Judy to run off with Max, and Michael to marry Sonia.

After the death of her Prince, Celia, with her sudden appearance, begins the reversal of the comfortable pattern in the Bottle household in a manner evocative of Shaw's *Major Barbara,* in which a father returns to reacquaint himself with his family. Like Undershaft who is unsure whether Stephen or Adolphus Cusins (Dolly) is his son, Celia is uncertain about which of the two women, Judy and Sonia, is her daughter.

Some of the wittiest lines, which evoked tumultuous applause at the return of Irene Vanbrugh (as Celia) to the stage, are illustrated from the scene in which Celia introduces herself to her family. After being reprimanded by George for kissing him and for calling him George, Celia responds: "Mr. Bottle has never seemed to me a very sensible thing to call anybody; least of all one's husband. Husbands should be treated with more respect. Now suppose you introduce me to my children."[1]

George: I'm not at all convinced that I ought to.
Celia: But surely there were only two?
George: Don't be affected. You know there were only two.
Celia: I certainly thought so. But my memory's not what it was. *(With a glance at Sonia)* That's a pretty one. Is that mine?
George: No, it is not yours.

Celia: What a pity. *(To Judy, who has been staring at her in admira-*
tion) Then you must be . . . I believe I'm quite a lucky woman. Nice
straight back and nice straight eyes. I should say you were a nice
person altogether, aren't you?
Judy: *(delighted)* I don't know; I hope so.
Celia: And thank God, you know how to dress yourself.
Judy: My mother's daughter, perhaps.

. . . .

Celia: . . . What's your name? . . . I'm sorry, George, but I really have
forgotten and it would be silly to guess.

Celia, however, does remember Michael's name, but not his age:

George: I congratulate you on at least remembering his name.
Celia: Ah, you see I knew him longer. He's twelve months older
than Judy.
George: *(snappily)* He's twelve months younger.
Celia: *(unperturbed)* Is he? I knew it was one or the other. (35–36)

Celia questions further:

Presumably they have some knowledge of their mother?
George: They have; but until this afternoon they had been brought up
to believe that I was a widower. . . .
Celia: So you killed me off. And this afternoon when the corpse
showed signs of walking you told them everything. (38)

The curiosity of Judy about her mother, whom she evidently
admires, and, conversely, Celia's curiosity about what Judy knows
dominate the dialogue:

Celia: Did George mention Prince Nicholas to you?
Judy: Yes.
Celia: Not many weeks ago he died. He would never allow me to make
a return visit.
Judy: Was he nervous of losing you?
Celia: He was nervous of losing his dignity.

. . . .

Judy: Were you with him long?
Celia: Sixteen years.
Judy: What were you called?
Celia: Madame Bottle. *(whimsically)* I'm sorry, George.
Judy: But after sixteen years? Don't people ever call you Princess?
Celia: Sometimes, but only as—a kind of discourtesy title. (40)

Celia, discovering that Michael wishes to paint rather than join his father in business, informs him that he could make more money in the sanitation business:

Michael: I know and with less hard work.
Judy: Michael is artist enough to realize that there are other things more important than money.
Celia: You mean he is rich enough to realize that. (41–42)

It is soon evident that temperamentally Judy is her mother's daughter. As scene 1 ends with a conventional cliffhanger, Celia discovers that the middle-aged Max Lightly, the famous artist and her former lover, is now the object of Judy's romantic inclination.

The remaining two acts are concerned with Celia's successful attempts to redirect the lives of her children toward a conventional middle-class lifestyle, which consists of Celia's return to George, based not on her love but on her liking and respect for him, Michael's decision to join his father's firm, and Judy's return to the studio as she attempts to recover from the devastating departure of Max from her life.

Celia's solutions of family problems are convincing when the comically witty dialogue is maintained consistently. When, however, Levy's wit takes on a sermonizing tone, the didacticism, sometimes strident, changes the play. Arguing the merits of practical considerations versus those of the bohemian life, the puritan has returned (Levy's subtitle for the play), and the play becomes a series of moral disquisitions.

Herein lie the play's weaknesses as both plot and dialogue turn mawkish. Even Sonia, for example, is part of the social morality in her rejection of Michael's love for that of a traditional suitor from a baker's family like her own: "Of course it's an awfully good match for me. The Figginses have been bakers nearly as long as we have. But you see I never thought he'd ask me: really I never. I mean me being a model, and his mother so very old-fashioned and, as you might say, aristocratic. And of course they're ever so comfortable" (92–93).

Some of the most awkward passages are those like Max's explanation of love as the excitement of the chase: ". . . but after the chase what an anti-climax is the kill! Dull and shameful. It's the eternal problem: what we do with the body? Solve that and all the huntsmen and philanderers in the world will be your debtors." To

George, Max defends his "unmorality." "Alas, I am, as clever Celia has pointed out, a true, a great artist. My shamelessness does not deceive Celia; for she—how blessed—is wise as well as good. It's merely that I have gone past shame; below it" (111). The effect is sheer melodramatic sentimentality.

Celia further explains away her daughter's claim that as an artist Max is not like other men:

> Art and Love! Love and Art! God, when shall we have swept away those two delusions? The two impregnable excuses of every malingerer that chooses to clog the wheels of Life. I tell you, my child, that one of George's drains is worth more than all the Rembrandts in the world, that one of Charlie Dawes' farm laborers is worth more than the whole of Montparnasse with the Slade thrown in. And it's taken me half my life to find that out. (84)

When Judy accuses her mother of judging art by moral standards, Max mischievously injects his "Art for art's sake, you know," to which Celia responds with "but drains for God's sake. The glory of America is that she has no artists but the finest plumbers. She thinks it is her shame, but, I tell you, it is her glory" (84–85).

Thus the argument of the play—art versus business or the bohemian versus the conventional lifestyle—ends, with Celia's warning to Judy that for twenty years Max has been a professional lover and she (Celia) has also been a professional lover. As farce turns moralistic, the result is sentimentality.

Critics faulted the play for the melodramatic ending of act 1, which then directs the play into an uncertain stylistic mode. When Celia is stunned by the revelation of Judy's romantic attraction to Max, her hand shakes, and as the tea drips from her cup, she attempts to regain her composure in a response to Judy's concern: "[I'm] Perfectly all right. I never did like China tea" (52). Valuable as artifice for farce, the gesture may have worked by itself, but the attempt at a joke at so serious a moment in the play rang false for a *Times* critic and rings false in the reading. Celia has been preparing for a transition to a serious mode, "by her tenderness toward her daughter, by her gentleness for her son, by a hundred delicate shadows of seriousness passing and repassing over the tight surface of comedy," but the moment when it comes is "ruined by the falseness of mood with which Mr. Levy is to destroy his own play."[2]

In a similar ending to act 2, Celia after a confrontation with Max smashes a vase, a gift from him during their time together in Paris, and the effect is serious as intended. This use of an object (e.g., Sardou's *A Glass of Water*) to advance or predict the ending of a play was a popular device in the Scribean *piece bien faite*.

The moral tone progresses uncertainly, evident especially in the reminiscences of Celia and Max, meeting after sixteen years:

> *Celia:* A kept woman, my friend, is usually a woman who cannot keep herself. Nicholas was a very amiable person, rather humorless, very kind and almost ostentatiously generous. Besides, I too, since we parted have acquired in my own small way a little fame. *(bitterly)* I used to play at the Big Tables. (70)

Max assures her that his memories of their affair are without regret or self-reproach:

> Should I regret my best six months? Paris was still a new fairyland, a city of adventure. I was a failure, but a light-hearted one. We were frequently hungry but always happy. (71)

In the long series of meetings planned and executed by Celia, first with her family, then with Sonia, Charlie Dawes (Judy's conventional suitor), and, finally, Max, Celia, as a wittily comedic and self-possessed character, is convincing. As a moralist, her nostalgic reminiscing and serious sermonettes do not ring true.

The play is an interesting treatment of characters and themes that appear again in later plays. *Cupid and Psyche,* also about the younger generation, is situated in a photographer's studio, although the topics of debate roam over a variety of issues: art, psychology, feminism, and so forth. In that play an unmarried woman does return to reveal one of the characters as the father of her son. In *Return to Tyassi,* a realistic play, a middle-aged wife changes a conventional second marriage to right a wrong she committed in her first marriage. Most important, however, is the growing emphasis on women who break social barriers beyond those in, say, Barrie or Pinero.

The Devil: A Religious Comedy in Three Acts and a Prologue (1930)

With its return to a familiar Levy setting and situations—a country house, guests with a common bond, a test to which the characters are put, debates, and a romantic couple who are a variation of Polly and Solomon in *Mud and Treacle*—*The Devil* is an unabashedly outright modern morality play. Choices, responsibilities, God, fame, money, ambition—all these are issues strangely reminiscent of those in the medieval play, *Everyman,* and at moments, the characters seem as much allegorical as realistic. In *Everyman* it is a stranger, Death, who appears unexpectedly, and in *The Devil,* a newly arrived curate, Nicholas Lucy (whose two names are not accidental) functions in a similar manner.

At the modernized old farmhouse of one D. C. Magnus (a commercially successful novelist and self-styled professional egotist) are gathered the host and his mistress, Paul (a name chosen by her in preference to Elsie), along with their guests, all of whom have unrealized aspirations: Dorothy Lister, an actress; Louis Kisch, a painter and Dorothy's husband who seems to be capable mostly of missing trains; Cosmo Penny, critically approved but commercially unsuccessful novelist; Mrs. Messiter, a conservator of commonplaces, who wants only to do her duty as a minister's wife; the Reverend Mr. Messiter, who wishes to become a leading church dignitary. Finally, there is Messiter's curate, a newcomer, Nicholas Lucy, who, strangely, has qualifications that enable him to offer means of advancement to the guests. He has some legal knowledge so that he can help Dorothy in her contractual problems. He owns an unfinished Conrad manuscript whose completion may be Cosmo's path to fame and fortune. He is the nephew of an influential bishop who may help the Reverend Mr. Messiter to realize a higher position in the church. To complete his qualifications, he is young, handsome, and romantic, providing for Paul (at least temporarily) the kind of complete love in which she could lose herself without the smallest speck of a fly in the ointment to spoil that love.

Nicholas places his qualifications at the disposal of the guests by a game he suggests they all play, a game of truth telling in which all tell what they wish most in life. His suggestion is the result of a bantering semiserious debate about romantics and realists, the conclusion of which seems to be that the former tend to degenerate into hypocrites and the latter into blackguards.

In the prologue to his play, Levy establishes the basis for the weekend houseparty in a conversation between Magnus (fifty-one) and The Girl (later identified as Paul, twenty-four) whom he has brought home after a party. Her reasons for being a virgin have nothing to do with morality or religion, for she sees God as does Hardy: "an opponent who holds all the trumps in his hand, who loves to tease you and trick you and bait you and make you caper for his inane sardonic amusement."[3] God, then, is one whose thunderbolts only cause her to "scramble on to my feet as best I can, snap my fingers and trudge along till the next one drops" (18). Her view of God reminds Magnus of the local Vicar, whose opinions strongly resemble Paul's. Magnus tells her of the Vicar gone half mad from God's thunderbolts and grown "to hate God with a kind of maniac sincerity. It was then that he took Holy Orders" (19). Their discussion ends with Paul staying on as Magnus's mistress and his promise to introduce her to his Vicar who loves him (Magnus) and hates God. The three acts of the play, then, with Nicholas as catalyst for the action, serve as a vindication of the wittily articulate honesty with which Magnus and Paul deal with each other in the prologue.

Within this May-December (perhaps June-November) realistic romance, the play's argument is set. The last of the guests to appear in the Magnus household is the Reverend Mr. Messiter's new curate, who informs the group that as a sceptic and one who has "no sense of the future or of the past: only of the present . . . ," he believes in God and the devil, the basis for his belief "the Devil's complete failure being the proof of God's success" (54).

Like the pilgrim, Luka, in Gorki's play, *The Lower Depths,* Nicholas encourages each guest to make a choice to realize the dream each has. Unlike Luka, however, he offers his good services in showing them the way to realizing their aspirations. The decision that each makes involves a matter of personal morality in the way of necessary sacrifices. Only one character, the Reverend Mr. Messiter, is willing to make the hard sacrifice. In a climactic moment in the play, he arrives, having delivered himself of a sermon that would decide his promotion. With the outrageous courage of his convictions, he had renounced the dogma of his church and expressed his hatred of God, justifying his rebellion in the name of his function as "the King's jester, the King of Heaven's? Can't you let God's fool cut his capers in peace?" (81). Assuming that his honesty is also his defeat, he repeats the sermon to the guests, with an explosive force that borders on insanity.

In an equally melodramtic move, however, he is appointed by Nicholas's uncle, the Bishop, to the new parish he desires on the grounds that "a man who would publicly proclaim his hate of God rather than achieve his own heart's desire, must love God well indeed." Queried by the Reverend Mr. Messiter as to who he actually was, Nicholas merely responds: "Why, just a poor devil striving to do his appointed work" (89). Nicholas's function throughout the play is to confront each character with a choice. As a devil he does God's work.

The choice for Paul, to leave the kind, generous Magnus after he had sacrificed for her or to give in to her "untainted" love for Nicholas, is difficult. Her indecisiveness is ended by Nicholas's announcement that he is leaving his current position to go elsewhere to do God's work. Her angry response to his desertion of her is that he must be the devil himself in his attempts to get Dorothy to "ruin that poor young author," to get Cosmo "to steal a dead man's work," and to get the Reverend Mr. Messiter "to profit by a blasphemous hyposcrisy" (103). Nicholas admits to the charge, adding that only the Reverend Mr. Messiter, in his honesty and insanity, was wise among the blackguards, the realists. Condemning her broken heart as grotesquely trivial, Nicholas responds to her query about their love as meaning nothing to him—"Nothing: less than nothing. Every little tinpot philosopher has been able to see that fame and money are blind alleys: but it took a Plato to discover that so also is beauty: and a Jesus of Nazareth to point out that personal love is a mere wasteful, distracting nuisance" (104).

The play concludes with the departure of Nicholas, who is ready to take on the next romantic, who happens to be the painter Kisch, late as usual, whose desire to create beauty instantly sets off an idea in Nicholas's mind. Nicholas begins yet another game of truths with the arrival of the character whose habit of arriving after the party is over remains intact to the end.

The character of Nicholas, like that of Gorki's Luka, is a shadowy one. He remains unsubstantially developed except as an idea. When he leaves, "his face [is] utterly without expression," as he "takes up his hat, smooths away a dent in it, adjusts his ring to the right angle . . ." (105), and sets off to continue doing God's work. His theorizing about Plato and Jesus seems imposed, since what he talks about—the blindness of fame and money or the wastefulness of personal love—is primarily an abstraction. The characters, however, are flesh and blood in their involvements in personal chases for fame, money, beauty, or love. Although they come alive momentarily, they exist as examples of Nicholas's theories, particularly as tests of the choices he offers them.

With near unanimity critics spoke highly of the prologue, one reviewer describing it as "brilliant . . . , sharp, clear, perceptive, and amusing"[4] and another as a "prologue that might well stand alone."[5] For example, Magnus and Paul establish their personae in a most Shavian equality. In admitting her virginity, Paul asserts that "some people hoard up their money for their children, so I hoard up my—purity for the man I shall fall in love with" (20). His hoard of money and her hoard of purity undergo a test in which his self-proclaimed "sentimental fatuity" in writing her a larger check than he can afford and her equally sentimental refusal of that check result in a micro-Faustian pact, sealed and signed by an equally matched debate of wits. As a result, she stays with him for the two months preceding the house party that is the subject of the play's three acts. Both compromise, Magnus having given up his rich aunt's legacy rather than give up his living in sin. A realist, he has also arranged an endowment for Paul, regardless of her decision. Paul, by default, stays with Magnus, thus having had to give up her ideal—her self-styled "untainted love" for Nicholas.

The three acts of the play, partly personal confessions and partly debate, dissipate the sharp wit of the prologue under the weight of moral issues (what people do or do not do to realize their aspirations) and religious beliefs. Had the level of brilliant dialogue struck in the opening scene been sustained, the ideas may have taken wing.

Largely responsible for not doing so is the enigmatic character of Nicholas, who in his affair with Paul seems human, but who, otherwise, behaves as the abstraction that he is. Unlike his literary forbears—Luka in Gorki's *The Lower Depths* or Gregers Werle in Ibsen's *The Wild Duck*—moralists who have missions in life—Nick Lucy remains a dramatic device rather than a fleshed-out character. Only Magnus has no aim beyond the good universe God has made for him. He is not tortured by the jealous god:

> I don't know what he wants or doesn't want, what I should do or shouldn't do, what to expect or not to expect, but I do know that Goya painted good pictures . . . , that Wren built good buildings, that Mozart made good music, that Corot can play good music . . . ; that there are some very good books in this vale of tears, that there are good brains to wrestle happily with one's own, that friendship is good and laughter is good and life, life is good. In short, God has made me a very good universe. I couldn't have done it better myself. (20)

Except for Magnus, each character voices an ideal, which then is tested by a willingness to make choices that involve potential hypocrisy or immorality. In their verbal sparring, they, as characters, take on the abstract quality of Nicholas. The one exception is the Reverend Mr. Messiter whose explosive moment in the play confirms and humanizes him according to expectations set up by Magnus in the prologue.

When Levy's witty dialogue is in control, as it is in the prologue, the characters are real. When the argument of the dialogue is shaped into sermonettes, its edge is removed. The personal dilemmas created by the game of truths exist to prove Nicholas's belief in God, a belief he states, early in the play, as "the one simple obvious reality." In his final exchange with Paul, Nicholas spars with Paul, who bitterly claims that "if there were a God, he wouldn't let you [Nicholas] draw another breath," Nicholas delivers a defense that, although a theme throughout his work, is the rationale for Levy's penultimate drama (in verse), *The Tumbler:*

> When you are told that God is omnipotent, it merely means that in the long run he has you all on the end of a string. He may hold some on a longer, looser string than others, but the string is always there. It is a mistake to strain at it: it only hurts. That much I think I have been able to demonstrate. A circle of distinguished blackguards, Messiter said. Poor little blackguards! (103)

This direct descent into a statement of morality is in sharp contrast with the convincing and unsentimental reality illustrated in the prologue as Magnus and Paul discover each other:

> *The Girl:* Lawrence once told me that with the exception of Norton Douglas, you're the wickedest old scamp in Europe.
> *Magnus:* I protest. He does me an injustice. I'll swear I'm wickeder than Douglas.
> *The Girl:* You haven't told me yet why you were content to spend three hours with me. Was it simply your preference for nonentities?
> *Magnus:* Not only that?
> *The Girl:* Then what was the attraction?
> *Magnus: (teasing her)* Physical.
> *The Girl:* Of course: but only that?
> *Magnus:* Othello liked Desdemona because she listened to him patiently while he showed off to her.
> *The Girl:* Doesn't my brain or personality interest you at all?
> *Magnus:* Very much. But it wouldn't if you were ugly. (14)

The self-characterizations of Magnus and Paul are convincing whether they spar about matters of sex or of God. Similarly convincing is the Reverend Mr. Messiter's working himself into near insanity in his sermon. All three are made of flesh and blood. Along with Louis Kisch, a painter whose Chekhovian inability to be on time causes his absence from most of the goings-on, they are the four characters who are more alive than abstract.

As the second of Levy's morality plays, *The Devil* contains stylistic and thematic threads of earlier plays. Again, there is the country house gathering of an assortment of artists or professionals, as in *This Woman Business* and *Mud and Treacle*. Magnus's admittedly comfortable chosen lifestyle, the Reverend Mr. Messiter's wild behavior, Nicholas Lucy's mysterious arrival and departure—all these reflect Levy's continuing interest in bizarre behavior, beginning with the thieving young Crawford, then in the strangling of Polly by Solomon, in the fantasy of Mrs. Moonlight, and in the sudden leave-takings of their families by middle-class, middle-aged married women. Facing their own truths, Paul and Nicholas are variations of Polly and Solomon. Choices that involve personal lives and professional goals are confronted by the remaining characters. All converge in Levy's concern with the "Hound of Heaven" theme embodied in the person of Lucy and central to Levy's morality plays.

With its cast of famous names, such as Sybil Thorndike, the play garnered praise for the performances of Diana Wynyard as Paul and Norman McKinnel as Magnus, particularly the former who "dazzled the audience by her beauty and played a long and difficult part, if not yet with all the fire that is in her, with a charming discretion and control."[6] Warning about the danger of modern morality plays, one critic saw the play as needing "the courage and genius of a Strindberg [to fulfill] the desire to have the best of both worlds." The play begins firmly with an "extremely impressive first act" [which] became lost in clouds of overmuch significance.[7] Another reviewer was "grateful that Mr. Levy is sufficiently 'old world' for a study in ethics."[8] Still another, "having torn Mr. Levy's play to shreds" character by character, admits to its "brilliant nonsense . . . [and to its being] one of the best pieces of playmaking wit, and entertainment that I have seen in the theatre for many a long day."[9]

In New York where it ran concurrently with *Springtime for Henry* to full houses, John Mason Brown described Benn Levy "at his best when introducing his characters—clear, interesting, sparkling," but "heavy with the need of proving the text upon which it is based, and begins to flounder."[10]

The arguments posed in the play are progressed in Paul, Magnus, and the Reverend Mr. Messiter, and tend, in other characters, to repeat rather than develop the idea of the hounding of man by ideals higher than he can achieve. Going the distance successfully in a full-length morality play is a challenge by which Levy has been consistently hounded. As with his other moralities, the play did not enjoy the critical or popular success of his comedies and farces.

Topaze (1930)

Marcel Pagnol's *Topaze* proves to be fertile ground for yet another morality play by Levy, this one in the form of a devastating satire that involves the conversion of a simpleminded but honest schoolteacher, Topaze, into an unscrupulous scoundrel more corrupt than his corruptors. His conversion is dramatized in his behavior in the classroom, a behavior, which, when he is fired, he easily transfers to his new position with a duo of crooks, one a municipal councillor, Monsieur Castel-Benac, and the other, Suzy Courtois. The third member of the trio is a front man, whose demands for a larger share of the take create a vacancy into which Topaze falls by virtue of his convenient propinquity, joblessness, and honesty.

The premise of Pagnol's popular comic drama, *Topaze,* is the corrruption of institutions, represented here by education and local government. The Rousseauistic "tabla raisa of Topaze's character" metamorphoses swiftly into corruption in the form of a black comedy. The focus is on the society into whose net Topaze is drawn without hope of escape. His gullibility—taken advantage of by his pupils, colleagues, headmaster, civic leaders and local entrepeneurs—propels him to a position of power. The means to that power is his accumulation of knowledge about connections that extend even to a newspaper ironically titled the *Public Conscience*. What emerges in Pagnol's satiric romp through a world of unvarnished greed is a series of fast-moving vignettes and unforgettable comic portraits. The play ends with Topaze, at the top of his confidence game, extending the corruption schemes to an international plane.

Thus the comedy of act 1 gives way in the remaining acts to unrelieved social satire more akin to Ben Jonson's than to Moliere's or Shaw's.

In a depressingly dingy private school, Topaze tries to inculcate moral virtues in his pupils, his attempts reinforced by walls covered with "maps, tables of weights and measures, and glazed 'moral' pictures illustrating, for example, the respective livers of a teetotaller and a drunkard. Higher still are a series of gigantic texts: 'Poverty is not a crime.' 'Laziness is the mother of all vice.' 'A good name is worth more than a golden girdle.' 'Money does not mean happiness.' et cetera."[11]

Of limited intelligence, Topaze teaches by dictating moral precepts and questioning students on these precepts. Unaware of student mockery, he repeatedly dictates the proper spellings of words such as "laughed aloud." When a pupil insists on pronouncing the last two words "lawed aloud," Topaze gives up, saying, "Well have it your way" (6).

Topaze is surrounded by colleagues who, like his pupils, also take advantage of him, in particular, Ernestine, the daughter of the Headmaster, Muche. In love with her, Topaze gives her his hard-earned new bottle of ink, his calendar, and colored chalks, and he corrects her papers for her, apologizing for being "gross-fibred." Tamise, another colleague, joins the greedy conspiracy when, for his own gain, he informs the already outraged headmaster of Muche's attentions to Ernestine. Topaze's status in the school is summed up in the words of Ernestine when her father confronts her with Tamise's story: "If I can find an ass to correct my exercises, why shouldn't I?" (35).

Topaze, in the opening scene of the play, dictates to uncomprehending pupils: "And so for twenty days . . . at the mere sight of mortal man, the gods laughed aloud" (6). The irony of Pagnol's use of this quotation from the Trojan War epic contrasts with the meanness of its context. Ironically, the gods here are the characters surrounding Topaze—pupils, colleagues, and headmaster. They laugh at him, even as they feed on his gullibility, honesty, single-mindedness, and insensitivity to the greed around him. Though his honesty in refusing to change the grade of a student and his generosity toward his colleagues in act 1 seem to be the only moral force in the entire play, they are also the means of his propulsion into the corrupt world that surrounds him.

They are also the source of the humorous dialogue in the play, the kind of dialogue for which Levy has earned a strong reputation. For example, Ernestine, having just been offered Topaze's hard-earned bottle of red ink and wanting more from him, exploits his attraction to her by suggesting that he has not been as warm to her as in the past:

Topaze: Warmer, Mademoiselle? In what way?
Ernestine: Well, well you brought me boxes of coloured chalks and everlasting calendars.
Topaze: Oh! Mademoiselle, would I not do the same today?
Ernesting: And you came into my classroom and corrected my exercises. You don't offer to do the same today.
Topaze: If I had offered, would have you allowed me?
Ernestine: Oh! that is another point. I only say that you did not offer. . . . But one must not be ungrateful.
Topaze: (much moved) Mademoiselle, mademoiselle, you hurt me. (5)

Topaze, completely gulled by Ernestine's wiles, reassures her that even when he "was alone in my little room in the evening, bent over those exercises of yours, wondering why Debusson Major could never realize that the square on the hypotenuse of a right-angled triangle is equal to the sum of the squares on the other two sides, at the back of my mind it made me feel . . . somehow . . . I cannot tell how . . . that I was still near you" (5).

Among a long series of episodes with pupils, colleagues, and Headmaster Muche, which repeat the innocent stupidity of Topaze, is the funny and ironic confrontation with both the headmaster and a rich mother who complains of her son's poor grade. He is told by Muche that the Baroness "has no less than three children in our school, not to mention three other children not in our school. I consider myself under great personal obligations to her, and should be extremely surprised if your report was not a mistake" (27).

Topaze: (bewilderedly examining the report) Well, I don't understand I am sure. These are certainly the marks I gave the boy.
Baroness: (snatching the report from him angrily) French, Algebra nought, History 2, Ethics nought.
Muche: Look well Monsieur Topaze, look well with all your perception.
Topaze: But there is nothing to look at. Except for the history, they're all noughts. I will show you my notebook *(He takes an open notebook.)*

Muche: Listen to me my friend, anyone can make a mistake Errare humanus est, perseverare diabolicum. Will you kindly go over this child's marks again? (27–28)

After additional haggling, Topaze, insisting that "no mistake is possible," is asked by the Baroness why her son is at the bottom of the class.

Topaze: Because he has nought.
Muche: *(to the Baroness)* Because he has nought.
Baroness: *(to Topaze)* And why has he nought?
Topaze: Because he failed to understand anything about the problem.
Muche: (to the Baroness) Failed to understand anything about the problem.
Baroness: And why has he understood nothing of the problem? I will tell you that, Monsieur Topaze. *(angrily)* My son was bottom because the administration of your class was dishonest. (29)

Explaining her dishonesty charge, the Baroness accuses Topaze of choosing a problem that favored the child of miserable Gigond, a contractor, and she winds up her argument by insisting on the impossibility of admitting to her husband "that his child should ever be at the bottom." Heaping further insults on Topaze, she describes him as "a half-starved wretch scavenging for private lessons and academic degrees" (28–32).

Topaze's refusal to change the grade or to apologize to the Baroness is only one of additional criticisms that Muche has accumulated, the final one involving Tamise's revelation to Muche of Topaze's designs on the headmaster's daughter. So Topaze is fired.

What follows as a result of his dismissal is a reverse "bildungsroman," as he is transformed by the people and institutions around him from moralist to corrupt realist. Choice is no longer his to exercise, and in its place people and events make choices for him; hence, unlike Levy's earlier plays, there is no moral battle between good and evil nor is there an intellectual debate carried on by antagonists. Knowledge and experience do not lead to wisdom as in traditional tragedies nor to restoration of social morality as in traditional comedies, nor to societal reformation as in the customary satire. Instead, individual greed and institutional corruption triumph.

Headmaster Muche, who is interested only in attracting pupils from rich families, pays Topaze pitiable wages, and not only scolds him for giving free tutorials, but also insists on being paid a percentage of the going rate for tutorials, even when these are free.

Reduced to financial desperation, Topaze arrives at the home of one Suzy Courtois for a tutorial with her nephew, only to become enmeshed in a net of far more devastating circumstances. He arrives in the midst of an argument between Suzy and Regis Castel-Benac (a municipal councillor) over Roger de Berville, who is demanding a larger share of the spoils of bribery schemes by which all three have enriched themselves. Roger has been the front for the trio in their phoney deals. As Regis questions the merits of Roger's new demands, the latter calls attention to his well-established reputation for integrity and that "integrity is something that has to be paid for. It has a rarity value" (46). Pagnol-Levy's devastating satire on municipal corruption in acts 2 and 3 is an intensification of his satire on the rote pedagogical practices and institutionalized education in act 1.

Besieged by financial woes consisting of demands by his wife and his mistress, Regis is now threatened by Roger's possible exposure of Regis's having "for years amassed a fortune by persuading his colleagues on the council to undertake unnecessary commitments, and to lodge the contracts with an imaginary contractor who is really himself" (38). When Roger leaves in a huff, Topaze is conveniently recruited as his replacement. His major qualifications are his honesty, gullibility, and ability to sign his name. Thus his education into his new duties begins, that education consisting primarily of signing his name and being kept ignorant until it is too late.

In a series of bizarre episodes (including one involving two secretaries whose idleness leads to behavior that attracts crowds and the police), Topaze finds himself ignorantly rising to a position of invulnerability. He enjoys his new position and even takes on a new garbage removal scheme all on his own.

Now involved in more than merely signing checks as a front man, he moves into wider spheres of influence such as the manipulation of a newspaper that is on the brink of exposing the municipal scandals. His total control is guaranteed by his one weapon, knowledge of the connections.

Events come full circle for Topaze when Headmaster Muche and his daughter, Ernestine, having heard of Topaze's prosperity, arrive to invite him to speak at the school and to inform him of Ernestine's pining away for him. Topaze easily dismisses headmaster and daughter. Able to win Suzy's love, not so much by her love for him as by his power over her, he bargains with her for their respective cuts in the latest scheme, agreeing to split the difference in a hard-won contest of equals.

The humorous dialogue of act 1, changed only by the cynicism of which Topaze becomes a part, is wittily sustained throughout the rest of the play, especially in the final scene in which Topaze wins Suzy on his own terms as an equal contestor. Having earlier replaced Roger, he is now in a position to fire Regis. Turning down Regis's offer of ten percent of the take, Topaze responds:

> I am sorry; it wouldn't pay me. Besides I have been watching you at work very closely, for some time now, and, frankly, I have been disappointed. *(With a patronizing hand on his shoulder)* You are not really a very interesting example. *(He shakes his head kindly)* You're a crook, I grant you, but in no sense a great crook. Your ideas lack vision, lack breadth. (99)

The play concludes with the typist's announcement of the entrance of Monsieur Duhamel, even as Topaze and Suzy have split the difference between her request of eight percent and his offer of six percent. Topaze's metamorphosis is complete as the curtain falls on the two laughing happily as they embrace.

Lacking any moral antagonists, Pagnol's play is a satiric allegorical tale that "presents the contemptible alternative to the obvious remedy for the ills of society."[12] For Levy, the play, even though lacking the customary morality debate between good and evil or the experience in which the devil serves as an instigator of the good, suits his talent for witty dialogue. Although not as bitterly humorous as the original, Levy's adaptation received a positive review in the *New York Times* as "mild and sunny, running to sly humor and gentle irony as, in always literate dialogue, it pokes its fun at an almost stupidly idealistic schoolmaster and the corrupt government officials with whom he finds himself involved."[13]

A major criticism of Pagnol's play has been the invisibility of Topaze's conversion, having occurred "somewhere between acts 3 and 4 [of the original play] [when] he steeled himself to the task, with love as the spur. Only the consequences of the conversion are observed, and the effect derived from the contrast between 'before' and 'after,' with the intervening conversion suppressed, is extraordinary."[14]

Frequently referred to and written about by Pagnol himself and recognized by critics as the "superb culmination of a cycle of development in Pagnol's theater, *Topaze,* with its "sparkling dialogue, tightly controlled structure, and cutting irony,"[15] has also caused confusion about the moral of the play. Seen as "ironical from beginning to end" and as an "allegory which presents the contemptible alternative to the obvious remedy for the ills of society,"[16] the play then lays claim to being a morality play. Without benefit of allegorical assumption, *Topaze* may be seen as Pagnol's view of his society, his version of Dante's "Abandon all hope, ye who enter here."

In contrast with the bitter satire of Pagnol's play, Levy's version, produced in New York, was a mildly humorous, ironic, and literate comedy. To a London critic, Topaze, was played by Raymond Massey as one of the "divine fools of the world—who loses his place as schoolmaster because he is too innocent of worldly intrigues to recognize their existence, and who becomes the dupe of a rascally municipal councillor because dishonesty, even when it is explained to him, runs off his gently credulous mind like water off a duck's back." The reviewer acknowledged the brilliant "separated performances" of Massey's portrayal, though the "connecting link . . . might have made of them a representation of one continuously recognizable human being."[17]

The contrasting views of the London and New York productions of Levy's adaptation might well find their explanation in the two opposite views of the morality of the original version: Is it an allegory as a contemptible alternative to the reformation of society, or is it, as Pagnol's last play of strong social protest, a darkly realistic view of society?

The second of Levy's adaptations of other writers' work, *Topaze* can be seen as a continuation of his interest in the psychopathic character. Both Crispin and Topaze share in common the medieval humors that were carried over into the Renaissance comedy of humors as practiced by Ben Jonson. A straightforward character and an orderly construction of the story, in one case Hugh Walpole's and in the other Marcel Pagnol's, provide Levy with a structure that enables him to adapt both works to his own talents, particularly his style of comedy with its witty dialogue, without the risk of the divided or dispersed nature of some of his original dramas.

Hollywood Holiday (1931)

Subtitled *An Extravagant Comedy, Hollywood Holiday,* co-authored with John Van Druten, is just that—a situation comedy so extravagant that any potential satire on the Hollywood of the early talkies era soon loses its bite as it gives way to hilarious episodes and character caricatures in the Hollywood movie industry. Both Van Druten and Levy had been involved in writing for early films, Levy in particular having written five films that appeared between 1929 and 1935. Pitting a semieducated English spinsterish movie-fan–governess against greedy Hollywood moguls and a temperamental actress, the coauthors put together "a witty affair, with some very amusing situations."[18]

The play has two casts of characters worlds apart—inhabitants of a lower-middle-class Bayswater boardinghouse in London and members of Phenomenal Pictures, a movie company in the throes of problems created by the tantrums of a famous movie star, Hedda Maelstrom. Among the usual problems confronting the variety of boardinghouse residents, this Bayswater group comes to life in the continual battle between Miss Pinnet and Mr. Lintish for the blue room, which he occupies but that she claims had been offered to her. There is also another skirmish among the residents every Friday night as each scrambles to be the first to read *Screen Fun,* the Hollywood gossip publication subscribed to by Gladys Pinnet, a spinster who seems to spend most of her time interviewing for temporary positions as governess. The situation that brings the two groups together and the one on which the entire comedy turns is the verification of Miss Pinnet's claim that for three weeks, seventeen years ago, she had been governess to Hedda Maelstrom, the featured star of the current issue of *Screen Fun.*

The Hollywood group of characters—producers, directors, actors, and hangers-on—are as caricatured in their loutishness and greed as Miss Pinnet is in her polite, English lower-middle-class spinsterism. The collision of these two worlds is accomplished by the extended use of a commonplace Hollywood joke—the changes that a script undergoes until a film is completed. It is this series of changes that constitutes the main plot, with a minor plot that involves the love affairs of Hedda.

Miss Pinnet is wooed and brought to Hollywood by a theatrical agent, Sam Bird, in a movie mogul's attempt to control his temperamental star who gets her way by constantly reminding others of her cultural superiority, allegedly because of her short-term alliance with her erstwhile governess. Le Mosenthal, head of Phenomenal Pictures, thinks that in a confrontation between Hedda and Miss Pinnet the former would finally meet her match and that the Damocletian sword hanging above his head would be removed. His hopes are realized when at a party Miss Pinnet, in a most uncharacteristic action, engages Hedda in a face-slapping incident, for which she is named Battling Pinnet and jokingly invited by a director named Bantor to be the studio's bouncer-in-residence.

The plot complications multiply when Miss Pinnet, movie fan and herself an aspiring writer with a talent that matches her bland personality and her naivety, becomes entangled in a sometimes repetitively farcical series of changes in the script currently in production of a film about Jezebel of biblical fame. There is debate about a happy ending, but more important there is Hedda's insistence on an ending in which she is thrown through a window to her death.

In the midst of this argument, Miss Pinnet appears and in her straightforward, innocent manner, she asks them to listen to a summary of her story entitled *Bitter Willows,* an imitation of Hardy's *Tess of the D'Urbervilles.* To appease her they do so and then get her out of the way by installing her in a Beverly Hills residence. She is given a hearing and assumes that her story will replace the biblical saga as the main interest in the play. As additional considerations affect it, the script changes from its English Wessex setting to American Western. When Hedda falls in love with a young member of the Balkan royalty, the plot shifts to a Ruritarian romance, then to an Antarctic epic, and to an exotic Moroccan romance entitled "Ladies of the Legion." By the time her fellow boarders in Bayswater read of the film in *Screen Fun,* the "super epic" has become an aviation picture entitled *Sirens of the Air.*

The adventures undergone by Miss Pinnet's script are complicated by subplots that involve the purchase of Phenomenal by Phantastic, by Hedda's sundry romantic affairs, and by the socialization of Miss Pinnet at wild Hollywood parties. She eventually returns to her Bayswater boardinghouse with the same characters whose routine lives continue to be punctuated by a "fight" every Friday as to who will first get to Miss Pinnet's copy of *Screen Fun*.

The play's pace begins quickly with the instrusion of Bird on the routine but relatively polite squabbles of the Bayswater group to offer Miss Pinnet an exhorbitant sum for both her services and her story. He mistakes her inability to respond, except in the most hesitant and vague manner, as a ploy for even larger sums of money. Mr. Petch, another boarder, capitalizes on the misunderstanding and, serving as financial advisor to Miss Pinnet, is successful in winning for her a much more lucrative contract than originally offered her.

The humor, however, consists primarily of the misunderstandings caused by the halting and digressive speech habits of Miss Pinnet, who deflects attention from her main points (or who has no main points) as she tries unsuccessfully to make herself understood. Hers is the type of humor that Nabokov in his distinguished study of Gogol's satire calls the humor of the irrelevant. In each of Miss Pinnet's comments, irrelevancies creep in, beginning with her reaction to the invitation of Bird to come to Hollywood at the request of the head of Phenomenal Pictures, Le Mosenthal. Her linguistic style is illustrated early in the play in her reaction to Bird's offer to come to Hollywood:

Well—well—I don't think I can. Of course, it would be lovely—I mean it would be an adventure, and all that—and they say the climate is wonderful—oranges and lemons in the open air—but there are many things. To begin with—there's Mrs. Archibald—she's the lady I saw this afternoon—oh, you didn't know I saw a lady this afternoon, did you? Well, I did—quite a nice lady, too—at least she seemed so—though, of course, you can never tell—as I was saying only this afternoon to Gladys—about Mrs. Maelstrom—Hedda's mother—that is, or was, rather—oh dear, what am I talking about? Two little girls, she had—Mrs. Archibald, I mean—one dark and one fair. Of course, I didn't commit myself definitely—I mean it wasn't anything I couldn't get out of. But I always think the letter of an agreement is just as important as the spirit, don't you? or rather vice versa, I mean.[19]

Her disarming innocence and confusing speech reaches its heights when she is given an opportunity to describe the plot of her story, *Bitter Willows:*

Sycamores, pollards, aspens, larches and poplars dotted the Dorset landscape, shivering in the autumn air. In the hedges larkspur and celandine, honeysuckle and wirrrel-weaver, Jews' harps, little ease and children's torment clustered in melancholy profusion. Anyone passing would have meditated on the brevity of life and the irony of fate. But no one was passing. *(She looks up tentatively for approbation.)* (58–59)

After a brief urging from the bored Le Mosenthal to "give us a quick treatment," she continues:

Well, I'll do my best, though, of course, it's a little difficult, like this. You see, it's quite a simple, little story, really—just a little village idyll, I suppose you might call it. Or do you people say "iddle"? *(She giggles: the others look at each other in surprise)* I'm funny. I sometimes say idyll, and sometimes iddle. But, after all, it is *Idylls of the King,* isn't it? Though, on the other hand, quite a lot of people DO call it iddles— well, anyway—*(She pulls herself together.)* Well, the story really rather derives from Thomas Hardy. You see, Hardy has always been my master, in a way, so of course you couldn't really be surprised could you? *(No answer)* (59–60)

Having confused and bored her audience with her self-interrupting, eight-page-long summary, she tries to explain some omissions:

They're really essential—Oh dear! Now I suppose I shall have to go back to the beginning again. Oh, but I couldn't do that, could I? Oh, no, I really couldn't and you wouldn't want me to, would you? *(On the verge of hysterics)* Please, you mustn't ask me to do that—not this afternoon. You'll just to have to imagine.

Her plea is rewarded with stares from all "while she goes into peal upon peal of uncontrollable laughter, mounting, mounting, mounting. *(Everybody rises, gaping in astonishment)*" (67).

The contrastingly broad and slangy Runyanesque language of the Hollywood group is established early by Bird in his negotiations with Miss Pinnet:

Miss Pinnet: But Mr. Bird, I don't understand. Why should I want to go to America?
Bird: Because they want you?
Miss Pinnet: America wants ME? Oh, do make yourself clear.
Bird: Well, I'll begin at the beginning. I had a cable from Le Mosenthal asking me to dig you up. Well, I've dug. Forty-eight hours is not such bad work; looking for a Pinnet in a haystack, eh? Ha, Ha. . . .

No offence, Miss Pinnet.

. . . .

Miss Pinnet: But what have I got to do with Phenomenal Pictures?

Bird: I don't know. . . . All I know is I got a cable telling me to dig you up and bung you across. So bung I to am going, as they say in the classics. (26)

The repetition of the illiterate and jargonized linguisms of Bird, Le Mosenthal, Bantor, and so forth, after a time call attention to themselves, so that they lose their effect, whereas Miss Pinnet's retention of her innocence keeps her humor fresh.

The one long joke on which the plot rests occupies a large portion of the play, and one of the many "new slants" on the Jezebel story serves as illustration:

Well then, you start the picture proper with a great banquet with Jezebel and Ahab (that's the king and queen), Maelstrom and Clive Brook, if we can get him seated at the head of the table with dancing girls and eunuchs, and niggers with fans and what have you, and a whole lot of guests, including four hundred Prophets of Belial . . . then, of course dancing girls in and out of veils, and a good deal of local hoochey makooch. Well, then in the middle of all this suddenly you get a voice coming through on the sound track. . . . And we learn that Jezebel is a floozey. (52–53)

When the eventual demystification of Hedda's lexical superiority over her colleagues is accomplished, however unintentionally, by Miss Pinnet, she returns to London, and her first words of greeting to her fellow boarders are "How wah yuh?"—her adopted racy language a tribute to and validation of her experience with the American film community. Levy's final bit of hilarity appropriately satirizes the British *Screen Fun* audience as throughout the play he has enjoyed an extended joke on the language and greed of the Hollywood talking-picture industry in its early days.

Critics found the play entertaining. "Laugh at this performance [by Jean Cadell] all playgoers must, so ridiculous is Miss Cadell's politeness, so impertinent her vanity, so sublime her tactlessness in a wonderland of sophistication; but the play would be more entertaining if it did not run the risk of wearying us with the too frequent repetition of a very good thing."[20] Although there is not "quite enough spontaneity and sparkle to excuse its charadelike formlessness," . . . "there is . . . fun in Miss Cadell's return to her Bayswater boarding-house where she gives prime utterance to some of Hollywood's more vivid bits of slang."[21] The richly witty contrasts of the speech habits of two contrasting cultures are the farce's most compelling raison d'etre, and, thus, "all playgoers must laugh,"[22] especially at Miss Pinnet.

The farce belongs to those plays of Levy's that at their best retain the dialogue of wit and are intended primarily for laughter as their main concern. His comic successes, begun in *This Woman Business* and perfected in *Clutterbuck* and *Springtime for Henry* exist in abundance in *Hollywood Holiday*. In this farce, however, one long joke as the comic premise—the unlikely connection between a three-week stint as governess and an American star—feeds on itself and results in replication rather than progression of the premise.

As in *Topaze, Hollywood Holiday* is about the role of innocence in an age of greed, but the satiric edge is stronger in the earlier play because of the predetermined ending by Pagnol. Also, Miss Pinnet returns uncorrupted, except in her proud and deliberate acquisition of Hollywood slang. Unlike *Topaze,* the normal order of things is restored on her return home. As variations of one joke, the play may seem more like a comedy series in the television age rather than a satisfying stage farce. Yet, as with many of Levy's plays, audience applause defied critics' judgments.

Springtime for Henry (1931)

Among its several distinctions, *Springtime for Henry* claims an acting history that merits special comment. Premiering in New York in 1931 with Leslie Banks and Nigel Bruce and in London in 1932 with Ronald Squire and Nigel Bruce, the farce was revived in New York in 1951 with Edward Everett Horton and Hugh Wakefield after a phenomenal eighteen-year tour of the United States. According to Brooks Atkinson, the play was "still a funny antic and the most skillful farce written in English for many years." Making virtue odious and turning accepted moral values upside down, the play in this later production garnered lavish epithets from Atkinson, such as "hilariously impudent," "enjoyably unscrupulous," "crackbrained and uproarious."[23]

For Horton, the play was a career, just as in the nineteenth century, *The Count of Monte Cristo* had become an acting career for James O'Neill, the father of Eugene O'Neill. In its peregrinations, the farce continued to evoke laughter, the difference between the original production and that of Horton's touring company being one of "comically glum" performances of the former as contrasted with the "more genial" role interpretations of the latter.

Another claim *Springtime for Henry* can make, as in the production of *Mrs. Moonlight,* is the reaction of critics as they reluctantly, even apologetically, confess to their enjoyment of the play—"a knockabout farce, outrageous in every respect, and none too skillfully written, yet more satisfying to the innards of man than most of its betters."[24] Brooks Atkinson continues:

> How are we to maintain the dignity of intellectual authority when the silliest sort of prank the theatre performs can give us so much pleasure? But the effect of such farces as *Springtime for Henry* and *Hay Fever* [by Noel Coward] . . . is to make us profoundly dissatisfied with the dullness of purposeful artistic endeavor.[25]

As pure farce uncontaminated by satire or morality, Levy's play goes beyond the traditional aim of comedy as a social corrective, beginning and ending with a topsy-turvy status quo in the lives of two rakes. "Mr. Levy's ideal citizens are crowned with vine leaves and dancing like bacchants down the primrose path."[26] Energized by the morality of a prim secretary, the libertine existence is temporarily halted by the conversion of both men to a socially correct behavior, but only temporarily, for wonder of wonders, "when the final curtain falls peace and sweetness have returned to Mr. Levy's comic world."[27] The outrageously asocial nature of that world is once more in place. In one of the many kaleidoscopic turns in the play, even the murder of her husband by the platitude-spouting Miss Smith is concluded to have been "the decent thing," her constantly repeated theme.

No subjects are more amenable to farce than sex and money. This farce is about both. Two libertines with old school ties, Jelliwell (married) and Dewlip (single), enjoy romantic profligacy and are also engaged in business ventures, Jelliwell having newly acquired a firm, Caribona Carburettors, and Dewlip in Dewlip Motors, the largest car-producing concern in Great Britain. Jelliwell tolerates and even encourages his wife, Julia, in extramarital activity, and Dewlip freely accommodates both. When Dewlip simply and directly tells Jelliwell, "I want your wife," the latter, incredulous, replies, "But whatever for?"[28]

Enter one Miss Smith, the temp whom Dewlip has hired, and as she falls in love with Jelliwell and tries to reform Dewlip, dislocations follow in the lives of the two men and Jelliwell's wife, Julia (the mistress of Dewlip). The entanglements are eventually straightened out and the restoration of the rakes' lifestyle accomplished. The two men also resolve their business problems as, in the interest of old school ties, Dewlip repents his decision not to give his friend a carburettor order and asks him to submit a bid, even though Caribona's carburettors may be inferior to others.

The first of two geometrically designed farces with a small cast (the other, *Clutterbuck*), *Springtime for Henry* is characterized by devilishly roguish wit, accompanied by fast-moving actions of exits, entrances, and slammed doors. Observing time-honored comedic traditions, such as the primacy of plot over theme; mechanical progression of the plot by opportune exits and entrances; well-placed repetitions of dialogue, situations, and habits of characters; secrets revealed in the course of the action, culminating in the scéne à faire; and a final return to the normal order of things, the normal here, however, being anything but societally approved behavior, even if universally practiced.

A device used frequently by farceurs is the letter to propel the action. Here it is used in Dewlip's reformation. Irritated with Miss Smith's challenge to mend his ways, he dictates a love letter to be mailed to some of his women friends, his irritation changing to a physical tweaking of her nose. Even he, however, cannot resist being moved by her tears, and act 1 closes with his tearing the letters to bits. Levy handles the beginning of her romance with Dewlip with a convincing deftness. Three months after his conversion, Dewlip's business has prospered, but the attraction of his reformation has begun to wane. He misses Jelliwell and is confronted with questions from an angry and indignant Julia. It takes merely Miss Smith's confession of her marriage and child to complete his dissatisfaction with the state of things, and he quickly withdraws his offer of marriage, returns to Julia, to the delight of Jelliwell, for whom there is an upturn in both business and romantic matters.

In the final scene of the play, Dewlip, audaciously quoting Ibsen to "be yourself," calls Julia to himself, evoking Jelliwell's delight

that he (Dewlip) is in love with Julia again. Dewlip gallantly rises
to the occasion with a final declaration of the rake's creed:

> Love? I would not sully our relations with that tawdry word! I *want*
> her; simply and honestly, as primitive man wanted his mate, as any
> decent, self-respecting animal today wants his fellow-animal, . . . Do I
> want her because I love her? Is this a pure love for a pure woman?
> Not it: not she. I want her because she has the best figure in London.
> Divorce her, if you like. Indeed I wish it. You may even cite me as
> your co-respondent. . . . I am so revolted with my last three months
> that nothing, I believe, will take away the unclean taste from my mouth
> until I have been through the relatively wholesome mud of the divorce
> courts. (107)

Jelliwell, likewise, responds to the knowledge he has just gained
of Miss Smith's marriage, child, and murder of her husband: "Andromache [his pet name for her], darling, you hear what he's saying! He says you're a murderess, old girl! Is it true?" When she
asks if he minds, he replies, "Of course I don't mind, old girl. You
shoot what you like. But I would like to have been told" (110).
Jelliwell's is the penultimate line in the play.

In the obligatory scene in Act 3 when all characters are assembled for the final revelation of secrets, the blame for marital mis-
conduct is laid squarely at the feet of English divorce laws. The
reason for Madame Tantpis's (Miss Smith's married name) exon-
eration in the murder of her husband is the difference between
French and English rules of behavior. For, as Dewlip explains to
Jelliwell, "when they [Madame Tantpis and her husband] were married, they had [his] mistresses for tea. There was therefore no
alternative. It was the 'Decent Thing.'" With her further assurance
that murder of one's husband is "hardly the kind of thing one
chatters about socially" (109), Miss Smith elicits Jelliwell's promise
that he doesn't mind, and the two are gone before Dewlip has time
to comfort his friend with "Perhaps she'll promise to tell you next
time" (110). Julia and Dewlip then go toward the bedroom.

The consistently maintained outrageousness of behavior and the
matter-of-fact manner of that behavior never falters, and this "gorgeous world to which we can only aspire . . . gives our admiration
gusto and ruddiness."[29]

It is obvious from the opening scene that Dewlip has had difficulty keeping his secretaries. His "evil temper" he explains to Jelliwell is caused by having just been thrown over by a secretary who

had been with him longer than any of her predecessors—three weeks. Their conversation introduces the audience quickly to what to expect in the way of behavior and to the delightfully simplistic humor characterized by the deflecting of real issues. Jelliwell, for example, informs Dewlip about his purchase of Caribona Carburettors; therefore, "I AM Caribona."

Dewlip: The devil you are! Since when?
Jelliwell: Since last Tuesday, to be exact. Me and one or two pals, we bought it up.
Dewlip: My dear Johnny, you can't possibly say that.
Jelliwell: Why not? It's true.
Dewlip: It may be true, but it's not grammar. "Me and one or two pals bought it up." (9)

The wit sometimes turns in on itself in its doubling. If Jelliwell questions Dewlip why he is sitting down when playing the gramophone, Julia, arriving for a rendezvous a scene or two later and finding Jelliwell in so odd a position, repeats, "But why were you sitting down to it?" (15). Dewlip, sulking and angry at his latest temp's departure, has no real answer and merely deflects the issue.

When Jelliwell returns to find his wife with Dewlip, the latter bluntly tells Jelliwell that he intends to steal his wife. Jelliwell responds, "Who steals my wife steals trash. Who said that?" (25). When Dewlip pressed his point that he wants Jelliwell's wife, Jelliwell reacts similarly with "Whatever for?" (26) and then calmly agrees to Julia's request to drive her home. Thus the farcically amoral ambience is established for the entrance of Miss Smith whose intent is to reform her boss, her pronounced theme being the decent thing. Her appearance set in motion a series of hilarious dislocations culminating in the revelatory scene at the end.

Another convention used by Levy is the cognomen syndrome, in particular, the assumption of aliases. When she accidentally meets Jelliwell, who nearly runs her over on her way into Dewlip's office, he (Jelliwell) introduces himself as Mr. Brown. Impressed by her, Jelliwell objects to calling her Miss Smith and promptly makes up a name, Andromache. When she admits ignorance of the name, he launches into his erratic memory of the story:

Well, the story of—er—Perseus and Andromache was a little like *our* story. Andromache was about the fastest girl they—er—ever had in Greece: a runner, you understand. She used to run after golden apples.

So one day—er—Euripides offered a prize of half a pound of golden apples for the girl who—er—got there first. Well off they all went, hammer and tongs, tooth and nail,—er—Hades for leather, with Andromache leading the course by a good four lengths, when she suddenly caught her toe in something and tripped—just as you did just now in the street. Now it happened that Perseus was flying by at that moment with his Golden Fleece—just as I was now, so to speak—and said to himself 'By Jove, that's a—er—a maiden and a half! Poor little devil, she's crashed!' And down he swoops and picks her up. But no sooner had he set her down, top-side up, than I'm blowed if Juno, who was always a bit of a cat, doesn't turn her into an oak tree! And an extremely elderly oak tree, too. So of course they've called the place—er—Clytemnestra ever since. (33)

Because of his "divine story," Miss Smith informs "Mr. Brown" that her name for him will be Perseus as his for her is Andromache.

The above mis-telling of a story is a comic convention used well by Levy in his earlier farce, *Hollywood Holiday*. The opposite of this fantasized variation on a myth is illustrated in Miss Smith's blunt relating of her murder of her husband, the result of his giving into a temptation to invite not one but two of his mistresses to tea at the same time:

I argued with him very nicely, and pointed out that it would be bad for little Pierre [her son] to grow up thinking that mistresses for tea was in the natural course of things. So I bought a second-hand revolver and said that I was most terribly sorry but, if he did it again, I really would have to take the law into my own hands. Well, poor darling, he did it again. That's all. (93)

To the charge that in England her crime would result in her hanging, she responds that in France "the judge declared that in a way I had performed a public service. If husbands began thinking they might bring their mistresses home to tea, he didn't know *what* would happen." Dewlip's comment—comic deflection—is that "No doubt the demand for tea would very soon exceed the supply" (93–94).

The abundance of witty dialogue knows no bounds and is resumed even when one thinks it has exhausted itself, as in the scene in which Julia confronts Dewlip with his "elaborate buffoonery . . . [as] no more than the outward manifestations of a reformed rake?" (66). Having answered three of her questions, he is unwilling to respond to the fourth: "What precisely has reformed you?" (66). He averts the truth by speaking of his anticipation of an extremely interesting evening at the Everyman Theatre "where they are presenting for the first time in English, a play from the Jugo-Slav: 'Three Sisters in Search of a Character'" (66–67). When her fourth question reveals Miss Smith as his companion for the evening, name-calling follows, Julia with "Reptile!" and Dewlip with "God, you little swine!" (68).

The zaniness in the play largely stems from the directness of Jelliwell who admits that his domestic happiness depends on his wife's extramarital affairs, of a Miss Smith who admits bluntly to her real identity as a murderess, and of a Dewlip who claims passionately that his aberrational "pure" love for Miss Smith was not worth the wrecking of other people's lives. "The world well lost for love! What craven, abject, pettifogging cur invented that most disgusting phrase? Some men are wolves and some are sheep, but nothing is more deplorable than the one masquerading as the other" (106).

The play runs on witty dialogue dear to English (and, as well, to American) audiences. Many of Levy's first acts have been described as the best, with both pace and wit diminishing in the remaining two or three acts. *Springtime for Henry* is no exception to this description. Brooks Atkinson has described act 1, like the prologue to *The Devil Passes,* as his giddiest.

"Its dialogue though crude, is nearly always lively, and the acting wrests from it all the liveliness and laughter that it has to give,"[30] writes the *Times* reviewer. To Brooks Atkinson, Levy writes "with the skill of a solemn philosopher" and "has made a wonderful prank out of nothing."[31] *Springtime for Henry* remains the one play in which Levy, occasionally mistaken for an American, appeals to both English and American audiences. Its plot and wit are universal.

Unlike *Hollywood Holiday,* which was criticized for its repetitive prolongation of one joke, *Springtime for Henry* contains the complex construction of a farce, its parts smoothly progressing the twin themes of sex and business without disruption or even interruption. The prospering of Dewlip's business, spurred by his designing of a successful carburetor, could very easily have been an extraneous event. His conversion to clean living could have run the danger of mawkish sentimentality. His mother's arrest and his own uncomfortable night in the rain are incidents that could have been a distraction. The success of the play resides in the smoothly woven farcical actions and the unfalteringly convincing wit. There is no striking of a false note, and the farce stands on its own as well as being prelude to Levy's two other major farces: *Clutterbuck* and *The Rape of the Belt*.

Springtime for Henry, Bijou Theater, New York, 1931. Left to right: Helen Chandler, Leslie Banks, Frieda Inescourt, Nigel Bruce. (Photograph by Vandamm Studio, reproduced with permission of The New York Public Library for the Performing Arts.)

Springtime for Henry, Apollo Theater, London, 1932. Left to right: Ronald Squire, Joan Barry, Nigel Bruce, Isabel Jeans. (Photograph by Stage Photo.)

Young Madame Conti, Music Box Theater, New York, 1937. With Patrick Barr and Constance Cummings. (Photograph by Vandamm Studio, reproduced with permission of The New York Public Library for the Performing Arts.)

Madame Bovary, Broadhurst Theater, New York, 1932. Constance Cummings with other cast members. (Photograph by Vandamm Studio, reproduced with permission of The New York Public Library for the Performing Arts.)

Madame Bovary, **Broadhurst Theater, New York, 1932. Constance Cummings as Madame Bovary. (Photograph by Vandamm Studio, reproduced with permission of The New York Public Library for the Performing Arts.)**

Clutterbuck, Wyndham's Theater, London, 1946. Author and cast: Benn Levy, Patricia Burke, Constance Cummings, Basil Radford, Naunton Wayne. (Photograph by Angus McBean.)

Return to Tyassi, Duke of York's Theater, London, 1950. Left to right: Constance Cummings, Helen Haye, Hilda Bruce Potter, Alexander Knox. (Photograph by Angus McBean.)

The Rape of the Belt, Picadilly Theater, London, 1957. Left to right: Richard Atten-borough, Kay Hammond, Constance Cummings, John Clements. (Photograph by Houston Rogers.)

The Rape of the Belt, Martin Beck Theater, New York, 1960. Left to right: Joyce Redman, Constance Cummings, Philip Bosco. (Photograph by Friedman-Abeles, reproduced with permission of The New York Public Library for the Performing Arts.)

Public and Confidential, **Duke of York's Theater, London, 1966. Left to right: John Gregson, Constance Cummings, Ian McCulloch. (Photograph by Mark Gudgeon. Courtesy of Constance Cummings.)**

4

1936–1940: Women and the Social Structure

Young Madame Conti: A Melodrama
(1936)

Written in collaboration with Hubert Griffith and adapted from a play by Austrian Bruno Frank, *Young Madame Conti* illustrates Levy's reworking of techniques and themes from earlier plays. There is, first of all, the use of a prologue as in *Mud and Treacle*. As a cliff-hanger to create suspense and as a structural prop, the prologue is one of a pair of bookends within which the main action is contained. At the end of the prologue, a woman points a gun at a man. With her words, "Stay where you are! Stay where you are,"[1] she introduces a chilling and bizarre note that runs unrelievedly through the drama. The other bookend is an epilogue in which the action of the prologue is resumed. As the gun goes off, the woman collapses, and her whimper "melts into a kind of ghastly giggle," growing "shriller and shriller and shriller" (61).

Between prologue and epilogue, the trial occurs, but the audience remains unaware, until the end, that the trial is not a real one, but the mental processes of the woman vividly and thoroughly imagining what that trial will be. Envisaging the conventional attitudes of society on the role of the prostitute in society and, consequently, the questions to be asked by prosecution and defense, she clearly premeditates both the shooting and its consequences. Thus, she tells Horka, before her shooting, that she is not a fool and knows what will happen to her:

> I've thought all of it. I thought of how you would come in here, of how I'd kill you, of how I'll be hanged for it. I thought of all the horrors of the trial, of having the whole story dragged out of me in public. I thought of the final weeks in prison. I even thought of the hanging,

101

Stephen, the nightmare hanging, d'you see, and I'm still going to kill you. (59)

Demystified of its potential murder-mystery-thriller aura and even of the usual courtroom suspense, the drama is a study of the psychopathic reaction of a woman to the general injustice of a society. Like Crispin's in Levy's earlier work, Nella's is a form of madness that progresses logically, without relief, to its self-destructive end. The melodrama continues Levy's interest in a psychological dissection of character (as in *The Man with Red Hair*) and its intersection with the societal attitudes and structure of the times. There is, for example, the stereotypical oration by the prosecuting attorney in his focus on the immorality of a prostitute's life. Schonberg's address to the president of the court is filled with references such as the Whore of Babylon in the Book of Revelations, the Woman on the Beast, the Mother of Unchastity, and all Abomination on Earth.

The woman is Nella Weber, alias Madame Conti, prostitute, and the man is Stephen Horka, a married man with a family and a one-time actor, now an agent for British interests in Austria and Germany. During the three acts of the drama, Nella has opportunity to tell her story as well as to decide to kill Horka. Although Nella may at first seem like the nineteenth-century prostitute with a heart of gold—a Camillelike character—she bears no resemblance to the Dumas heroine in the manner of her telling. With an objectivity that sets the tone for the trial, she tells the court of her recognition of the familiarity of her story and thus cannot promise the court anything very original:

Just the story of a young girl of lower middle-class family; brought up in an atmosphere where every penny counted desperately and where appearances counted even more—two things which make people mean, narrow and poor-spirited. Like many other girls, I married the first presentable man who came along with enough money to keep me, and, like many other families, mine was only too pleased to get rid of me. But it was not really a good idea, because my husband had no illusions and never forgot he'd bought me—which to him meant that he could do exactly what he liked with me." (41)

In a legal system in which a frustrated romance may vitiate the nature of the crime, Nella refuses to be "the central figure in a romantic tragedy, instead of the central figure in a very sordid crime" (22). She could be spared the death sentence, as is common practice in European courts, should she so plead. Central to the understanding of Nella's refusal to give in to the "romantic tragedy" plea is her decision to be truthful at all costs. Her truth is that she no longer has an interest in living. In traditional fashion, she had found someone whom she loved and thought loved her. She had financed Horka in the comfortable lifestyle to which he had become accustomed, and she wished only that she could do more than merely provide necessary cash. In this Edenic context, one afternoon in a restaurant she overhears a conversation in which Horka relates to his actor-friend, Farenthold, a graphic, mocking description of his (Horka's) liaison with Nella. His betrayal gradually fixes Nella in her obsession with death. She insists that she has already died because of that overheard conversation.

The trial has its climactic moments, despite its de-romanticized nature, for example, when Nella turns inquisitor and proves Farenthold a liar in his insistence that he and Horka were discussing the play he was currently rehearsing, rather than Horka's and Nella's affair:

Nella: Herbert Muller was the author of the play, wasn't he?
Farenthold: Yes.
Nella: And he arrived back here from a visit to America only two or three days before rehearsals started?
Farenthold: (warily) Well?
Nella: Did you know he wrote most of the play on the way over from America?
Farenthold: I did not.
Nella: And that the last act was actually not written when rehearsals started?
Farenthold: (faltering a little) I certainly don't remember anything of the kind.
Nella: Don't you? You have not forgotten you are on oath, have you, Mr. Farenthold?
Farenthold: Certainly I have not.
Nella: Because there is quite a heavy penalty for perjury. *(He doesn't reply.)* I hope you haven't missed the point I am getting at?
Farenthold: (loftily) I'm afraid I have.
Nella: Have you? It's only this. If the author hadn't even finished the play by the time rehearsals started, wouldn't it have been very difficult for you to have been studying your part four or five weeks earlier? (47)

The trial provides both authors, particularly Levy, whose talent for writing dialogue is unquestioned, unlimited opportunity to employ that talent. After Nella's effective questioning of the prosecution witness, he can only respond with "It's so long ago. How can a man be expected to remember all these details accurately?" (48).

Aria-like orations give decided contrasts to the recitatives of questioning and also are a vehicle to carry the views of the authors, for example, Reuchlin's speech on the ugly nature of hangings in his attempts to persuade Nella to change her plea:

> It's not a pretty thing. It's not even a very brief thing. Don't imagine that all you are facing is a quick drop and then oblivion: the execution begins much earlier than that. As a people, Madame Conti, we are fond of tradition. And a great deal of medieval tradition still informs the ceremonial of our executions. And when I use the word medieval I do not wish it to bring romantic colours into your imagination. In a funny perverse human way, you know, we tend to romanticize executions just as we romanticize war. It is the only way to make either tolerable to our imaginations. You may have noticed that most romantic things are gross or terrible at close quarters. The executioner is not a picturesque gentleman of heroic build in black tights and a mask; he is a local tradesman and wears a hired evening suit and white cotton gloves. And after the day's awful work, he is pestered by anyone, who can scrape acquaintance with him to indulge their morbid curiosity with the more succulent details of how you died. (40)

Reuchlin, the defense attorney, concludes his warning with a reference to the Bell of Atonement, rung ostensibly "to warn the condemned that he should devote his last hours to repentance" and with a bizarre description of a condemned man seized with "uncontrollable exaltation" that resembled "in some strange perverted fashion . . . an obscene horrifying sexual quality" (40). The melodramatic pathology of Reuchlin's description and his commentary on the monstrous societal rituals at a hanging are designed to influence Nella to change her plea rather than to impose a moral on the events.

Even the president (of the three presiding judges) is a part of the unsentimental reality of the proceedings. He insists on the truth and on courtroom decorum despite the fact that his son, in his unrequited love for Nella, appears as a witness. He conducts his court without the slightest sympathy or antipathy toward his son or toward Nella.

Critics have faulted the play for the absence of some redemptive insight or moral affirmation, thus the lack of the positive nature of classical tragedy and the narrow skirting of the psychological analysis of the criminal mind as in Dostoevskian characters. An American critic wondered, "Where does melodrama end and serious analysis begin? When both men are describing events of criminal violence, where does the territory of Edgar Wallace become the territory of Dostoevsky, requiring of us a different response and a different critical standard?"[2]

The authors have also been criticized for being too manipulative in their use of the prologue and epilogue. Yet to the *Times* reviewer, the play is also a piece of many merits:

Ingenuity, strength of attack, an unusual power to make effective its own violent purpose, and sometimes genuine touches of sympathy that by no means depend on plot-spinning—but it remains an ugly play, ugly in the sense that its dominating motive is felt to be exploitation of human suffering, not pity for humanity.[3]

Yet other reviewers mention the sympathy evoked by Constance Cummings in the role of Nella "in the witness box pouring out at last the misery of this woman's life, [as she] communicates an agony that is much too fierce to belong to any mere puppet in a murder story."[4] In the first of many roles in her husband's plays, Cummings's performance was described as "supple . . . passionate and it has the assurance an actress needs for her most frenetic scenes . . . , a remarkably keen and spirited actress."[5] Although Brooks Atkinson sees the play and its production as a melodrama "more counterfeit than most," he lauds Cummings, as giving "one of the most resourceful and virtuoso performances of the season and [she] reminds us that now the time has come to reckon her among the actresses who are also artists and who have something more substantial than personality to give to the stage."[6]

And there is Arnold Zimmerman, son of the presiding judge, "with so powerful a suggestion of repressed passion and with so brilliant an avoidance of sentimentality that all the play's merits are remembered when this youth is on stage."[7]

In an odd twist, *Young Madame Conti* follows *Springtime for Henry,* an unlikely subject for comparison. Yet in Levy's popular farce about two rakes, there is the moral Miss Smith, whose real identity is Madame Tantpis who had murdered her husband and been exonerated. Nella's guilty verdict, however, is partly the result of her refusal to sentimentalize her case. The two sequential plays share yet another similarity, this one stylistic. Each remains purely within its genre, one a farce and the other a courtroom melodrama. There is no uncomfortable intrustion of morality on the farce, as there is no hint of comedy in the courtroom melodrama. Neither forces any message on the reader except as that message is contained in the actions of both plays. On the farcical level of *Springtime for Henry,* the happy ending for Madame Tantpis is in keeping with the delightfully amoral nature of things. In *Young Madame Conti,* the morbidly unsentimental ending is inevitable. In both plays, the cases are convincingly made within their respective genres.

Like *Topaze, Young Madame Conti* is a morality play in which no moral alternative is presented in the play, but which by its absence is left to the audience to consider. In the absence of the conventional poetic justice, the endings in both plays make them seem in the one case amoral and in the other ugly.

Above all other thematic considerations remains Levy's (and Griffith's) concern with women's positions in and treatments by the prevailing social structures. In the courtroom situation those positions are unremittingly, sometimes relentlessly, dramatized. They include a woman facing a skeptical all-male jury, the diversionary tactics of appeal to religious and societal biases, and, of course, society's judgment of the scarlet woman. Nella Conti is in the tradition of Levy's women who in their own right assert themselves actively rather than assume roles as the power behind the male.

The Poet's Heart: A Life of Don Juan
(1937)

Following his structure in *Madame Bovary,* Levy has arranged *The Poet's Heart* in ten scenes, spanning sixty-six years. Like *Mrs. Moonlight,* the play embraces the life of his main character from youth to old age. Levy's title, the last line in Shaw's *Candida,* is the epigraph with which *The Poet's Heart* begins: "They embrace. But they do not know the secret in the poet's heart." More directly, however, the tribute to Shaw is in the borrowing of characters and story from *Man and Superman:* John Tennison (Shaw's John

Tanner), Anne Duller (Shaw's Ann Whitefield), Otto Lovelace (Octavius Robinson), and, of course, the requisite General.

There are unabashed Shavian references, for example, in Tennison's reproof of his wife (now dead) in a dream scene in which he accuses her of having cheated him into thinking that she was a woman, when, in fact, he discovers that she is "merely an atom in the Shavian Life Force!"[14] On his eighty-ninth birthday Tennison confesses another discovery in words straight out of *Man and Superman:* "Seekers after love are seekers after happiness. I want more than happiness" (10.10).

Despite his use of the Don Juan myth, Levy stays within the framework of the realistic *Candida* more than that of the philosophically speculative *Man and Superman*. Although he calls for a composite and non-naturalistic set, he also asks that the set be indicated in naturalistic terms. Thus within the mythic outline, the action proceeds realistically for the most part.

Constructed in ten kaleidoscopic scenes, the play traces the . romantic episodes in Tennison's life from his undergraduate days at Oxford to his eighty-ninth birthday, when his forty-year pact with the devil, General Duller, is called in.

The early scenes are reminiscent of Schnitzler's *La Ronde* in the rapidity with which they move from one affair to the next: the first his abortive affair with an undergraduate siren, Isabel Moffat; the second with "The Lady," an older woman; and the third with "The Girl," a chorus girl. His first serious affair with a woman of his own class, Ann Duller, leads to his accidental killing of her father, the General. Disillusioned with Ann for trapping him into visiting her the night of the murder and then for withholding information (during his trial) about her part in the affair, he marries Ann's divorced sister, Eliza, honestly admitting to her that he could never love her nor any woman.

Levy's technique throughout is to mix realistic (Isabel Moffat) and abstract (The Lady) characters and scenes, paving the way for the dream sequences in scenes 7 and 10.

For example, four years after his marriage to Eliza, Tennison finds himself in a park (presumably Speakers' Corner in Hyde Park) listening to an "Old Lady," whose appearance and manner—"gentle, genteel, comfortable . . . neat, plump and gracious"—belie the radical movement she represents, The League of Marriage Reform. Her radical ideas—attacks on anti-Semitism and support of pacifism and feminism, stressing marriage reform rather than divorce—evoke heckling from bystanders. She berates a society "where men and women are jumbled up together and asked to lead a common life, to pretend that they have interests in common, to walk in step together when Allah made their strides of different length!" (7.2). Like the Amazons in a later Levy play, she likes men, "but only as fathers for my children" (7.3). When the heckling grows hostile, Tennison intrudes in her defense, and a policeman disperses the crowd.

During her subsequent conversation with Tennison, she is suddenly frightened by a voice from a Statue (the General) directly behind them. Tennison, however, welcomes his old friend and tries to quiet her fear. His invitation to the Statue to dine with him is turned down, in favor of a postponement of forty years. Levy easily mixes the real and dream worlds in this episode. The policeman walks away, warning Tennison to go easy or "one of these days you'll have an appointment in Colney Hatch," and Tennison, after being refused by the Statue, invites the Old Lady to tea.

Although just part of one episode in the play, the park scene marks a turning point in Tennison's life, simultaneously beginning the deterioration of his own life and his serious questioning of that life.

The next scene occurs in Tennison's house, where, in an action reminiscent of Mrs. Moonlight and Mrs Bottle, Eliza, having been with her husband for more than eight years, decides to leave with their young son. With the help of his friend (Eliza's ex-husband), Lovelace, Tennison discovers her reason for leaving—a terminal illness, which she chooses not to burden her husband with for the rest of his life. The suddenness of her action, as in the women of earlier plays, is touched with a sense of the bizarre and grotesque. Eliza's reason, however, is realistic rather than fanciful, yet the style of her answer suggests the latter. When asked by Tennison to stay if he could convince her that he loves her, she "merely smiles the wider" and replies: "No, Darling" (8.5) She has lived with her own secret of the poet's heart and has decided on a rational course of action.

Twenty years later, Tennison's life has become a parody of itself and as such has its measure of grotesqueness. He is now sixty-five and cohabits with Inez, a handsome woman of about twenty-eight. He now goes through the empty motions of the lover, as he presents her with a pair of diamond earrings on an evening when she is preparing to chaperone eighteen-year-old Miriam Lee. When Miriam arrives, she brings news that her own Granny, who has made a sudden appearance, insists on going out as her granddaughter's chaperone. Miriam, in the meantime, has already provided a suitable escort for Inez, "the king of reach-me-downs," who couldn't be more amiable in doing whatever he's told and who "simply hasn't got a will of his own" (9.5). The scene is strangely evocative of the three generations represented in a play of the 1950s by Edward Albee, *The American Dream,* in which the "then" generation (the elderly), the "now" generation (the middle-aged), and the "nowhere" generation (the young) depict the moral wasteland of the time.

The arrival of Granny, however, is Levy's means of having Tennison's life come full circle, for she is the Isabel Moffat of his Oxford days, the same Isabel who had given him a blank manuscript book in anticipation of his becoming a writer. The blank book has taken on significance as a record of Tennison's life. Mocked by the memory of the remaining blank pages of the book (he has torn out the few written ones), he throws it at her.

In a dream scene on his eighty-ninth birthday, Tennison consummates his pact with the Statue, Ann Duller's father whom he had killed in a duel. Now a Nurse waits on him. Even his old servant, Albert, from his Oxford days has died and been replaced by Fisher. As Tennison rings for Fisher, the music of Mozart's *Don Giovanni* is heard, and Albert enters, followed by the Statue. Rounding out the reunion is Eliza, peering around from a chair in which she had been sitting unnoticed. She informs him that she, like the Statue, had never feared him, "for I was a woman and part of an eternal cosmic eye that could outstare you any day" (10.6). Finally, Lovelace appears, still Eliza's faithful ex-husband. His heart yet bleeds from Tennison's having stolen Eliza from him, and he is advised by Eliza to throw it away and get instead a heart of stone from which some immortal sparks could yet be struck.

Weaving in and out of reality, this final scene is interrupted by the return of Inez, Miriam, and Granny from the party, and then again by the Nurse, whom Tennison allows to unlock his book of blank pages. The waking and dream worlds unite at his approaching death, even as he sips the water Nurse has brought him.

Emerging in this scene is a reality that runs like a thread through most of the play: the inequalities in human relationships, especially between males and females. His first love, Isabel, rejects Tennison. Ann, the intellectual of the two sisters, finds herself trapped in her affair with Tennison, an affair which has paled on him, only to become a physical necessity for her. Then Eliza forsakes her conventional marriage with Lovelace for Tennison, whose inability to love she accepts. The friendship between Tennison and Lovelace suffers, and the fencing ties between Tennison and Duller have ended with the latter's death.

Levy's recurrent theme, the conflict between the jealous god who demands much of man and the human who attempts to fill that demand, remains unresolved. In this respect, Eliza draws a clear contrast between Tennison and Lovelace when she, in defense of the former, reproves the latter who is judgmental of his friend's wasted life. She reminds him that it is Jehovah who "wrote the Ten Commandments and that Moses only waited and prayed on the mountain" (10.15). Tennison, still envied by Lovelace for winning the love of Eliza, the princess, can only say of his friend: "A beachcomber, a beachcomber to the end" (10.15).

Basic to these inequalities are the conflicts created by the jealous god (a title for one of Levy's plays), a demanding god-in-man, to whom references occur throughout *The Poet's Heart:*

> They're so damned pretty when the sky's pale. They do their sparkling without effort, without haste. A million million miles high and a million million years old. The implacable indifference of infinity: serene and above all impersonal. The only beauty is impersonal. All that serenity must have been hung there to make us prickle with shame! . . . And yet, and yet, Princess, the Lord God isn't there, but here in our tiny hearts. (6.7)

Tennison continues his reflections, more to himself than to Eliza: "Thou shalt have no other gods but me, for I, Thy God am a jealous god" (6.8). Acknowledging his "wanting the moon," Eliza is advised by Tennison to run from a religious maniac who "once he has felt the icy heat of religious emotion . . . knows all others are as candles to the sun! The emotion that makes a man climb mountains without stopping for breath, without need of applause or encouragement save from his own beating heart, that needs no lover's flattery to warm it and no pale love-light to illumine it. *There's* an enemy to strike terror into a woman's heart" (6.8). The exception to his advice is the woman who is a "great princess and prefers pain with the mountaineers to peace with the beachcomber" (6.8). Lovelace is the beachcomber; Tennison is the mountaineer.

Tennison has lived his eight-nine years with the heart of the poet, who unlike the seekers after happiness, sees through the ephemerality of things. In summing his life at the end, he speaks of fishing for fishing's sake and of liking to do what he does well, "even if it is only fishing: the little uncertainties, the choice of bait, the emotion of conflict, the triumphs and defeats. But when the defeats no longer made me sad, the triumphs no longer brought me joy: so in the end, when I was hungry, I would as soon buy my fish as catch it" (10.11). What makes him proudest is that "no fish, not even the loveliest or strongest, ever dragged me into the sea. And the flow of the sea . . . is strewn with the contented corpses of drowned fishermen; drowned and dead and damned into eternity" (10.11). When asked by Lovelace whether it may have been nobler to "cultivate his garden," Tennison concedes the possibility, but insists to the end that the world is still young and that he may yet write.

Levy's Don Juan is not consigned to a fiery hell as in traditional versions of the myth, nor does he achieve the philosophical heights of Shaw's Don Juan in hell; instead he becomes increasingly aware of the jealous god. His last duel with the jealous god occurs when the Nurse informs him of the multitude of women knocking at his door. Tennison smiles fondly: "Tell them, Albert, . . . I love them dearly—and lock the door" (10.13). Aware of the unwritten pages of his life, yet aware of the "contented corpses of drowned fishermen," he dies in the knowledge of himself. There remain those few written pages which, torn out and burned, did emit some sparks. This is his best as he reminds the Nurse: "Would you have had me satisfied to provide graceful literary confections for cultured drawing-rooms?" (10.14). He returns full circle to the initial scene in which he refuses to write for Lovelace, editor of *Isis*. Tennison's jealous god, minimal though his influence may seem, refuses to let him rest in a contentedness with his life. The conflict between the god and the human, between soul and body, between the ideal and real continues within him while he lives, a testament of his unwillingness to compromise.

In its epic sweep, *The Poet's Heart* occupies a unique place among Levy's comedies, fantasies, and moralities. It is his dream play in which realistic and dream scenes are linked thematically by the metaphors of the blank manuscript book and Tennison's weekly fencing matches with the General. Disdaining the writing represented by Lovelace as clever things said prettily by an artist who is "stirred to music by the breath of life," Tennison questions life itself in favor of a higher morality—that in man which demands his utmost honesty and results in a Faustian restlessness that must struggle with contentedness. When his fencing matches turn deadly in the gunfight between Tennison and the General over the violation of the latter's honor, Tennison turns philosophical in his recognition of the duel as an illusion rendered superfluous only by death.

Only at death's door is he convinced that the foils he asks for in his last fencing match with the Statue are useless. Rebuffed by the Statue's "You don't need me, John" (10.15), Tennison is reinforced in his awareness of the futility of outmoded chivalric stances. Now there is only the Nurse to whom to say: "It's too soon to cry, my dear. Other men have books: they shall not be empty" (10.16).

Within his mythical structure, Levy airs contemporary issues, expressed directly in the Old Lady's speech in the park. Tennison's rejoinder to the Tall Man who heckles the Old Lady is a call to struggle (Levy's jealous god again): "If we fight not for a belief, if we fight for profit, or for glory, or excitement, or because we're afraid to fight against fighting, then are we surely damned for murderers, weaklings, conscipts and paid assassins" (7.7). Mocked by the blank pages of his own life, Tennison is comforted by the few written, though torn out, pages and by the thought that he is unlike Albert and his wife—Mr. and Mrs. Dough, who "crouched . . . securely, listening to the whistling storms above . . . had shut out the spring days as well as the winter nights" (10.5).

Unlike the philosophical realists of Shaw or the moral idealists of Ibsen, Levy's Don Juan character has no system of philosophical thought nor any consuming drive to fight social injustice. His conflicts are personal, aloof from the intellectual debates of his time or from engagement in societal reform. His conflicts remain unresolved, except for his increased consciousness of choices he has made over his long life and the consequences of those choices. The final consequence is his realization that he had not "shut out the spring days as well as the winter nights." His dimensions in the play, whether one sees them as affirmative or negative, are finally those of the characters of Levy's other plays, human in the personal struggles that cease only in death.

Levy's jealous god haunts the main character, even when his life seems existentially driven rather than one engaged actively in social problems or absorbed with philosophical or moral questions. These matters are left to other characters in the play. They do slowly emerge to the surface of his consciousness and come to a sharp focus in his ruminations in the last days of his life. The issues in which Levy engages his characters directly in his morality plays, although not obviously affective in Don Juan's life, have never deserted him, and his early differences with Lovelace have remained and are witness to the stirrings of his moral sense. This is the secret of the poet's heart. Without the profundity of Shaw or Goethe, the secret in Tennison's heart is Faustian—a restlessness that continually drives one beyond contentedness.

As one of Levy's few attempts at a poetic drama, *The Poet's Heart* combines elements in other plays, such as the episodic structure of *Madame Bovary* and the fantasy elements of *Mrs. Moonlight*. The use of dream reality weaving in and out of realistic events and the unifying poetic symbols of the manuscript book and the fencing duels expand Levy's dramatic territory beyond the timely and topical to the universal. *The Poet's Heart* is to Levy's other plays as *Heartbreak House* is to Shaw and *The Cherry Orchard* is to Chekhov.

Madame Bovary (1937)

A double adaptation—of Gaston Baty's dramatization of Flaubert's novel—*Madame Bovary* is yet another of Levy's structural experiments. In seventeen scenes, rather than acts, the fast-moving episodes, akin to Levy's film-writing style, make possible the inclusion of the major events in the life of Emma Bovary.

Like Nella in *Young Madame Conti,* Emma Bovary is on trial, not in the legal system but in the ugly atmosphere of small-town societal attitudes and rituals. Unlike Nella, however, Emma enjoys literary stature as a nineteenth-century major fictional heroine. Thus, Levy's play runs not only the usual risks inherent in an adaptation of an adaptation but, more important, that of the inevitable comparison with Flaubert's famous heroine. The immensity and intensity of detail by which Flaubert builds his main character and his themes can at best be only suggested in a dramatic adaptation, with the inevitable loss of the power of the original.

In the Baty-Levy arrangement of the main events in Emma's life, Flaubert's graphically detailed metamorphosis of Emma from romantic dreamer to suicide victim of the blackest sort makes for a different Emma. Particularly this difference is noticeable in the absence of any intellectual or moral weakness in the Baty-Levy Emma and in an accompanying de-emphasis of the devastating meanness and middle-class tawdriness of the town inhabitants, whose vise slowly tightens around Emma with their every thought, word, and act. The loss is felt in the chronologically sequential scenes that dramatize an event without the convincing contextual verisimilitude of the novel, in which Emma's early days in the convent school are described in detail, providing the reader with a contrast between her drab life and her yearnings for romance, partly gained from her reading of French novels and, during a church service, from her mystical reveries caused by the music and stained-glass windows.

In the play, scene 1 thrusts the action immediately to the wedding night of Emma and Charles. On the balcony of her bedroom, having left the coarse merrymaking below, she indulges in her romantic dreams of life away from her father's farm. Leaning against the door jamb, her eyes half closed, she soliloquizes from *The Merchant of Venice,* in itself a contradiction of her underdeveloped mind and overdeveloped yearnings for romance:

> The moon shines bright: in such a night as this,
> When the sweet wind did gently kiss the trees
> and they did make no noise, in such a night . . .
> Troilus methinks mounted the Troyan walls,
> And sigh'd his soul towards the Grecian tents,
> Where Cressid lay that night.[8]

Her father, puffing his pipe, intrudes on her reverie, bringing with him the noise and smells of the drinking wedding guests into her sanctum. He leaves when Charles Bovary enters, "a gawky well-meaning thickset man of thirty, swaying slightly. His square fleshy face is scarlet with alcohol and shiny with perspiration" (5). Emma verbalizes her dream of life with Charles. "People will be dazzled by the string of Orders on your coat, and they'll take me aside and ask me how you did it, and I shall smile, for only I will know how night after night you worked with silent passion at your books" (8). In a state of near rapture, she speaks of future memories of this night, and as she looks down at her husband who has fallen asleep, "there is a loud snore from Charles. Every muscle in her body contracts. She moves away from him. . . . Without thinking of what she is doing, her fingers take the sprig of jasmine from her bodice and start to pluck at it. The moon still shines bright. Her eyes go up towards it emptily, shining with unshed tears" (9). The pattern for her life is in place.

In scene 2, realities have begun to take their toll, and the scene shifts to an inn, the Lion D'or in Yonville, where the Bovarys have arrived because of Emma's boredom with life in a smaller town, Tostes, in which Charles had practiced medicine. Again in a brief scene, most of the residents are introduced by way of their arriving at the inn, the main gathering place for the inhabitants, on the very day the new doctor and his beautiful young wife make their appearance. The townspeople include the innkeeper, the local curate, a prominent merchant, and the most despicable of the lot, Homais, the local druggist who aspires to a reputation that vies with the town doctor's. It is through Homais's smugly critical eyes that we are first introduced to the other inhabitants, most of whom partake of some of his evil genius, but in not quite so offensive a manner. The Yonville residents also include Leon, the youngest of the inhabitants, and, like Emma, the most bored. He and Emma at first carry on a platonic affair that begins at one of Homais's biweekly Sunday soirees. Emma plays the piano, and Leon sings. Both read romance novels and entertain dreams.

Despite the presence of Leon and later, Rodolphe, with whom Emma enjoys temporary liaisons, the pattern established in the opening scene repeats itself incrementally for the rest of the play. The contrast between Emma's romantic expectations and the sordid realities around her sometimes resembles more that of characters in some of Levy's other plays, particularly Mrs. Moonlight and Mrs. Bottle, than of the Emma of Flaubert.

The events of the Baty-Levy adaptations follow closely those of the novel. One of several scenes that resemble the unsentimentality of Flaubert's treatment is the famous fair scene, in which Rodolphe, the affluent young squire, makes romantic overtures to Emma, their conversation, in an ironic touch, interspersed with the voices of the dull orations and awarding of prizes. Rodolphe and Emma share a common dislike of the fair proceedings.

To dramatize the inner states of Emma, Levy uses a cinematic ploy, the off-stage voices in a scene at Homais's soiree during which Emma and Leon are alone. For Emma, Charles's coarse habits and his unromantic appearance contrast sharply with those of Leon. In the coolly detached prose style of Flaubert, the details are devastatingly effective. In the play, the use of voices to suggest Emma's inner thoughts and emotions glosses over the deadliness of the original. As she listens to Leon's talk of the few beauty spots of Yonville, Emma hears a "Woman's Voice": "Dream a little" (29). There follow other Voices:

> *Voice:* You love him.
> *Another Voice:* You love him.
> *Emma: (answering Leon)* After three weeks? That's not possible.
> *Voices:* Not possible? Look at him: see how he stands: elegant and slim.
> His eyes large and grave, his mouth sensitive.
> Now think of Charles: think of Charles slumped at your fireside after dinner.
> His gross hands crossed upon his stomach.
> His heavy boots sprawling on the fender.
> His great cheeks red with feeding and his eyes moist with a foolish contentment. (29)

In the scene in which both Homais and Charles fall asleep after the meal, Emma speaks of her convent school days and her school friends. As she does so, the Homais living room disappears into darkness, and two theater boxes light up, one on each side of the stage, occupied by her friends wearing hairdos, luxurious dresses, pearl earrings and necklaces. Emma carries on a conversation with them in what seems partly like a Greek chorus and partly like the Senecan-ghost scenes in Renaissance plays—both devices used to dramatize the conscience of a character:

> *Emma:* We are too far apart. I am nothing: you are fulfilled.
> *The Companions:* Are we? How do you know?
> *Emma: (strongly)* I know, I know!
> *The Companions:* Why are you so sure?
> *Emma:* How can I doubt? Life must dance and glitter somewhere; everyone is not in prison; everyone is not Madame Bovary. (31)

The Companions continue to raise questions about the beauty in renunciation, sacrifice, virtue, and about the comfort of religion that they had been taught. When the vision disappears, "Emma is alone, head lifted, exalted" (32). Then reality asserts its ugly head, as the Homais living room reappears. Levy's cinematic ploy enables him to dramatize Emma's inner states. Her wedding-night solo dancing and the voices at the Homais soiree are two episodes that provide a dramatic contrast between her real and her longed-for worlds. Only in these two incidents does this quality of Emma's oversized romanticism appear.

Flaubert's coolly detached prose, on the other hand, details this difference with a deadly force, beginning with Emma's school days when her yearnings for romance found escape in the music and colorful windows at a church service.

The play covers the three major aspects of Emma's adult life: her marriage to Charles, her affairs with Rodolphe and Leon, and the developing sense of desperation that leads to her suicide. One by one, her romances end in ashes. Like the novel, the play focuses on the townspeople's strangleholds on Emma: the insensitivity of the curate to Emma when she goes to him for advice; the cruel gossip of jealous wives; the financial vise of Binet and L'Heureux as they close in on Emma for her debts; the rakish use of Emma by Rodolphe; her reduction to poverty that results in the selling of the furniture; the monstrous amorality and hypocrisy of the town's leading and most powerful citizen, Homais, in particular, his attempt at fame by encouraging Charles to perform what turns out to be a botched-up operation on the leg of Hippolyte, Homais's clerk—all of these leading, finally, to Emma's use of Hippolyte, her loyal admirer, to obtain poison. As in the novel, no one emerges in a positive light, unless it is Emma's maid and Charles, who to the end, loves Emma, but his love, like Emma's over-romanticized nature, lacks the firmness of an intellectual and moral stance. It remains for the strong to survive, but the strong are the greedy and the hypocritical.

Emma, in scene 1 on her wedding night, is described as dancing by herself "round and round the room . . . in time to the fiddle; untaught, improvised steps related to no tradition, related only to her own spontaneous vitality and ache for movement" (1). Undirected by an intellectual or moral sense, she never grows into any realization of the realities of life. She remains the convent schoolgirl whose dreams derive from her reading of romance novels (not Shakespeare) and from her daydreaming in church as she loses herself in the music and the images and colors of the stained-glass windows.

Intended as a character flaw, her romantic inclinations take the vague form of escape from the confines of her small family village to Tostes, where the young doctor has a practice; then to Yonville, from whose boring life Emma seeks escape through her affairs with Rodolphe and Leon. Her final escape is a horrible death. The tragedy, if one may use the term here, is the unreality of her school-girl dreams, headed for self-destruction and collectively symbolized by the blind man who haunts the carriage on which Emma travels in her escapes to Rouen. The carriage, La Hirondelle, functions symbolically as Emma's journeys between the two worlds in which she lives, worlds that converge only in her suicide. Flaubert's Emma does not have the strength of mind of Levy's Nella Conti, and therein lies her weakness.

It is Emma's romanticism as a weakness that escapes the Baty-Levy adaptations of Flaubert's novel and reduces her dimensions to those of a Mrs. Moonlight or Mrs. Bottle. Critics called attention to the play (directed by Levy) as not showing the "human disintegration," but rather "surrendering to actors of the English school of drawing-room comedy manners,"[9] a fault partially that of the production by the Theater Guild.

In her second role in a play by her husband, Constance Cummings again garnered critical praise in "giving the finest performance of her career. Beautifully costumed and made up with a kind of cameo daintiness, she moves through the play with the loneliness of a woman whose hopes wither away wherever she places them. It is a deliberately planned study in the graces of despair, and it is reticently stated, except in the death scene, which is crammed with morbid details. If this is not precisely the Emma of the novel, the fault is not entirely in Miss Cummings's acting, for the play discreetly omits the malevolence of the character." This praise, by Brooks Atkinson, is accompanied by a faulting of Baty in his selection of scenes from the novel that "are prudish in the interests of pretty theatre. Flaubert's novel would not be a classic if his passion for the truth went no deeper than that."[10]

Although the scenes in the play may have seemed superficial to one critic who described them as postcard scenes and Emma's characterization as a "chromo portrait,"[11] Flaubert's dramatic scenes, such as the local fair, were fair game for Levy's skill in writing dialogue. In addition to Levy's flair for staging, mentioned earlier, the use of a variation of the Greek chorus, there was also the effective "double stage set—Emma in her bedroom preparing for flight with Rodolphe: and her lover in his sitting room composing the letter which puts a period on their romance."[12] In Washington, "the audience "gave Miss Cummings [as Emma] many rounds of applause at the conclusion of the play."[13] Levy himself directed the play with outstanding actors in supporting roles: Harold Vermilyea as Charles Bovary, Ernst Cossart as Homais, Ernest Thesiger as Lheureux, O. Z. Whitehead as Justin, and Eric Portman as Rodolphe.

In taking on the dramatization of Flaubert's classic heroine, Baty and Levy have demonstrated, as have many others, that the nature of most adaptations precludes the possibility of faithfulness to the original and risks, as well, the inevitable comparison with that original. Thus, the Shakespeare-quoting Emma of Baty-Levy is a deviation from the Flaubertian heroine whose reading consisted of French romance novels. Levy's Emma can also be seen as yet another portrait in the gallery of feminine characters that Levy has created. As such, Levy's Emma shares the fantasy of a Mrs. Moonlight and the sordidness of a Nella Conti, but lacks the balancing intelligence of Kate Settle, Martha Cotton, or Liza Foote.

The view of Vincent Canby on the 1991 French film, *Madame Bovary*, might well apply to all dramatizations of Flaubert's novel: "Mr. Chabrol errs on the side of understatement. His *Madame Bovary* is not to be dismissed. It is so good in so many details that the wish is that it were better. See it. You won't be bored, but you may want to talk back to it."[14]

The Jealous God (1939)

The year that World War II began and the Spanish Civil War ended witnessed an outburst of plays directly or indirectly reflecting and questioning the spirit of the times. Levy's *The Jealous God,* no exception, joins other dramas in depicting that spirit: Shaw's *In Good King Charles' Golden Days,* O'Casey's *The Star Turns Red,* Yeats's *Purgatory,* Eliot's *The Family Reunion,* Coward's *This Happy Breed,* and Rattigan's *After the Dance.* In dealing directly with the personal problems of the middle class, Levy's play is akin in its realism to the plays of Coward and Rattigan in their dramatizations of the stalemated mood during the time of England's entry into the war.

In the context of his own plays, *The Jealous God* can be seen as a defining play in that it brings together a number of themes of his serious plays. The very title of the play is the focus of the

debates in *Mud and Treacle* and *The Devil,* and, although indirectly, a theme to be found in most of his plays, as varied as *A Man
with Red Hair, Topaze, Springtime for Henry,* and *Young Madame
Conti.* In *The Jealous God,* the conflicts in the private lives of
people are engendered by the divided self, an old Arnoldian theme.
At one point, a character quotes from Levy's source—the Old
Testament: "Thou shalt have no other gods but me: for I thy God
am a jealous God."[15]

The play's argument is the same as that dealt with on a much
broader and more philosophical scale by Ibsen and Shaw: the place
of ideals in a realistic world in which life forces people into compromises with their ideals. Debates of ideas, although they exist in
this play, are taken beyond their verbal level and subjected to the
tests that a jealous god demands of men and women.

The idealists are summed up by a character, Muriel Shufflepenny, who has undergone a bit of a conversion to their life
views:

> God, you know, has one great trick that he never tires of playing: to
> start us off in life with hopes too high for our strength or purity—too
> high for most of us. My own was to marry romantically and bring up
> a son to be great and good. Instead I married—or rather remarried—
> prudently and struggled to make my son a "success." William once
> meant to uncover traces of dead civilizations, but somehow he would
> always start next year. Jim dreamed of being a historian of deadly
> scientific impartiality, instead he writes snappy little lies about ladies'
> underwear. Walter Byways was to have raised up the oppressed; he
> has raised up only himself. Only the very pure get what they intend.
> The rest all fail by trying to make the best of both worlds, this world
> and the next. (137–38)

Levy's idealists are a loose family of characters going their respective ways. In a country cottage, a little untidier than most, Jim
Settle, a copywriter for an advertising firm, and his wife, Kate,
maintain a household composed of Rod Shufflepenny, an artist,
and Jim's elderly father, William Settle. Except for Jim who must
settle for his job to provide for the family, all have given up any
possibility of compromise with the outside world, all pursuing their
interests and living in accordance with their ideals. The meals that
Kate prepares on the days the maid does not work consist of
heated food from tins and leftover cold leg of mutton. Jim is bored
with his job at Premier Publicity Limited where he is limited to

"thinking out an irresistibly seductive trade name for Messrs. Thyme and Wattlebury's new bust-bodice" (13). William devotes his entire time to birdwatching, and Rod, detesting the ambitious life of his father and mother, Sir Ernest and Muriel Shufflepenny, paints, Kate asserting that he is unhappy as a painter because his work never stops tormenting him. She maintains as well that because Father William, who has for financial reasons been unable to pursue his interest in archaeology and thus has settled for photographing birds, is not alive because he is happier than most. Contented for nineteen out of twenty days, she worries about that twentieth day when she sees her own long-range prospects of warming up tins for the men as hardly exhilarating.

The idyllic life of the household seems ripe for a change, and the catalyst for that change is a visitor, Walter Byways, the righthand man of the hotelier, Sir Ernest Shufflepenny, Rod's father. A second catalyst for change, like that in Virginia Woolf's *To the Lighthouse* is war, here, World War II.

Changes in this idyllic existence of the four characters happen on the personal, business, political, and moral levels. Kate recognizes Byways, now forty, from her "finishing" days in Paris as a pimply schoolgirl of twelve when he used to talk to her as though she were thirty. Additional information from the past emerges early in the play about the purpose of Byways' visit. At the same time that Sir Ernest Shufflepenny had absconded with William's wife, he (Shufflepenny) had engaged in unsavory business tactics to wrestle control of Associated Hotels Limited from Oscar Settle, whose death had left his share in the business to William. In an ironic repetition of Sir Ernest's actions, Byways, developing his own creative ideas for the hotel business, attracts Kate personally and professionally. Her romantic interest in Byways, however, soon ends, and eventually she gives up even her work (after a reconciliation with Jim who has enlisted) to return to the country. Here she confronts a new set of situations: Father William in a senile state, Rod's return from a catastrophic jail term as conscientious objector, and, finally, news of Jim's death in the war.

Mere summary of events is deceptively melodramatic, for the ideals that drive them are more important than the events. Kate, for example, though in love with Jim, is attracted to Byways by his apparent ideals and by the thought of his doing something to implement them. She remembers her first taste of freedom during her Paris school days when he was a "roaring young revolutionary, planning salvation for a suffering but reluctant mankind" (41). Now he is a successful businessman. As such, in his new plans for the hotel business, he would supply not only the *Times* and the *Mail* for guests in the houses, but the *Worker* as well, and not only the Bible, but *Das Kapital,* as well. Thus "the twelve million people who vote Left can go into the bar or lounge without sitting off in a corner like pariahs" (43). In the tradition of Ibsen's and Shaw's women, Kate finally finds some outlet for her feelings of uselessness and boredom experienced on that earlier-referred-to "twentieth day."

Throughout, Kate not only remains firm in her ideals but acts on them. Informed by Margaret Byways about Walter's decision to leave the business and accept an offer from the government to serve as Minister of Food, she interprets that decision as disloyalty to their ideals, reminding him of his aim, "if ever a war came, . . . [to] use the opportunity to pitch the old gang out of the window, not support them" (105). Rod also is true, labeling Walter the Garibaldi of the business world, "still making the best of both worlds. The imperial lion, but the workers' colour" (109). Byways now incurs the disillusionment of both Margaret and Kate. Even Muriel Shufflepenny, an individualist in her own right, although maintaining a social facade as wife of Sir Ernest, describes Rod and Kate, survivors, as stronger and purer and thus luckier than most of us. She (Muriel) wanted only to raise Rod to be great and good, but found herself struggling to make him a success by her remarriage to Sir Ernest; Jim's dreams of being a historian gave way to his copywriting; Walter Byways raised only himself, not the oppressed. God is indeed a jealous god, who demands a high cost from those loyal to him.

From the battlefield, Jim, in his final letter to Kate shortly before his death, echoes Muriel's thoughts: "Dying to preserve the England of Milton and Hampden and Cromwell, of Burke and Shelley and Fox, of Bright and Gladstone, is no bad bargain; . . . He [Rod] and I are struggling for the same thing" (144). He concludes with a reference to a return to his interest in writing a history of English liberty.

The play may well be subtitled "A Battle on the Left and Right" on issues of business, education, and attitudes in general. Prevailing business morality is framed in language that seems strangely familiar more than fifty years later when words such as *arbitrage* and *leverage buyouts* have become public currency in a way that even the average nonbusinessperson understands them. To Kate, Walter explains Shufflepenny's genius "in discovering precisely what is legal":

> For example, supposing there's a hotel or suitable country house or building somewhere with a mortgage on it, he has a habit of buying up the mortgage through a nominee. Then when the interest on the mortgage falls into arrears, the nominee is instructed to exercise his power of sale and sells the whole property to Shufflepenny at a sacrifice price. Shufflepenny then re-sells it at a normal market price to Shufflepenny Hotels Limited, and pockets the difference. (32–33)

In a business war in which William's sudden inheritance of part of Shufflepenny's hotel shares becomes a negotiating factor, William, like Topaze in Levy's earlier play, outmaneuvers his would-be victimizer in a deal, hoping to help his daughter-in-law even when it involved her decision to leave Jim for Walter. And like the debates in *The Devil* between capitalism and socialism, the conflict here is between capitalism and an idealistic anarchy as practiced in the Settle family before the intrusions of Walter Byways and World War II.

This morality is played out even in the matter of education, where left-right issues are seen in a comment by Byways to the Shufflepennys on the merits of the contemporary behaviorist psychology that has replaced the old "subjective academic back numbers like James and Adler and Freud" (55).

Thus the play packs some plot lines that, although eventually merging in the reconciliation of Kate and Jim before he goes off to war, disperse the conflict between ideals and the real world among the many lives very differently. The effect at times, is a loss of dramatic focus, most obvious in the three changes of locale. In act 2, the scene is moved from the secluded domicile of the Settle's (in act 1) to the annual community cricket match at the affluent Shufflepenny's estate, where the main event turns out to be not the cricket match, but the maneuvering between old Shufflepenny and old Settle in an attempted buyout deal. Kate's resultant decision to leave seems to make the act a complete playlet in itself. In act 3, with the shift to a London locale, Margaret Byways enters the play, appearing unexpectedly, not to confront Kate with her (Margaret's) knowledge of Kate's affair with her husband, Walter, but to inform her about Walter's decision to leave his profitable

Red Lion Hotel venture to take a position in government. Both women are disillusioned with his decision. The rapidity of events—Margaret's appearance, then Rod's, then Jim's (along with Jim's departure for the war)—are melodramatically paced. Finally, in act 4, the play returns to the Settle home, and like the final chapter of *To the Lighthouse* in which surviving characters return to a cottage made empty by the death of Mrs. Ramsay and desolate by the ravages of war, Levy's play concludes with the reunion of four survivors whose ideals, though tattered, are intact, despite the devastating tests of the jealous god.

When Kate returns home, she finds a senile father whose bird watching has been replaced with writing letters to every name in the telephone directory, apologizing for his responsibility for the deaths in World War II. His ex-wife, Lady Shufflepenny, still lame from a train wreck, now helps him seal his envelopes. Rod returns that same day, broken from his four months in prison as a conscientious objector, and he anticipates a further term eventually. Finally, Kate receives news of Jim's death at the front. The play closes with William's last lines as he licks envelopes:

> My son is killed. What of it? . . . Thousands are dying every day. Trillions are dead. This aged earth contains the dust of more dead men than there are live ones. Am I to pause and weep because MY son is dead? Because he is mine? . . . I've work to do; I'm in a hurry. At seventy you're in a hurry. (145)

As a dramatist whose subject and technique depend on debate, Levy does not build a plot up to the conventional climax. Instead, the effect is one of story lines more appropriate to fiction than to a three-hour stage drama. The absence of dramatic impact is there even in the moving reconciliation scene between Jim and Kate before the former's departure for the war. Their brief confrontation with each other and with their respective ideals seems an exigency of wartime as much as a passionate reunion.

Some of the time characters seem to inhabit the ideas, rather than vice versa, particularly in the first two acts, making the story and characters seem secondary to their ideas. This impression is reinforced by the telling names: Settle, Shufflepenny, and Byways.

The reviews of *The Jealous God* were mixed, calling attention to the serious issues dealt with in the play, but the presence of "too many threads, woven [into] too indeterminate a pattern."[16] Both the *Times* and the *New York Times* reviewers refer to the main theme, the divided purpose, as an idea that did not emerge clearly until late in the play. Still another critic, F. Majdalany, refers to Levy and to Karel Capek *(The Mother)* as two *angry* playwrights, a term that became popular in the 1956 stage revolution begun by John Osborne's *Look Back in Anger.* Leading the distinguished cast were Constance Cummings (whose "personal grace and vitality . . . accomplish much")[17], Irene Vanbrugh, C. V. France, and Frank Allenby.

Levy's own career as a dramatist with liberal views would follow the curvature of the careers of Jim and Walter, the former as demonstrated in Levy's own service in World War II (and in his earlier role, along with others in his profession, to persuade the United States to enter the war), and the latter in Levy's entry into the political arena as M.P. from 1945–50, followed by a return to the writing of plays.

In its realism, *The Jealous God* is precursor to Levy's tightly constructed last play, *Public and Confidential.*

5

1946–1966: Playful Philosophical Debates

Clutterbuck: An Artificial Comedy (1946)

With its run of 366 performances at Wyndham's Theatre, *Clutterbuck* enjoys the distinction as the longest London run of any Levy play. Belonging to the group of Levy's pure comedies and farces—such as *This Woman Business, Springtime for Henry,* and *Hollywood Holiday*—it pretends to nothing more than a highly entertaining evening. If *This Woman Business* is based on the idea of *Love's Labour's Lost, Springtime for Henry* written in the tradition of the Restoration comedy of manners about two rakish gentlemen, and *Hollywood Holiday* constructed as a situational Hollywood farce, *Clutterbuck* is a variation of the geometrically designed comedy made famous by Noel Coward in *Private Lives* (1941).

Coward's literary geometry consists of a series of symmetrical situations and conversations that provide the author with opportunities to create laughter and to comment ironically on the contradictions of married life. When the husband, Elyot, of one honeymooning couple in France discovers his former wife, Amanda, occupying with her new husband an adjacent room, he insists on leaving. His wife, Sibyl, however, protests. Similarly Amanda, catching a glimpse of Elyot, asks her husband, Victor, to move to another hotel. Like Sibyl, he refuses. What then happens is that the dullness of their current marriages glaringly asserts itself to both Elyot and Amanda, and they run off to Amanda's Paris flat. Pursued by their current spouses and discovered by said spouses in an exhausted condition after a battle that had turned physical, they sneak off, suitcases in hand, with the arguing voices of Sibyl and Victor trailing behind them.

Coward's thin and artificial plot gives way to the even more contrived but entertaining series of dialogues as the old relationship between Elyot and Amanda returns, stimulated by the return of the tempestuous verbal and physical wrestling that had been the cause of their divorce and the reason for their remarriages to relatively calm spouses.

Everything in the play is arranged symmetrically: precisely matched terraces and terrace furniture and similar doors through which characters conveniently enter and exit, one person or one couple at a time. With equal precision, Sibyl appears on the terrace, calling to Elyot in almost the same words that Victor, later appearing on the terrace, utters to Amanda. Again, Sybil and Victor in similar ways inquire of their spouses about their previous marriages. If Sibyl tells Elyot of her dislike of suntans on women, Victor relays the same dislike to Amanda. It is this mathematically precise doubling—one of the oldest devices of comedy—that creates Coward's laughter. The precision is just as easily undone, even as it is maintained, in the furious arguments in Paris, between Amanda and Elyot and, as well, between Sibyl and Victor.

In his play, Levy adds to the Cowardian quartet a third couple who are there to help move the plot. He adds, also, a dimension of caricature to the Edwardian speech habits and manners that in one character at least echo more the stereotypes of P. G. Wodehouse than the stylish wit of Coward.

Some distinct artifices serve to make a thin plot more intriguing than it really is. One is the title character, Clutterbuck, who makes three very brief appearances and never utters a word. Another is the aforementioned increase from a quartet of characters—two couples—to a sextet. The plot of the play involves the discovery by two of the husbands that each had enjoyed, previous to his marriage, an affair with the wife of Clutterbuck (Melissa) and a similar discovery by two of the wives that the other had had a liaison with Clutterbuck.

On a four-week cruise and already bored with each other after four days, two couples—Deborah and Arthur Pomfret and Jane and Julian Pugh—find their attempts at civility reaching the breaking point. Arthur runs a rubber plantation, and Julian is a novelist. Julian is a straight man to the Wodehousian Arthur, a fathead by his wife's straightforward description. The two men have little in common, and Julian is obviously bored. When Arthur is addressed he automatically responds with a question—"Who? Me?"—or an indefinite "Yes. What? Yes. Well-um . . ."[1] Not knowing what to say to each other, Pugh and Pomfret in the opening dialogue of the play, finally resort to saying together: "Where's Deborah? Where's Jane?" Their conversation through much of the farce runs in a kind of dead-end inanity:

> *Pomfret:* I'm sorry. What were you saying?
> *Pugh:* Oh, nothing. I just said where's Deborah?
> *Pomfret:* Oh, Deborah. I expect she's in her stateroom. She went back after dinner to powder her nose.
> *Pugh:* Oh.
> *Pomfret:* Where did you say—er—Jane was.
> *Pugh:* I—I think she's in her stateroom. Powdering her nose. . . . Now, I suppose we commit a pungent aphorism on women.
> *Pomfret:* What's that?
> *Pugh:* Nothing.
> *Pomfret:* Oh. Thought you said something.
> *Pugh:* No. Not a thing. . . . Well, see you later.
> *Pomfret: (cheered)* Yes. Cheerio, Pugh.
> *Pugh:* So long, Pomfret. (6–7)

As the Wodehousian character, Arthur combines dullness and predictability in both speech and manners. He wishes to discuss only serious subjects, such as Julian's novels, whereas novelist Julian prefers to watch the Marx Brothers. Julian also has an instinctive hostility to Arthur's pretense at culture. In one of his vain attempts to involve Julian in a discussion of his novel, Arthur wants to know if there is a bicycle in the novel, whose title is *Cicero's Bicycle*. When Julian assures him there is no bicycle, Arthur responds, "I see. One is being slow." In the continuing dialogue, Arthur repeatedly refers to himself as "one." "One merely ventured to inquire about the title." He is open game for Julian's devastating comments.

Arthur's fatheadedness is at its funniest during moments such as the silence between Deborah and Jane after each has hurled insults at the other. When he appears, running after Melissa, he stops dead in his tracks and fumblingly tries to cover his embarrassment:

> Well, well, well! You two having a good time? Delightful spot. Ten years since I was here last. That must have been in . . . No, it wasn't: it was the year before. Because old Beanstock was still alive. More or less! Poor old Beanstock. You two never knew old Beanstock. Delightful chap. Like a mother to me when I first went out East. We were inseparable. They used to call us Arthur and the Beanstock! Ha, ha,

ha! Reference to the old fairy story, you see. Very amusing! Crawshay-Parsons thought that one up. He was always quick. No, come to think of it, it wasn't old Crawshay-Parsons, either. It was young Finkelstein. He was quicker still. I say, what a heat! It was never much hotter in old Pubgore itself. How about a nice cold drink, eh? *(He claps his hands.)* Waiter! Or better still some hot tea. That's the stuff to cool you off. *(He claps again)* Funny, it's pouring off me. Just shows you: get away for a few weeks and what happens? It just pours off you. *(He claps)* (39)

Deborah pours cold water on his monologue with her "Darling do stop applauding yourself." (39)

In geometrical fashion, the wives in some respects serve as doubles of the men. Although married to Arthur, Deborah is the smarter of the two and informs Jane, married to the highbrow author, that she (Jane) has a lot in common with Arthur. Jane agrees, and the women form a bond of sympathy in their understanding of their husbands. When Deborah mentions Arthur's morbid hankering to do what he calls interesting things and to meet interesting people, the women exchange views:

> *Jane:* He's crazy. Our life is infested with interesting people and they're so dull. That's why Julian was looking forward to meeting Arthur. He knew Arthur wasn't interesting. I assure you the disappointment's mutual. Arthur tried to talk to him about the art of John Gielgud and "Mourning Becomes Electra." Poor Julian was at a loss. Highbrows only go to see the Marx Brothers.
> *Deborah:* It is a shame. There are hundreds of things in Julian's new book that Arthur keeps trying to discuss with him.
> *Jane:* I know. Unfortunately Julian's a rather peculiar author; he doesn't enjoy talking about his books.
> *Deborah:* You mean with fellows like Arthur?
> *Jane:* No, with anyone; but especially with Arthur.
> *Deborah:* What do you mean by "fellows like Arthur"? Go on, be natural.
> *Jane:* I was going to be. I mean people who haven't the foggiest idea what he's writing about or why. You know; like Arthur. After all we don't have to pretend. Arthur's whole charm is that he's fatheaded.
> *Deborah: (romantically)* I know; he's the most fatheaded man in all the world. (12)

When Deborah first appears, she is immediately established as lovely and beautiful, sighing wistfully at the moon as she repeats

Lorenzo's lines from *The Merchant of Venice,* lines, incidentally, which Levy, in *Madame Bovary,* used to dramatize the romantic mood of Emma, alone on her wedding night:

> The moon shines bright. In such a night as this
> When the sweet wind did gently kiss the trees
> And they did make no noise, Troilus methinks . . . (7)

Her mood of romance is undercut by the voice of Jane, also enchanted by the moon, "Crikey, what a night." Deborah returns: "All right, darling; you needn't exert yourself. I've done all that and there's nobody here" (7). Thus the characters of the two wives and their husbands define themselves. What they do have in common is that they know who and what they and their husbands are— in the tradition of the women in Barrie's plays. Lifelong friends, they discover that since their marriages they have lost count of each other. Deborah speaks of her "moral contract" to Arthur: "He wanted a woman of sensibility. I said, here you are. He wanted the kind of woman who sighed and quoted poetry in moonlight. I quoted. He wanted a woman who choked with emotion at chamber music that he'd have liked to like. I duly choked. He wanted a woman who gurgled with delight when bestial little children dragged their jammy fingers over her fresh make-up. I duly gurgled" (8). Jane, as well, has her own moral contract with Julian, who wants her only to be natural. To him, being natural included belching explosively at least twice after dinner. Comparing notes on their disparate husbands, they acknowledge that after four days on a four-week cruise the husbands already are driving each other crazy.

Two characters, Arthur and Melissa, are sheer caricatures, Arthur in his fatheadedness and Melissa in her schoolgirl speech habits, consisting mostly of adding the syllable *le* or *el* to words: "All rightle." "I had a nasty shockle." She is in full fashionably linguistic glory as she compares, in their presence, her two former lovers:

> Besides, the funny thing was that my tastes were different when I was with Artie. With Julie I should have loathed smoked salmon and champagne, while a toasted herring all mixed up with Artie-Partie would have made me positively ick. It's funny how men turn you 'round their little finger; you find yourself being exactly what they want. (48–49)

Melissa, like Deborah and Jane earlier, knows her men and asserts her knowledge in her behavior.

The plot consists primarily of the discoveries by the two husbands that the other has, before his marriage, been a lover of the wife (Melissa Clutterbuck) of the third couple and by the two wives that the other has been at one time the mistress of the husband (Clutterbuck) of the third couple. The two wives, however, retain their fantasies with fleeting glances of Clutterbuck, whereas the husbands actively engage in conversations with Melissa.

The geometric pattern of the plot includes the mechanical formula of having everything that is said and done turned upside down not only once, but sometimes twice or thrice. Whatever the women hate, the men like and vice versa in the manner of traditional farce. However friendly the two women are at the start, they turn into farcically clawing creatures, and then return, each to her own conversational style, as at the end when Deborah once again indulges herself in her romantic "How beauteous the sight from here, How beauteous the morn" and Jane utters her customary "Crikey, what a view!" (74). Similarly, the early husbands resume their civilized modes, with Arthur's reassuring fatheadedness, "I hope I'm not boring you, old man?" and Julian's more reassuring "What makes you think that, my dear fellow?" (72–73).

Another geometrical device is the time-honored doubling of a situation. If Jane has gastronomical problems that end in belches, Deborah has her convenient headaches. Even Melissa, abandoning her composure as she plays her childlike games, bursts into uncontrollable boohoos, warning that the next time the men knock on her doors, those doors will be unlocked.

The doubling motif is there in the use of the bedroom doors, so essential in a Feydeau farce. Here a variation of that ploy is used in the scene on shore in which Melissa's bedroom is located between those of Julian and Arthur. Each husband is convinced that the other had gained entrance to Melissa's room. The doors, however, never open, as Melissa has locked them. Thus, nothing comes of the two husbands' maneuvers. With the wives, the possibility of a renewed romance with Clutterbuck hardly exists as he makes brief appearances, is given no dialogue, and exists only in the fantasies of the two wives.

Though its reliance on the artifices of farce is nearly total, *Clutterbuck's* success is essentially due to the caricatured speech patterns and manners that result in the necessary recognition by an

English audience. Despite its contrast with the more complexly plotted action of *Springtime for Henry, Clutterbuck* shares with that play some of Levy's best comic dialogue. The earlier farce was more popular with American audiences; obversely, *Clutterbuck* entertained English audiences to give Levy his longest run in London. In New York, Brooks Atkinson described *Clutterbuck* as a "sophisticated farce by an impish playwright." The New York production, however, did "not sip much of the cream of Mr. Levy's jest."[2] The difficulties for American actors and audiences consisted of the in-jokes and popular English slang such as "mad dogs and Englishmen," and "stewed prunes," whose lack of recognition by American audiences renders the thin plot even thinner. Absent in both farces is any hint of moral, psychological, or philosophical issues. Absent, also, are those touches of the grotesque found in earlier plays.

Despite its thinness of plot, considered by some to be too stretched-out for a whole play, *Clutterbuck* has its compensations in the thoroughly Edwardian character types whose habits of speech and behavior evoked instant recognition from an English audience. In London, the *Times* reviewer called attention to the "brightest moments . . . [as] those which see the inarticulate stolidity of Mr. Radford [as Pomfret] blocking the demon verbal deliveries of Mr. Wayne [as Arthur] disguised as a highbrow novelist." Singled out for special praise was Constance Cummings's taking "with splendid assurance the one chance she has to throw some romantic weight about, and her faint in the third act is superbly sudden and complete."[3]

Of all of Levy's plays, *Clutterbuck* seems the most British with its nearly total dependence on the types of middle-class British who populate the stories of P. G. Wodehouse. Critics have been in near unanimity in their recognition of dialogue as Levy's distinctive talent. In *Clutterbuck,* this talent is given free rein as perhaps in no other of his comedies and dramas. The result is a very funny collection of English stereotypes that easily explain the popularity of the comedy.

Cupid and Psyche (1952)

Yet another farce based on distinctive speech habits, *Cupid and Psyche* relies on the fashionable jargon of a Freudian, a biologist-anthropologist, a Pankhurstlike feminist, a bookie, and a Calvinistic Scotsman. In this respect the farce is a variation of the source of humor in *Clutterbuck* whose Edwardian characters wallow in the fashion of current slang—a slang, however, empty of ideas. More like *This Woman Business, Cupid and Psyche* is clearly a debate-of-ideas farce, about art (photography), science, psychology, anthropology, sociology (feminism), and sex. Though with a larger cast and more complex plot, *Cupid and Psyche* is akin also to *Springtime for Henry* in its dependence on the amorous and gambling adventures of two rakes, whose story is the frame for the debates.

In a dedicatory note to his son Jonathan, Levy refers to the "topicalities" in *Cupid and Psyche*. These, he continues, include fashionable freudianisms, surrealist idiom, clothes, slang, and theatrical convention. Levy qualifies the topicality of the farce, however, by commenting on the truth underlying the topics—that they spring from human impulses which defy change, except for the forms that they adopt in a given time. Some of these impulses include Miss Thompson's self-contradicting feminism, Mildred's caricaturing of her betters, Thompson's fear of the responsibilities of free will, Deptford's adaptive sexual talents, Gabriel's resentment of pain, and Mac's fear of a mechanical universe. The Cupid and Psyche myth (eros and soul) is a convenient structure within which the fashionable feminist, psychological, and scientific positions are argued.

When the Earl of Deptford (bookmaker, rake, and recently made Earl) arrives at the studio of a photographer, Gabriel, to have the customary photograph taken as befits a newly titled person, he finds himself, a self-acknowledged philistine, in a bohemian world to which he adapts on his own terms. Those terms involve his instant attraction to Mildred, an amazingly informed and articulate model whose qualifications are her having worked for a psychologist at one time. Cupid's arrow finds its mark, and that very night she moves in with the Earl—thus the title of the play.

Complicating the situation is the surprise arrival of Thompson, a Canadian genetic scientist (and Gabriel's young, virginal friend), whom Deptford decides to initiate into the rites of Cupid by offering him his mistress, Mildred. For Thompson the rites prove unsuccessful, and he returns to his happy existence in a sexual desert, acknowledging as he does so his success in sublimation, if not sublimity. Deptford, renouncing his rakish life, reclaims Mildred and announces his reformation as monogamist.

The catalyst for the action is a second arrival—that of Thompson's unmarried mother, whose ideas are in the feminist mold of the Pankhursts. In the scéne à faire, she reveals the big secret of the farce, her having chosen Deptford, in their Oxford student days, to be the father of her son. As a result, Deptford, now fifty-one, can no longer pass for thirty-one. Reluctantly admitting to his age, Deptford informs Thompson that father and stepmother (Mildred) will always make him welcome. With secrets now in the open, normal patterns of life are resumed with the exception of Deptford's change to monogamy and Mildred's marriage to a philanderer.

Despite the dispersed actions of the plot, the dialogue keeps the comedy intact throughout the play. In act 1, in an attempt to explain Deptford's conventional behavior, Mildred and Thompson vie with each other in offering, respectively, their Freudian and scientific analyses of the personality of Deptford—a philistine clearly out of his depth with the intellectuals and bohemians, although even he is infected by their ideas. When Mildred tries to find symbolism in the subjects of Deptford's dreams, he confesses his commonest dream: "Winning the Derby on a donkey from Margate Sands." Triumphantly, she exclaims: "Aggression, fantasy! Self-aggrandisement! Inferiority trauma! Roaring psychic-castration complex! Riding his father, with whip and bridle, to an ignominious victory! . . . . The donkey was his father-substitute."[4]

She and Thompson egg each other on, with Thompson summing up their comic debate:

Whether I diagnose infantile insecurity or a defective chromosome or Mildred diagnoses a deranged libido or whether we decide the patient is merely overeating or has contracted a lesion of the brain when playing Oranges and Lemons in his nursery or suffers from too little oxygen or too much sugar, or, even, as Professor Otto Rank would maintain, has never recovered from the terrible initial shock of being born, whatever we decide, the whole groping paraphernalia of diagnosis and treatment does somehow and sometimes help to relieve the patient, even though it may well be the wrong diagnosis and the wrong treatment.(33)

If the laughter of act 1 is primarily due to the witty exchanges of ideas, that of act 2 is based on farcical plot actions at Deptford's

party. These include the appearances of two women of questionable social status; of Deptford's rakish friend, Fox, and his female
friend; and, finally, of Thompson's mother, whose surprise entrance is the catalyst for the revelation of secrets that not only
enliven the action, but also bring all to a most happy conclusion.
The major secret of the play is the affair between Miss Thompson
and Deptford when both were students at Oxford, the result of that
liaison, unknown to Deptford, being a son, Thompson. Deptford
finally confesses to his real age, like Miss Thompson's, fifty-one.
Both, however, even with signs of aging, are resilient and as lively
as any of the younger members of the group.

Miss Thompson, feminist par excellence, has refused to marry
the father of her son and has insisted on reversing tradition in the
professions by being a man's tailor. With Shavian aplomb, she
admits to learning two things:

> . . . first that the difference between one man and another was so tri-
> fling that ready-made suits were more than good enough, and secondly,
> that men were so corroded with what is usually termed feminine vanity
> that they didn't think so. . . . I therefore invented a system whereby
> prefabricated sections of a suit were woven by thousands in the mill
> and sewn together later after . . . a fitting with the customer. It brought
> a great deal of happiness into a great many little manly hearts and a
> great many dollars into my till. (78)

On the matter of her entrance to a man's trade, she utters a
reprimand to her questioner:

> Have a little self-respect, girl. Once upon a time only men were secre-
> taries—or bus conductors or painters or business executives or bur-
> glars or politicians or matadors or doctors or all-in wrestlers or lawyers
> or agitators. (76)

Now there are "male cooks, male milliners, male nurses, male
tailors for women; and I decided it was high time there was a female
tailor for men" (77).

The topicalities debated in the play eventually merge in a confrontation between Mildred and Thompson—when she is supposed
to be initiating him into the rites of Cupid—about the relative merits of patriarchies and matriarchies. The real matriarchist turns
out to be Thompson, not his mother or Mildred. Matriarchy, he
argues, is more than feminism. He explains that feminism is too

frequently a male ruse to lure renegade women "into forgetting the wisdom of the female in the hope of acquiring the lesser talents of the male" (101). "The true feminist is one who repudiates masculine standards rather than emulates them" (102).

Deptford's philistine contribution to the topical debate consists of reproaching himself for defaulting in his duties as father to Thompson. His temporary effort to rectify the situation by marrying his son's mother ends when he discovers that Mildred and Thompson enjoyed "the delights of intellectual parity" rather than of a sexual encounter. He is reminiscent of Henry in *Springtime for Henry* whose reform is only a temporary aberration. Even as he proposes marriage to Mildred, he sees for the first time Blanche, Gabriel's secretary, appealingly clad in her boss's pajamas.

Among the many debates, that between predestinarian Mac and the scientific Thompson is doubly comic for the Scottish accent brought to it by Mac:

> *Mac:* Tell me, professor; are ye here of your own free choice?
> *Thompson:* What? Of course I am.
> *Mac:* Interesting. I thought it might have been the force of genetic predisposition. We must na' underrate the gene.
> *Thompson:* Ah, I see. You know, I never denied that choice, whether real or not, is at least a convenient fiction.
> *Mac:* Aye; Mildred will be flattered. He didn't really choose to come haime wi' ye. That was a polite and convenient fiction. The choice was made for him. It was made by his genes and his chromosomes, by his upbringing, by his ancestry, by his environment, by circumstances beyond his control. (95)

Still another Shavian style confrontation is that between Miss Thompson and Deptford, sparked by an innocent question by Crystal (one of the questionable ladies at the party) about Miss Thompson's choice of Willie Deptford as a lover:

> *Thompson:* Yes. Why in the world?
> *Mother:* Because I was unwilling to accept the indignity of a mere seduction. I was not prepared to become somebody's scalp. Willie may not have had much to offer; but at least he could and did offer me respect. He had no vulgar notions of male superiority. How could he? On the contrary he was surprised and grateful that I even noticed him. We could proceed upon a basis of equality and dignity. It was for this reason that I decided—

Deptford: (exploding at last) You decided! Of all the presumptuous nonsense! I decided!

Mother: You? Don't be silly.

Deptford: I remember the whole thing most distinctly, what I said and did and how you reacted and how in less time than I ever dreamed of—

Mother: (really cross) You impudent blusterer! Are you presuming to claim that you took the initiative?

Deptford's explanation of his initiative is that his poetic instinct to steer by the stars rather than by cold calculation directed him to concentrate on admiring her intelligence rather than the customary feminine traits, thus justifying his modus operandi and, as well, gaining the support of young Thompson. Yet his support of Thompson was also his final humiliation: "All these years I had been led to think of myself as the living emblem of free love in all its fine rebelliousness and proud equality. Now I find myself no more than a corporealized leer" (85).

In a *quid pro quo* reversal, Deptford suffers financially even as Thompson's scientific authority is put into question. Having persuaded Deptford, by a genetic argument that he should not invest in a race horse (Lily White), Fox announces that Lily White has won the race. Deptford's consolation, however, is that despite his loss, he has gained Mildred.

Levy's gallery of feminist, Freudian, and scientific caricatures is augmented interestingly by the lesser characters: Gabriel, the artist-photographer, in whose studio the group coalesces; his Scottish assistant, Mac, who expresses his view of modish ideas on predestination and free will; and Blanche, Gabriel's "general factotum."

Although Gabriel, a self-styled misogynist of sorts, does not participate seriously in the witty debates, he functions more importantly as a part of the plot mechanics, providing the setting and the situation in which the others meet. At times, however, he has some of the perennially comic function of a Jacques-style misogynist. He sees no need to smile. "You can't smile often! In a world of poverty, starvation, hatred, disease, cuelty, injustice, greed, and atom bombs, what in the name of all that's bestial is there to smile at? Children smile for joy, schoolboys smile at jokes but grown men know there's nothing joyful and nothing jocular in this vale of tears. They merely smile, in desperation, because it makes a change" (24).

Later in the play, in response to Fox's unease at finding himself in "a funny kind of party," Gabriel responds: "Life, my dear Harry, is a funny kind of party, so funny that sometimes our laughter drowns the screeching of the ravens and the whirring of the carrion winds; but not for long" (89). Following, as it does, Levy's poignantly realistic *Return to Tyassi, Cupid and Psyche* can be seen as Levy's recognition of the need for laughter or "a party." Gabriel's comments on the world situation reflects Levy's direct participation in politics and in the causes he embraced—the fight against poverty, the atom bomb, injustice, and stage censorship.

The pastiche of characters and attitudes assembled in *Cupid and Psyche,* like those in *This Woman Business,* are contained within a conventional plot structure built around a secret withheld from the audience until the second act. The themes, especially feminism, are handled as issues of the time. Issues that create problems in the serious plays take the form of fantasies in the Barrie-like dramas and are the basis for the plot and witty dialogue of the comedies. Levy was accurate in his description of the underlying nature of his character types as those who will continue in their chosen attitude and modus operandi.

As a discussion/debate of ideas, *Cupid and Psyche* marks a return to the comedy-of-ideas style that Levy perfects in *The Rape of the Belt* (1956). Shavian wit permeates the play. An abundance, at times overabundance, of reversals in ideas, plot, and wit, so essential to comedy and farce, is in clear evidence from beginning to end without the distracting intrusion of morality.

The Rape of the Belt (1957)

In *The Rape of the Belt* Levy has come full circle in returning to the theme of his first play, *This Woman Business.* Reversing the patriarchal setting of the earlier play, he now fights the battle of the sexes on matriarchal territory, in the context of the Greek myths of Heracles' ninth labor: the wresting of her girdle from Antiope, Queen of the Amazons. In the 1925 comedy, the playing field is a male bastion, a country house to which the characters retreat to enjoy the peace of an all-male society or to get away from a variety of personal problems caused in part by women in their lives. In 1957, Levy expands the subject in three ways, by changing the geography to a political entity, the "beetling city of

Themiscyra"; the personal battles to political ones; and currently feminist attitudes to their mythical counterparts, involving even the eternal domestic wrangling between Zeus and Hera. The two comedies share the subject of matriarchy, which is only one of many themes in the earlier farce but the central and sharply focused idea in *Rape of the Belt.*

In *Cupid and Psyche,* Thompson berates his mother for the superficiality of feminists who emulate rather than repudiate male standards. "The feminine lady who regards boxing as a male brutality is a better feminist than the lady who seeks to establish equality by becoming a boxer herself."[5] And in descending to a domestic metaphor, Thompson responds to Mildred's query about the renegade woman who uses her nails rather than her fists: "I'd much rather Joe Louis scratched me than hit me. If you give up scratching for hitting, you play into my [male] hands. That's what happened to Mrs. Pankhurst."[6] In elevating the arguments of Thompson from the prankish situations in *Cupid and Psyche* to the sustained high comedy of ideas in *The Rape of the Belt,* Levy joins the ranks of Wilde, Shaw, and Giraudoux.

Again using a prologue as an introduction to his debate, Levy launches his battle of the sexes immediately in a scene that depicts Hera and Zeus as spectators of a play about the legendary rape of Antiope, a play "of which we [Hera and Zeus] form the somewhat undisciplined prologue."[7] The prologue begins with set speeches by each of the two gods, speeches that deteriorate humorously into the domestic squabbles for which they have become famous. In a niche on either side of the playing area, Hera and Zeus accuse each other of marital infidelity, the consequences of which are their respective bastard sons, Hephaestus and Heracles. Their initial fight concludes with a victory by Zeus who insists that the players skip the introductory scene in which "King Eurystheus imposed upon my ill-starred son for his Ninth Labour the task of wresting from proud Queen Antiope her glittering royal belt, most prized possession of her fierce subject Amazons" (4). His victory in the argument foreshadows that of Heracles over Antiope at the end of the play.

Arriving late after Hera had delivered her part of the opening monologue, Zeus is queried by Hera about where he has been and with whom—"Leda, Io, Europa, Semele or some new strumpet?" He responds by wondering what she does with her time, reminding her, in turn, of her infidelity that led to the birth of Hephaestus.

One quibble leads to the next, including Hera's charge that the rules are different for the sexes and Zeus's countercharge that her defeatism could end in her defeat. Why, he asks, must she rate feminine patience below male valor? Levy concludes the argument in the prologue with the implication that the desire to be like a male will only lead to defeat, as the ensuing play goes on to demonstrate.

The involvement of Hera and Zeus, begun in the prologue, grows as the events they are watching on stage remind them of their own domestic grievances. They not only provide a running commentary during the performance, but also eventually desert their roles as spectators and interfere in the events they are watching. When Zeus, apologizing for his flatulence, belches wind to propel the Greek ships, Hera, not to be outdone, enters the body of Hippolyte, thereby gaining a personal revenge on Zeus for his famous Amphytrion escapade. The last laugh, however, is Zeus's, for Hera precludes her hope of victory when she enables the peace-loving Amazons to imitate the militaristic actions of the Greeks as a means of settling disputes.

Commenting on his own lot, even Zeus is sad: "That's one of the troubles with eternity; it is so unavoidably repetitious. No wonder we Gods envy you your mortality. Life without end. Yes, and without surprises. How I sometimes covet your almost impenetrable ignorance! In a God's eye there are no new visions; in a God's ear no new turns. Listen! To you tonight, that was a new tune. To me? *(He shakes his head)* It has indeed ancient words" (63).

The plot proceeds from the prologue in an incremental reversing of centuries-old male attitudes of governance to a point at which Heracles and Theseus eventually find themselves without something to fight for or against. Only when Hera, in answer to Antiope's prayer for help (and, thereby, hoping to avenge Zeus's fathering of Heracles) enters the body of Hippolyte to mobilize the Amazons for war, are the two men able to recover from their apparent defeat. Ironically, it is Antiope's choice of Hera rather than her traditional Ashtoreth that initiates Hera's action. The Amazons themselves, then, are responsible for changing the rules of the game, now having to fight on male rather than feminist terms. Recognizing her error, Antiope sadly describes the change to Theseus:

It is a deep change, deeper than I can explain. It will not last but meanwhile the mischief will have been done. We shall have betrayed ourselves, we shall have lost faith, and, if WE sink, there may be left only a world of barbarism a world of men, with women as their corrupted satellites. I am not rancorous at you, my lord, but where you dominate there must be degradation. In the name of equality, we shall be tricked into descending to your level. Oh, my Lord, we, too, have faults, grave, ugly faults and follies, but at least—you must see this—we are not worshippers of death. (66)

From this sense of self-betrayal Antiope refuses to accept Heracles' inclination to return the belt, saying, "Even if I took it, it would no longer be ours. We have betrayed it" (75). In Shavian style, they exchange good-byes:

Antiope: You—are a man, a true man. You carry the heavy past on your back, so yours is a world of fear and you must be brave.
Heracles: You are a true woman. You carry the future under your heart, so yours is a world of hope and must be faithful.
Antiope: Two worlds.
Heracles: Two half worlds.
. . . .
Antiope: Your half is waiting.
Heracles: Yes.
Antiope: And mine: or what is left of it.
Heracles: May the gods one day join them. (75–76)

Hippolyte, on the other hand, accepts the traditionalist position on the role of women in a patriarchy in her decision to leave with Theseus. She rationalizes her decision:

Mind you, *he* [Theseus] doesn't *know* they have power, but obviously they must, mustn't they? I mean if they didn't, there would be chaos? (76)

The opening scene of act 1 establishes the play's situational wit in a meeting between Hippobomene and Theseus. The counterpart to the Greek Haphaestus, Hippobomene happens also to be aunt to the two sister queens, Antiope and Hippolyte. She is their equal in enjoying the respect of the community. Her name suggests her size, and she is referred to by one of the visitors as a hippopotamus. As his hand clutches the wall over which he peers, Theseus is mistaken by Hippobomene for one of the studs escaped from the "Farm." She pins his hand painfully to the wall and sets in motion a rapidly accelerating series of contrasts, most of which are put-downs of the civilized behavior of the Western world.

She admits, much to Heracles' chagrin and discomfiture, that, no, she has never heard of his name. When Antiope appears, she too, does not recognize the heroes nor has she heard of Theseus' lineage: Aegeus and Pittheus. Antiope further rattles Heracles by returning his compliment on her beauty, thereby establishing a bond of equality between the sexes. She is more impressed by his telling of his legendary feats than by the feats themselves, and she acknowledges that Theseus and Heracles are men by gender and heroes by profession. As he relates the murders for which he is doing penance, Heracles' growing unease is noticeable. To shift some of the embarrassment, he calls attention to Theseus' deeds that in the glare of a peaceful civilization are, like his, anything but heroic.

One by one the assumptions of superiority by the Greek visitors are dismantled. They discover that men are kept in hygienic sheds at the Farm and that they, Heracles and Theseus, had been mistaken for escapees from the Farm. They are told that the Minister of Defense, Queen Hippolyte, has nothing to do. So when the men find themselves politely proposing conditions for war, Antiope replies that "even the proposal to slaughter each other in a civilized way does not attract me. Forgive me" (18).

The explosion of perpetuated myths about Amazons occurs in a witty exchange about pectorectomies. Based on the theory that "nothing is too wild for masculine credulity" (20), a great-Aunt Euphemia had conceived the rumor of the amputation of right breasts "so as to further our skill with the bow and arrow" (20).

This myth is one that Antiope has especially enjoyed. It is only one of many stories about the fierce, warlike civilization that evoke giggles from the women. The men become exasperated at not being taken seriously by the women, even as they are enamored of the golden beauty of their hostesses. Anachronistically Heracles assumes chivalric manners as he boasts of success in subjecting women.

Act 1 ends with Hippolyte's acknowledging that "it sounds a rather nice game" and with Hera's announcing victory to Zeus with her own bit of gloating: "Will you walk into my parlour said the spider to the fly." Zeus's response is "You may be right, my dear. We'll see. We'll see" (30).

Act 2 continues the hospitable entertainment enjoyed by the Greeks even as they plan to "pinch" the belt. Occasionally they feel the need to justify their attempt because historically they are "supposed to be heroes," and, after all, "one doesn't want to go down in history as a petty pilferer" (37). They discover, furthermore, after considering complicated techniques to unlock the tower in which the belt, they suppose, is contained, that there are no locks or keys in the country. They discover, finally, that the belt has disappeared and so decide to leave to consult the oracle for new directions. Because of his lingering good-bye to Antiope, Heracles is left behind by his men.

Zeus's and Hera's direct intervention (a deus ex machina ploy) in act 3, temporarily changes the playing field from ideas to action. Hippolyte is struck by lightning, feels dizzy on awaking, and has instantly changed from the idle, languid lover of baths to a militaristic female. Her transformation is the responsibility of her sister queen, Antiope, who, before choosing Hera, asks Hippolyte, "Do you think it would be very wrong—I mean, do you think Ashtoreth would mind if, just for this once, we tried another goddess?" (54). The responsibility thus, Levy asserts, lies with mortals, not the gods. Once more, as in other of his plays, the demands of the jealous god are crucial to the plot.

Although the gods' interference and the later battle in act 3 shift the comedic style from the flow of witty ideas to a farcical series of battle scenes, delightful verbal wit continues, as in the exchange among Amazonians as they view the behavior of the Greeks:

Thalestris: Men simply are not to be trusted.

. . . .

Hippobomene: Oh, they've behaved disgustingly. Whenever one of our side stumbled and fell, they calmly ran off with her weapons. Sometimes, they didn't even wait for accidents. They'd go up to our troops as cool as you please and simply wrench their arms out of their hands.

. . .

Diasta: Look! Look there—under the olive trees. What are they doing to them? Look, Hippo, can you see?
Thalestris: Well, really! (74)

When Zeus, explaining away the thunder and rising wind as mere flatulence, interferes to return the departing Greek ships to land, Hera gains her revenge for his Amphytrion escapade by deciding to enter the body of Hippolyte. The playing field is now even, as the Greeks, having forgotten Heracles, who was left marooned on land, return, and the Amazons suddenly become militarists.

From this point, Greeks and Amazons fight until Hera exits Hippolyte's body and the battle ends in shambles for the women, as Thalestris, the Minister of Maternity, advises the women to run. Hera responds to Zeus's mild acknowledgment of victory with "If I could have trained them for a little longer." Self-confidently, Zeus agrees, "No doubt. No doubt" (75).

For the short time that the Amazons enjoyed victory, that victory was gained by their ability to reduce the "heroes by profession" to a verbally fumbling, inept duo of lovers, and, in the process, reverse Western civilized customs and attitudes. While they fought on their own grounds of verbal debate, they were successful. For the first two acts, they had the upper hand in their contrasting of their way of life with that of the Greeks. In the gradual disarming of the Greeks, sexually and militarily, the matriarchal order of things is temporarily victorious. The heroes were about to depart in failure, when Zeus with his winds and Hera with her parody of Zeus's exploits with humans enter the fray. When the battle shifts from ideas to action, reversals occur for the Amazons, and the war ends in a sham single combat between Antiope and Heracles, which the latter wins.

It is in the prologue and in the first two acts, then, that the language of the play is at its wittiest. In the prologue, Zeus and Hera turn the Amphytrion adventure into a quarrel about the legitimacy of Zeus's fathering of Heracles:

> *Hera:* That's what I mean. Hercules! You brave boy! Instead of having the grace, the gentility, to deny his parentage, you are forever boasting of it.
> *Zeus:* I think it would be far more ill-bred to deny it, my dear. And my son's name is Heracles. Only to Romans and other upstarts is he Hercules.
> *Hera:* But *is* he your son? for all we *know* he is nothing of the kind.
> *Zeus:* Surely there can be little doubt?
> *Hera:* Simply because you stooped to impersonate his father?
> *Zeus:* But rather successfully, my dear. After all, his mother took me for Amphytrion and—she took me.
> *Hera:* Is that conclusive?

Zeus: Ah! You raise a novel legal point. You mean to say, when I
   borrow Amphitryon's body to woo his wife, is the resulting progeny
   fathered by the body or the body's occupant, by the ground-landlord,
   as it were, or by the tenant? Fascinating. It should keep the lawyers
   busy. (3)

In transferring her resentment of Zeus's boasting of his parent-
age to a fine point on the legitimacy of his claim, Hera only incurs
Zeus's accusation of parochialism as she complains of the status
of women as second class citizens: "My dear, a feminist is a lady
who makes the mistake of supposing that the war of the sexes has
been lost. Curb your defeatism. It could end in your defeat" (4).
   In yet another reference to the self-defeatism of feminist actions,
Zeus relates to Hera a fable of the giraffe who was taunted by the
monkey: "Why should you be treated as a second-class beast?
When will you emancipate yourself?" So the giraffe attempted to
climb a tree, nearly breaking her beautiful neck and never being
able to reach her full height again. Zeus's argument, like Thompson's in *Cupid and Psyche* and, perhaps, like that of Levy himself,
takes traditional feminism one step beyond itself.
   Some of the funniest scenes in act 1 include arguments between
Heracles and Theseus about how to provoke the Amazons to war
when it is clear that there is no will or intent to fight on the part
of their hostesses. Levy has his protagonists decide on the anachronistically medieval ploy of the chivalric glove. After much bick-
ering about who will carry out the challenge, Theseus is ordered
by Heracles to do so. In the context of the hospitality offered by
their hostesses and, in particular, of the bath-loving Hippolyte, who
enjoys nothing more than to lie about, Theseus is immobilized.
Both enamored of her and sheepish about his role, he is again
reduced to size as he can only say, "I adore women who just lie
about. . . . At home it is a dying art." Their exchange follows:

Hippolyte: What did you wish to say?
Theseus: Oh, Oh, of course (*He takes the glove from his belt but it does
   little to increase his confidence.*) I hope you won't feel—whatever
   happens—I mean as far as I am concerned personally—that is to
   say, there is a distinction, isn't there?
Hippolyte: I beg your pardon.
Theseus: What I mean is, some things are personal while others are
   not.
Hippolyte: Are they?

Theseus: No, they aren't—other things, that is.

As he fumbles through his explanation, he becomes inarticulate, asking that she not be outraged if he strikes her because he has loved her since their first meeting. She responds with "Of course you do?"

Theseus: Why "of course"?
Hippolyte: Well, don't you love everyone?
Theseus: Certainly not. I loathe most people.
Hippolyte: You horrid little man!
Theseus: Why horrid? Everybody loathes most people. If everybody loved everybody else, it would be a nice mix-up. It wouldn't be decent. Do you suppose I feel the same about that blacksmith creature that I feel about you? (29)

Theseus's attempts at an explanation of the glove ritual as his duty end in failure, having faded, from the first moment he saw her, into a desire to protect her. "By clouting me with a glove," responds Hippolyte (29). Almost weeping with frustration, Theseus hurls the glove to the ground and the two join Heracles and Antiope for lunch, unsuccessfully attempting to explain the rite of chivalry, a rite that to Hippolyte "sounds rather a nice game." Hippolyte is well on her way to her decision to leave with Theseus.

Custom after Western custom and attitude after Western attitude are grist for Levy's high comedy in the first two acts of exchanges between males and females on the matter of the sexes and on the relative merits of civilized (patriarchal) versus uncivilized (matriarchal) values.

In Levy's keen satire of war as a means to settle disputes, Antiope refuses to accept Heracles' invitation to a war because she likes him far too much. He inquires whether the war could be fought without rancor, for "we are not savages" (18). Antiope counters with "Even the proposal to slaughter each other in a civilized way does not attract me. Forgive us" (18). Heracles then reasons with her: "You can't both refuse a challenge and refuse to surrender." She finally sums up her refusal of his argument.

We cannot fight you, my lord, because, as we have said, it would only end in tears, our tears. If we were fortunate, we might score tears on your side, too; a few tears from a few of your wives and mothers. This seems to us an insufficient prize. We cannot fight for the satisfaction of making a few strange women weep. We cannot fight, moreover—to be blunt with you—because we should very certainly be beaten. (19)

On feminist concerns, the relative values of males and females continue the comic reversals in the play. Males are held and treated well in a stud Farm for reproduction. Thus it is not surprising that Hippobomene had mistaken Theseus as an escapee from the Farm. Then there is the incident of the fifth pregnancy of Melanippe, daughter of Hippobomene. Antiope excuses herself to attend to the delivery of the child, as her other four pregnancies had ended rather tragically. Theseus extends his sympathy and asks, "Stillborn?" Antiope replies: "No, no, all boys" (27). In a later episode, Antiope informs a befuddled Theseus of her relief on the birth of a daughter to Melanippe. Offering his view that now "she'll have four nice little brothers to look after her," Theseus was scolded for "a joke not in quite the best taste." Antiope clears up his misunderstanding of the situation by explaining that the four boys "were drowned, of course." Theseus can only reply, "Well, really" (43).

As Minister of Maternity, Thalestris then further explains that though she hates regimentation,

we shall have to insist that the men at the Farm are all properly labelled and numbered. And our girls MUST make a note of who they are mating with. If this were not such a happy occasion, I should really be quite cross with Melanippe. I had just given instructions that he was to be used extensively and now I find Melanippe hasn't the faintest idea who he was. (43)

This comment follows her observation to Antiope that "the father of this child is obviously a useful strain, strong enough to counteract Melanippe's unfortunate tendencies" (43).

The belt that Heracles has come for is in itself a minor part of the play, except as a symbol of what the crown is to the English and as demonstration that there is really no need for a crown tower in which to keep the belt safe from thieves, even if those thieves be heroes by profession. Consequently, there is no need for locks.

What is so effective in *The Rape of the Belt* is Levy's having found a subject from mythology that allows him free rein to satirize a variety of so-called civilized values whatever form these take, from personal views on love to political-philosophical attitudes on running a country and, indeed, a civilization. All are a piece of the myth that accommodates the views expressed in many of his other plays, but nowhere else with such wit.

Running for more than a year, *The Rape of the Belt* boasted an impressive cast that included Constance Cummings as Antiope, Kay Hammond as Hippolyte, John Clements as Heracles, and Richard Attenborough as Theseus, all impeccably suited to their roles.

The critic for the *Times* commented on the equality of actors with the opportunities of their roles:

> Mr. John Clements, as Heracles, speaks in anger with a voice that is like the clashing of swords and in tender mood with measure and tact. Mr. Richard Attenborough is delightfully naive as the slow-witted Theseus. Miss Constance Cummings brings a disarming manner and a shy sincerity to the highly civilized Amazonian queen who captures the heart of Heracles. Miss Kay Hammond is deliciously absurd as her sister queen who is obviously destined to flirt the time away carelessly in Athens for the rest of her life, and she has some good farcical moments as the incarnation of the fiery Hera. This goddess's bitter flavoured commentary on the action is spoken with bite and guile by Miss Veronica Turleigh, and Mr. Nicholas Hannen, a delicately amusing Zeus, surprises us by trotting out a melancholy little slave in splendid style.[8]

Kenneth Tynan wrote that "Benn Levy is writing squarely in the great tradition of Shaw and Giraudoux. The tradition of drama as playful philosophic debate. . . . The dialogue glitters with a levity that is never thoughtless, and some anachronisms are kept to a discreet minimum." Constance Cummings was singled out for playing Antiope "with a crisp nubility and a taunting intelligence that are entrancing to behold."[9]

Despite his objection to the sagging middle of the play, T. C. Worsley comments on the well-chosen theme, the splendid comic reversal, the laying out of the play "graphically, wittily and theatrically, bringing us to the impasse, Shavian in its excellence where the strong man is left absolutely baffled when there's no one for him to be strong with. . . . Adult and civilized comedy is a rare treat on our stage, and this comedy is both adult and civilized without being in the least precious."[10]

As Levy's last comedy, it is his best, and it represents the successful culmination of a long career in writing entertaining and serious plays. *The Rape of the Belt* has succeeded as none of his other plays have in its blending of the comic and serious, without either one a distraction from the other. The comic actions of the plot are focused on the belt episode; the themes of love and war are single-mindedly in control of the actions. The actions of Zeus and Hera in the plot and the many minor themes of political governance are seamlessly woven into the total pattern of the play. Most importantly, Levy's philosophical ideas and satiric wit, inextricably entwined, express his *Weltgeist* as no other of his plays, whether comedy, fantasy drama, morality play, poetic dramas, or dramatic adaptations of other writers' work.

In his combination of parodies of Pope's title ("The Rape of the Lock"), Greek myth, and contemporary attitudes, Levy, in his high comedy of ideas, has elevated the narrower morality of his serious plays and the prankish plots of his earlier comedies, so that comparisons with the best modern writers in this genre, Shaw and Giraudoux, are inevitable.

The Rape of the Belt bears comparison, in particular, with *Amphitryon 38* (1929), Giraudoux's comic-romantic fantasy about Jupiter (Giraudoux uses Roman names) as persistent wooer of Alkmene, even after he had already seduced her to fulfill the destiny of the birth of Hercules. His role is that of a god who yearns to enjoy the purity of a human love with Alkmene, who insists on fidelity to her husband, Amphitryon. Jupiter sees his eternity as a bleak void except for his occasional forays with humans. As a god, he is destined to seduce her by trickery in the domestic guise of her husband, not even in the more imaginative guise of a swan as in his love affair with Leda.

Levy's play, on the other hand, casts Zeus in the role of a husband whose jealous wife imitates his own strategy of entering humans in disguise as she attempts to gain her revenge.

The two plays further complement each other in a variety of ways. Giraudoux's version of the Amphitryon myth is the central story of his play, whereas Levy uses the legend as part of the structural framework within which to dramatize Heracles' adventure with the Amazons.

By profession a diplomat, Giraudoux, like Levy who spent five years in the House of Commons, plays out his own morality themes underneath his whimsical fantasies. In the fifteen plays he wrote, mostly based on history or myth, there is always a duel of angels (the title of his last play) fancifully and poetically fought between gods and humans, the ideal and the real, the pure and the tainted, sometimes outright good and evil as in his popular play, *The Mad-woman of Chaillot.*

Even if Levy's major theme in *The Rape of the Belt* is matriarchy and Giraudoux's in *Amphitryon 38* is romance, a minor theme provides a convergence of the two: that of Zeus as real husband in the former and as assumed husband in the latter. So Hera plays an active role in the action of Levy's play but is conveniently absent in Giraudoux's.

Stylistically, Giraudoux's conflicts consist of highly poetic verbal duels—between Jupiter and Mercury, between Alkmene and Leda, who (having had her own experience with Jupiter) has advice for her friend, and, most seductively, between Jupiter and Alkmene. His duels correspond to Levy's more prosaic debates.

Finally, Giraudoux's god (or angel) and Levy's jealous god serve not only as catalysts for the plots, but also as metaphors for an underlying morality, in the former a search for a purity of experience and in the latter a search for elusive truths. Giraudoux's search takes the form of a whimsically imaginative exchange of views between the divine and the human, Levy's the form of farcical actions and witty debates between warring sides. Both dramatists are part of a major twentieth-century tradition of mythological burlesque—British and French—whose writers have found in myth a medium for exploring the problems and contradictions of their times.

6

1946–1966: Tribalism and Myth

Return to Tyassi
(1950)

As Levy's first produced play after his retirement from five years as Member of Parliament for the Eton-Slough constituency, *Return to Tyassi* is an interesting reinvention of themes in earlier plays, added to which is his most explicit judgment of upper-middle-class English tribalism that is responsible for potentially problematic marriages. In the earlier plays, Levy handles the problem in fantasy-comedy style or in the serious morality play. Mrs. Moonlight escapes through a charmed necklace, and Mrs. Bottle suddenly departs one day for a bohemian life with an artist. In the morality plays, rationality rather than fantasy directs and determines the action—as in *Mud and Treacle, The Devil, The Jealous God* and in the adaptations: *Young Madame Conti* and *Madame Bovary.* The women debate and make choices in their lives in the context of the dualistic realities of body versus mind, the physical versus the spiritual, duty versus romance, and the individual versus society.

As a divided self, Martha Cotton in *Return to Tyassi* is in a marriage similar to theirs. She makes two major choices in her life: first, to follow her romantic inclinations at an early age and marry an anthropologist (Hugo Hubbard) and thus to live in an exotic country without the physical comforts of civilization; and, second, to return to her family in England to give birth to a child, a decision that leads to divorce from Hugo and a second marriage, this one to a civil servant, Gilbert Cotton, who provides her with those comforts.

For seventeen years, she has lived a life of ease, duty, and decorum. Her life with her husband and daughter (Susan Hubbard), along with her mother, who lives with them (Gracie), embodies all the advantages of a civilized society. Lately, however, she has seemed changed, as the Edenic surfaces of their lives are broken through by events from the past that have been haunting Martha since her marriage to Gilbert. Civilities break down as Martha's lying about the reasons for her divorce from Hugo affect both Gilbert and Susan. He is hurt beyond being able to forgive, and Susan is disillusioned to the point that she leaves home and wants no more to do with her mother. Only Gracie, the "concoction" of the tribe, remains intact.

Return to Tyassi reenacts the game of truths that is at the heart of earlier Levy plays. The devil or the jealous god in this play is Hugo's brother Francis, who arrives one day to inform Martha of Hugo's legacy to her and to request from her the literary remains of his brother in order to continue his brother's unfinished work. The game of truths that ensues is similar to that engaged in by Solomon and Polly in *Mud and Treacle;* directed by the curate, Nicholas Lucy, in *The Devil;* and dramatized in *The Jealous God* in the life of Kate Settle in 1939 in an England unsettled by the events of World War II. Martha's lies about Hugo's treatment of her, the generosity of Hugo's will, and her feelings about Hugo are revisited, catalyzed by the appearance of Hugo's brother that follows the death of her ex-husband.

To this variation on a theme in earlier plays, Levy adds Gilbert Cotton, whose civil service position as an aide to a government Minister, has made him the upholder of the civilized values of his class and a contrast with Hugo and Francis, who are engaged in the romantic profession of unearthing the rituals of old civilizations. Contemporary tribalisms, thus, as engaged in by the Cotton household seem empty. The stereotype of contemporary middle-class life is Gracie, who rises about noon and never appears until she is perfectly groomed to meet the day. Proper marriages, attendance at the opera for no other reason than that it is the custom, and her concern with curtains for the Portman Square residence are essential to the tribe to which Martha and Gilbert belong. The effects of his civilization on himself are seen in small details like Gilbert's constant concern with his digestive system and in his own questioning of why he joined the civil service: "Civility and servitude! One as onerous as the other."[1]

The hold of middle-class tribalism on Martha asserted itself strongly in Martha's life when she chose to stay in England after the birth of Susan rather than face the primitive conditions in Tyassi. The lies she tells about her treatment by Hugo equally illustrate the lure of those rites and have, over the years, convinced Susan of the beastliness of her father.

With Hugo's untimely death from tuberculosis, Martha's frustration, long repressed by the iron-clad respectability of upper-middle-class British life that had dominated the Cotton household, is unleashed. To Francis, Martha not only grants the literary legacy he requests, but offers him, as well, the financial bequest that she does not need and which Gilbert does not want her to accept. Then, overwhelmed by her feelings for Hugo and by the pain of her lies, Martha finds in Francis some of Hugo's qualities, and, after spending the night with him, chooses to go back to Tyassi with him.

When Martha confronts Gilbert with her decision to return to Tyassi with Francis, she acknowledges what they (she and Gilbert) have had together: "your consideration, your good company, the equal partnership you established even though you are so much cleverer than I. I may have joked sometimes about your favourite adjective 'civilized,' but we've had, I realize, a civilized marriage and I know that's a great deal more than most people have" (71). But, as she agrees with Gilbert, it is not enough for her. And it is not just her love for Francis. "There's love in me again; it's a pretty world again; I'm without armour again, like a young girl without fear, treading lightly, unhurtable; and loving you too, if you can believe me, more than ever before" (71).

Her defenselessness is cruelly used by Gilbert who cannot rid himself of his bitterness: "There's a devil in my entrails. May God give me the strength to forgive you" (82–83). To pray for a better universe, as Martha does, "would be less a prayer than a blasphemy" (83). So he offers her bottles of ephredine (which he takes for a gastrointestinal condition), a service revolver, or the fourth-floor window as choices for escape.

Gracie knows that Martha isn't as lucky as Gilbert: "The church can comfort him when things are difficult. You and I haven't got that" (83). Her solution is to forget unpleasant things and get on with the curtains in Portman Square and with her home in Antibes. Susan's is to leave home. Only Martha seems to have none, except for one of the three offered her by Gilbert.

At one point, Gilbert offers the wisdom of his own tribal principles to Francis:

She is my wife. If you take her, you will regret it. And if you regret it, she will regret it. You'll regret it because you've doubts about it even now. You'll regret it because she'll look like a misfit in Tyassi. She did before and she will again. You may not like it here, but this is her proper setting, this is where she looks her best. You'll regret it because she'll see through you. She'll know you've changed your mind as soon as she comes into this room. She'll know it whatever lies you tell her. She'll take one look at you and she'll know. (77–78)

When Martha reappears, packed and ready to leave for Tyassi with Francis, she responds to Francis's "I love you" with "I know . . . No. I don't know" (79). Helpless under the weight of her contradictory emotions, she looks to Gilbert for an explanation, which he provides tauntingly: "I told him he couldn't fool you. It appears the moon was full last night. There was also some auxiliary alcohol. This morning—is morning, a less illusory time of day. Tyassi's off. It's not for you: it never was. You can unpack" (80). Under the influence of the wisdom of the tribe, her will, reminiscent of Miss Julie's in Strindberg's *Dance of Death,* vanishes, and she reminds Francis of their talk the previous night: "It was not your fault. Nor mine. There was a conspiracy. We were its victims. Your tears . . . are just a protest; a prayer. Do you remember?" (80).

After a momentary return to her lost chance in life, Martha reverses that return "once and for all, for [she knows] there are no second chances in this strict universe" (62). Francis reminds her that when she sees beyond her "parish," she sees only another parish, for Tyassi is as real to Hugo as Regent's Park is to Gracie. Martha's response is that "our parish is dying fast." She remembers the excitement and spontaneity of Tyassi and now feels only the "many millions of light-years I'd travelled from Tyassi" (63).

Martha's third and final major choice in life, then, is to act on one of the suicide solutions proposed by Gilbert. An offstage report is heard by Gracie and Chris (a decorator-cousin of Martha's), who are in the midst of a discussion of the color scheme for curtains as the play ends.

Martha is reminiscent of Hester Collyer in Terence Rattigan's *The Deep Blue Sea,* a play about a loveless marriage whose societal correctness has turned into an emotional trap for the wife. Produced two years before Rattigan's play, Martha's story is not as taut and harrowing as Hester Collyer's, since the consequences in Martha's life occur swiftly near the end, whereas Hester's painful life occupies Rattigan's entire play. Martha belongs not only to the Levy gallery of characters like Polly Andrews, Kate Settle, Nella Conti, and Madame Bovary, but also to predecessors such as Hedda Gabler, Miss Julie, Anna Karenina, and to the women in the plays of Arthur Wing Pinero, particularly Zoe in *Mid-Channel.* Caught between the proverbial devil and the deep blue sea, Martha's suicide grows from the intractable desperation of her divided self.

A psychosociological rather than moral examination of a marriage without love, *Return to Tyassi* focuses on the tribalism inherent in middle-class English life and the lies born of that tribalism that are foisted by all three adult family members—Martha, Gilbert, and Gracie—on Susan, innocent victim of their lies, even though she is young enough to carry on in her life.

Half child, half woman, Susan is not yet a prisoner of custom. She still asks her mother's permission to do things even as she fashionably calls Martha by her first name. Similarly, even though she defies her father's warning about the company she keeps, she is young enough to repudiate her mother completely when she learns of the lies. The lies have spread to Gracie, who has known secretly of Martha's love for Hugo from reading her daughter's diary (without the latter's knowledge). In her own way she is part of the conspiracy of lies but without the guilt suffered by Martha.

Levy's recent experience in Parliament is reflected in the many references to politics. As aide to a politician, Gilbert describes the Minister for whom he works as someone who would be a

quite useful citizen behind a haberdasher's counter or even as a crossing-sweeper, but democracy, with its infinite sense of fun, puts him in charge of a national Ministry. Moreover, it warns him that it's undemocratic to be led by his officials. Plato, Aristotle, Cicero, Hobbes, Locke, Mill, Keynes, they're all at his elbow ready with advice—through an interpreter which is I. For this I spent the first four years of my adult life hobnobbing with the immortal dead; for this I acquired the handicap of a Double-First. But he looks at me with an Olympian god's eye and prefers to put his trust in the platitudinous half-truths he's contracted from other political hacks. . . . He is the classic illustration of the mystique of democracy. Well, it works: by and large, it works. No wonder we intellectuals can't understand it. (43–44)

Gilbert illustrates Levy's description of himself as someone who too often allows rationality to lead.

Although Gilbert takes comfort in the Catholic church, there is little comfort elsewhere as seen in his conversation with Susan shortly after her disillusionment with her mother:

> *Gilbert:* So you're bolting.
> *Susan:* There isn't really much to stay for. It would probably have been better for me if I had cut loose years ago.
> *Gilbert:* My child, you're seventeen.
> *Susan:* But I didn't because I hated to be away from her because I loved her so much. Now I don't love her at all. I loved someone who didn't exist.
> *Gilbert:* Those are the only people we ever love, Susan. Real people don't deserve to be loved. God in his mercy hides us from each other, so that we may enjoy the relief of loving and being loved from time to time.
> *Susan:* He hasn't hidden Martha from me: not any longer. I couldn't stay without loving her. Perhaps you can do without love because of your religion. It makes you independent and strong. But I can't do without it; I haven't any religion. (66)

Gilbert's realities of the civilized life are those he sees in his marriage, a "civilized relationship, considerate, self-respecting, gracious, without brainstorms, emotional crises, histrionics and juvenilia" (69).

Return to Tyassi abounds in references to the jealous god, the god in man who requires much of those who make demands on him—those demands that consist of nothing less than truth and the following of that truth in one's life. For Martha, weakened by having lived seventeen years of lies, the demands are overwhelming. Unprepared to reveal her secrets, she tells Francis that she had meant to do so for ages, "shivering on the brink: you provided the necessary push." In his response to Martha's reference to Susan's being upset, Francis explains: "Disillusioned, eh? You were God" (61). Only Gracie seems unaffected by the jealous god. In the view of Martha and Francis, Gracie is a concoction of society, and Hugo is "more alive in his grave than she in her shoes" (62).

The Guardian reviewer saw the play as a "penetrating study of a woman offered a second chance of romance who yet arrives at some saner and safer terms of reconciliation."[2] And, despite the *Times* reviewer's criticism of Martha's role as one of too few notes, possibly in the writing, the third act with its series of climactic scenes "creates a superb theatrical tension, and here the comparison [to predecessors such as Pinero and Jones] works to his [Levy's] advantage."[3]

Return to Tyassi is the second of Levy's three realistic problem dramas, the other two being *The Jealous God* and *Public and Confidential.*

The Tumbler (1960)

As Levy's third consecutive play derived from myth, *The Tumbler* reworks part of the Agamemnon legend. Electra, Clytemnestra, and Aegisthus are reinvented in the characters of Lennie, Nina, and Kell, respectively. The characters bear resemblance also to Hamlet, Gertrude, and Claudius, with the Doctor as both advisor to the family and Greek chorus that fears an ominous turn of events.

In a verse style that combines the tension-creating stichomythic Greek line with symbols and poetic language, the play has been likened by critics to that of his contemporary, Christopher Fry. The influence of the poet Gerard Manley Hopkins is directly invoked in Levy's use of the hound of heaven as the play's major symbol. In this extraordinary mix of influence, sources, and analogues, Levy has written a verse tragedy, an entirely new form for a dramatist sixty years of age when the play had its premiere in New York in 1960.

In this new form, Levy converts his jealous god to the metaphor of a hound, and references to the god abound in the play. Like Martha Cotton in *Return to Tyassi,* whose guilt drives her need for atonement, one of the two main characters, Kell, refers to his conscience-god in a drawn-out confession near the end of the play:

> We gods require our sacrifices, I
> No less than others. We must conform. How better
> Could I mock my colleagues than by aping them?[4]
> Must we be abject forever? (3.15)

In a barn where both seek shelter from a storm in which the thunder crashes around them, Kell, in response to Lennie's questioning of his identity introduces himself as a man haunted by dogs:

Yap, yap, yap.
We know you're there. Pardon
My little dog. He will not harm you—much.

(1.1.2)

So begins another of Levy's many games of truths, played out in a pseudoincestuous story of a daughter (Lennie) newly returned from Canada to a home in which guilt-infestation has taken its toll on her mother (Nina) and her stepfather (Kell).

Nina is in constant attendance by a physician for a heart condition, and Kell seems throughout a tortured man roaming the universe of an English village, frequently embroiled in fights in a local pub. Lennie's jealous god is the memory of her father, now dead, whom she had loved as much as she now hates her mother. The plot consists of Lennie's gradual piecing together the total truth about the death of her father from the fragments of information she is given during the events of the play.

On the night of her arrival, she decides to walk from the train station, and during a storm finds shelter in the family barn, where another refugee from the storm appears. Identified throughout the first act as The Man and The Girl, they converse in the language of poetic metaphor. He introduces himself as "a man," only one of too many men and one with "a little dog" whose "bow-wows" will not harm her but who hates to be forgotten. Recognizing his metaphor, she asks, "What have I found? / So you have the hounds of heaven on a string." (1.1.1) Varied references to the dog as the metaphor for guilt suggest not only Hopkins's hound, but also the dog from Goethe's *Faust,* a Mephistophelean force, operating to keep man from being content with the moment. The devil is the hound of heaven, keeping man in constant conflict with his conscience. The Man describes his devil as a hound that at times binds him and at other times gives him leash to challenge that force to which he is "linked most damnably, umbilically together." His response to further questions illustrates the Fry-like metaphors in which the two converse:

A man, a hound of heaven or a master of hounds,
A bear with a sore head, a butt but not
A beggar, a buffoon perhaps, I'm not sure what,
A tumbler by profession like us all
But one who will not practice merely at

The crack of a whip. They must trip me and send me
    sprawling
Or else my capers aren't for display.
Yes, come to think of it, I am a man,
A little man homonculus, for I stand
Upon my two precarious flat feet
As proud and impotent as Lucifer, as firm. . . .
    (the thunder roars again)
All right, all right! I hadn't finished! As firm
    as thistledown, erect as a cocoanut
Until they shie me down. *(to the skies)* Now are you
    satisfied?
Check me again while I'm bragging to the lady
And by heaven, I'll shorten the leash
And give you the rough side of my tongue!
Pardon my little dog, lady.

(1.1.2.)

Theirs is a language that produces an immediate understanding between them even as it provokes audience suspense. He introduces himself to her:

I work here. I have noble work.
I hew the wood and draw the water. I even
Order other little men to do the same.
We play at calves and milk our mothers,
We bring the bulls and stallions into school
And teach them how to conjugate.
We conjure barley from a wizard's test tube
And listen to the earth turn with envy,
We lead the brilliant sheep about—or they
Lead us; another controversial point
On this confused and most confusing farm.
But here for better or worse I stand and spraw.
This shallow hill serves me—or I serve it.
This dumb green eminence.
Is my green eminence—or I am its green eminence.

(1.1.2)

The thunderstorm continues as they converse in a pastiche of references to the Faustian homonculus, Lucifer, the hound of heaven, "little Prometheus"—all Levy's means of examining the moral questions posed in his serious dramas, questions that must be asked, regardless of consequences, until the whole truth is revealed and the jealous god satisfied. "Man in the image of God is the very devil, is he not? I wish it were not so, bull-dog. Give me your hand." Bandaging his hurt thumb, she draws close to him, acknowledging him as the first man to have "halted" her since her father died. The two spend the night together, as it is later revealed, in the location in which her father had died.

The remaining two acts are a series of verbal confrontations in which the whole truth slowly emerges, concluding in her final meeting with Kell, again in the barn. Before she leaves, she is able to tell him as they embrace, "I loved you, not for your tiny / Accomplishments but for your mighty hopes . . . / And for a dearer reason. . . . / That you wept for the world. Kell responds with "I am alive again!" (3.20). And as the thunder rolls in the distance, he starts to knot a noose in the rope in the very place in which he had hanged the body of Lennie's father after his death from a heart attack.

Reminiscent of the wandering Electra's homecoming to revenge Agamemnon's murder, Lennie's return and her quasi-incestual union are the beginning of a series of slow revelations involving her mother's lovers, one of whom was Kell, whom she (Nina) forced to marry her under threat of exposing him as her husband's murderer. Reportedly having hanged himself, the father had actually died from a heart attack suffered in a fight with Kell after discovering the latter in bed with Nina.

The truth that Lennie learns and for which Kell insists on paying the ultimate price includes Nina's charge of neglect by her husband, her many affairs with other men in addition to Kell, and the Doctor's responsibility for Lennie's homecoming. Like the Greek chorus, the Doctor fears what may happen if all is revealed. Well-intentioned, he is the innocent catalyst for the events, the result of his not mailing a letter to Lennie. For the audience, there is the revelation of the lifelong hostility between Nina and Lennie, caused by Nina's jealousy of the close relationship between Lennie and her father. Until she knows all, Lennie's search for the truth takes a tortuously labyrinthine path.

Levy's exploration of family relationships in *The Tumbler* illustrates again his technique of pastiche, the pastiche consisting of parts of various myths. Although the Electra story is the most obvious, there are also suggestions of the sexually reversed incest of Oedipus and Jocasta, Kell's Promethean challenge to the gods, the Faust legend, and allusions to writers, such as Hopkins, Herrick, Keats, and Shakespeare, for example, Hamlet's lines: "I did not think I'd meet his stature again," (1.1.14) and "so confusion chews upon its tail" (1.1.3).

A sometimes distracting feature of the play is the vivid contrast in the extravagant poetic language between Lennie and Kell, on the one hand, and, on the other, the terse stichomythic lines when Nina and the Doctor are present. Another contrast is that of the allegorical identities in act 1 and the use of realistic names in the remaining acts.

The contrasts extend even to the locales. In the barn during the storm at the beginning of the play and in the last scene when Lennie finds out that her sexual episode with Kell had taken place in the spot of her father's "suicide," the language reverts to metaphor. Here the context is nature, with the thunder symbolic of Zeus, against whose power "little Prometheus" wages his war. In Nina's home, where the remaining scenes occur, the dialogue for the most part is staccatolike stichomythia. When in act 2 the Doctor enters, Nina is surprised as she has been nervously expecting the arrival of Lennie:

Nina: Doctor! Why do you frighten me so?
The Doctor: Did I? Dear me.
Nina: You know I'm still not strong.
The Doctor: May I sit down?

. . . .

Nina: Doctor, I've dreadful news.
The Doctor: Bad news? Let's see if I can guess. Lennie is back. Is that your news?
Nina: Her bags are here! They're in the hall.
The Doctor: Ah, yes.

. . . .

Nina: How did you know?
The Doctor: I never know for certain how I know What I know. I think Joe Carter told me. Didn't he bring her luggage in the car?
Nina: From the station, yes. Did you meet him? What did he say?

The tension in the abruptness of the lines continues throughout the ensuing dialogues until all is revealed, reaching its peak in the scene in which the police officer appears and Kell tauntingly encourages Lennie to accuse him and Nina of the murder of her father. She refuses, and once more the metaphorical language takes over. Lennie tells Kell of his similarity to her father: both are "great fighters" although not "victorious ones." Tortured by his mortality, Kell has just provided Lennie with the last bit of information (no "saga" or "deeds of "derring-do," but yet "another skin to the onion"), describing the fight in which her father died, a fight in which "his [the father's] heart, not he, . . . had given in." In his moment of "ignominious terror," Kell then hanged the dead body from a beam, the same beam under which the incest occurs in the opening scene of the play. As he relates the story, Kell can still "hear the brave chattering of my Promethean teeth." Having lived with his torment, he now feels alive again. After their farewell kiss, he "watches her out of sight," and with the roll of thunder, as in their original meeting, he challenges the heavens for a final time: "You here again? Well, well, my little bow-wow! / I have a shot in my locker yet!"

As the rain falls and Lennie prepares to leave, Kell knots a noose in a rope. The Doctor on his usual way home, ever smiling, looks neither to the left nor to the right. Natural elements—rain and thunder—resume activity in both nature and the lives of humans.

The Tumbler was produced in New York with Laurence Olivier as director and Rosemary Harris, Charlton Heston, and Martha Scott in the leading roles. Even with such an illustrious company, the play received mostly negative notices, some even ridiculing. To Walter Kerr of the *Herald Tribune,* the words of The Man—obviously in imitation of Fry's *The Lady's Not for Burning*—are ghastly: "I am a man, a sack of skin . . . three yards of winding viscera. . . ."[5] Brooks Atkinson of the *New York Times* faults Mr. Olivier for a "heavy and flat" production and Levy "as a first-rate playwright . . . [who has] nothing in his record to suggest that he can write literary drama on an elevated plane of thought and style," despite "a few gripping moments."[6] Frank Aston of the *New York World Telegram,* however, while acknowledging the ultimate product as "ponderous" speaks of the play "leaping to life" in act 2 and of its "undeniable power in examining mankind's depravity against the soul's persistence."[7] And with some reservations as to its falling "somewhere short of greatness," John McLain of the *Journal American* discusses the play's "dimension and strength; its language is often soaring and it is wonderfully-well acted."[8]

In this modern verse tragedy, Levy once again poses the conflicts of the duality of man—body versus soul, human versus god (or fate)—conflicts whose ultimate goal is truth and whose condition is one of constant struggle for truth. The drama stands alone among Levy's work as a modern tragedy after the Greek style, both in its use of the Agamemnon story and its stichomythic dialogue that is more natural to Levy's talent than the sometimes awkward metaphors, as, for example, the mixture of Hopkins's hound of heaven imagery with that of little Prometheus' bowwow. Yet one wonders, given the right director and actors, whether the play would fare better than in its single New York production.

The Tumbler, a mixture of romance, melodrama, and tragedy, is one of Levy's two poetic dramas, the earlier one, *The Poet's Heart,* although not in verse, the more stylistically consistent of the two.

Public and Confidential
(Retitled in publication *The Member for Gaza*)
(1966)

Levy's fourth consecutive play to use myth, *Public and Confidential,* revamps the Old Testament Samson in the person of a politician, Joe Malkin, a Member of Parliament from the constituency of Gaza. At this juncture in his life he is Minister of Trade in the cabinet of a Labor government. The play's revised title derives from a despairing comment by Joe's brother-in-law, Duncan Doubleday, "Eyeless in Gaza! Oh my God!"[9]

Its genre is the realistic problem play in the tradition of Ibsen's *Pillars of Society* and *An Enemy of the People* or Shaw's *Widowers' Houses* and *Mrs. Warren's Profession.* Its subject is a scandal that leaves Joe's public life shorn of its power and his private life tattered but intact. The playing fields of the scandals are politics, press, and sex. The morality battles are played out in the private lives of Joe; his secretary of many years, Liza; his wife's brother, Duncan; and in two younger and lesser characters: Colin Jenkins, a political radical who has just been released from jail and his nonpolitical girl friend and popular television songstress, Gillie. All are caught up in complications created by Joe's attempt to get at the whole truth in the potentially corrupt granting of a secret military contract to the firm in which young Jenkins is employed.

All of the play's action occurs in Joe's office, which is located next to their bedroom, where his sick wife, Molly, lies. Without ever appearing on stage, she becomes, in her death, the catalyst for the private scandal that eventually determines the course of her husband's attempted investigation of corruption. The plot consists of a series of conversations—duets, trios, and quartets—and very little action except for the death of Joe's wife and his one-night sexual episode with Gillie.

Act 1 opens with Joe and Liza discussing the matter of his post-dated resignation as Minister of Trade, even as reporters are besieging his home to verify the leaked rumor of his resignation. Their discussion is joined in by Duncan, who arrives shortly, both as family friend and newsman, and, later, by Colin and Gillie.

Bent on exposing the corruption in his own party, no matter the levels of authority involved, Joe begins creating the trap out of which he cannot escape without damage to his public and confidential life. His current focus is Colin, fired as an M.1.5 security risk and newly released from prison, having served time on a trumped-up charge of causing a riot at a demonstration in Trafalgar Square. An angry Colin arrives, contemptuous of all establishment figures, even of Joe who is in a position to help him. His contempt drives Gillie, who takes offense at his crudeness, to her decision to stay after the others have left. Act 1 ends with what, in a mere summary, seems melodramatically convenient—the death of Molly. Gillie's attempt to comfort Joe ends in her spending the night with him, a minor incident in his life but one that will loom large in the crossing of publicly acceptable lines of personal behavior.

Act 2 shifts ground from the political to the personal in three conversational duets, between Liza and Joe, between Joe and Duncan, between Liza and Gillie, these followed by the arrival of a Colin angrier than he was in act 1, his political situation now complicated by Gillie's attraction to Joe.

This succession of arrivals establishes the characters in their relationships to each other. It becomes obvious that Liza is much more than just a hack secretary. It is her advice, rather than Molly's that Joe has followed in his political life, especially in his decision to resign and, later, to continue the investigation. For example, the idea of crossing the floor (switching parties, in American politics), which would be intolerable to Molly, the politically savvy wife, to Liza is not a matter of principle, either political or moral. To her it does not matter where one sits, "so long as you [Joe] say the right things. . . . You don't speak with your bottom." Joe's politics are attuned more to principle than to expedience, and so he agrees with Liza: "I think issues of personal freedom are [the most important in politics]. And that means cutting down the power of everybody except those that ordinary people elect and have the right to sack. It means no power except power on sufferance."

Liza: In other words, old-fashioned radicalism.
Joe: If you like. A freeman should have no master that he cannot sack. We've all become too damned interested in efficiency, and too careless about freedom. My god, we even put up with secret police, above the law and beyond our control, so that an anonymous head of M.1.5 can be more efficient. (48)

Joe's principles are those that Levy himself fought for, not only when he was in government, but also when he was out of government in his activist participation in the very kind of protest for which Colin was arrested.

It also becomes obvious that Duncan, despite loyalty to his dead sister, understands the longstanding affection between Liza and Joe and suggests that Joe do the right thing and marry Liza. At one time the relationship between the two had been more than just work, a romance that had metamorphosed, for Joe, solely into his dependence on her as a secretary and advisor. Remembering the high excitement of her early days as his secretary, Malkin concludes, "In the end she has become—merely indispensable" (55).

Liza, however, is in love with him still, and like the Mashas in Chekhov's plays is in mourning for her life, that mourning taking the form of whiskey. Duncan, who does not care for women sexually and who understands Joe's situation, is not an unsympathetic character, despite the compromises that he as a newsman must make.

In their different ways, both women—Liza and Molly—have been an important part of Joe's life, and his loyalty to both takes into account their differences. Molly's practicality is seen in her not wanting him to resign his Cabinet post. Liza's idealism, though soaked in whiskey and expressed in her cynical, street-smart wit, keeps Joe's conscience intact even to the end, when as matters close around him, he is tempted to compromise.

Liza's strength is illustrated in her advice to Gillie, who is having problems with Colin over her by-now purely social relations with Joe. Liza explains to Gillie that from Colin's "point of view you couldn't have made a more unfortunate choice than Joe Malkin. A straightforward case of 'Old Bull, Young Bull' would have been bad enough but this particular bull—wow! I wonder he's not foaming at the mouth" (72).

Like act 1, act 2 ends with the requisite cliff-hanger ending, as Colin angrier than in his earlier appearance confronts Joe in regard to the latter's liaison with Gillie: "How many other women gave you a free ride out of sympathy for the poor bereaved widower?" (78). His anger takes him to Duncan's newspaper with a sordid account of the night of Molly's death.

It remains in act 3 for Duncan to arrive to make Joe's choices clear. Either Malkin withholds his memorandum or Duncan's publisher, McKinley, bowing to his daughter-in-law's father, the attorney-general, prints Colin's story. Duncan's loyalty to the memory of his sister is challenged by McKinley's family loyalties. For Joe, now, private and confidential scandals intersect rather than run in parallel paths. Their crisscrossing forces Joe, encouraged by the tart wit of Liza, to his response that Duncan tell McKinley to "go and frig himself." Liza, crying, says her tears are not for Joe, but "for everyone, the poor bastards" (104). By this time even Mrs. Craig, as loyal to Molly as Liza is to Joe, has resigned out of her sense of decency. Only Joe and Liza remain, their principles intact, but their situation desolate, like that of Kate in *The Jealous God* and Martha Cotton in *Return to Tyassi.*

Levy's lifelong moral impulse and his political commentary derived from his own five years as Member of Parliament, are aired in some of the monologues that punctuate the witty dialogue. To Colin Joe pleads his idealism:

> Don't be insulted, Colin, if I say you and I have much in common. Even though you think it's a waste of time trying to put the world to rights and I'm still naive enough to think the opposite, we both still go on trying. Probably, the motive for us both is only what you call self-respect—which is just a fancy-phrase for putting on a show. And that's a civilised disease that corrupts not only you but everyone—except for a few stubborn savages like Liza. . . . and yet, occasionally, if we aren't too far gone, an emotion comes along strong enough to wash the foolish makeup off our faces—and we cry aloud. It isn't humiliating. That moment of truth is a moment of dignity. (77–78)

Faced with his faded idealism and reminded of his own youth, Joe finds it easy to talk to Gillie of both:

> You think Cabinet ministers inhabit the stratosphere, Colin thinks they inhabit the sewers. You're both wrong. We both live in a floor below you artists and scientists—if you're good—and a floor above ordinary

street level—when we're good. Most of us are only men-in-the-street writ large. The worst thing to be said of us is—we're representative! Which is bad enough but not incurable. Parliament is the mirror in which you all stare angrily at the reflexion of your own ugly faces. Of course people like Duncan still have dreams of a philosopher-king. Very nice no doubt but find him! . . . In the end who should he trust but himself? (34)

Earlier, patting Colin on the back, he agreed with him on his view of the tactics of the Air Ministry and of M.1.5: "I'm of your school; for me too, security has become a dirty word. Nothing has done more to eat away our system of civil rights and liberties than the blessed, God-sent word—security" (26). His idealistic political certainties, however, are shaken by the sudden realization of his aging—in contrast with the youthful energy of Colin:

He's made me realize for the first time in my life, that I'm no longer the younger generation! . . . Growing up is a slow process but growing old is a mighty quick one. Out of the blue—wham! It hits you precisely when you are looking the other way. You just meet a Colin Jenkins— or twenty years ago, a Joe Malkin—and lo and behold, you meet a foreigner. You don't know what fuel he runs on; there's some new mechanism. You're out of your depth. By God, no wonder I'm sore. (35)

Ex-politician for about fifteen years, Levy had legislated while in office for liberal causes such as the repeal of the stage censorship law. Now "a man-in-the-street" rather than a representative of all the "angry, ugly faces out there," he had spoken at a rally in Trafalgar Square on 30 March 1959 only a year before the production of *Public and Confidential*. His antiwar message was unilateral nuclear disarmament and the end of American bases in England. His portrait of Joe as a jaded politician yet includes an insistence on principles, even though his supporters in the end narrow down to only one person, Liza. More and more he finds himself trusting only himself, faintly reminiscent of the cynicism of Moliere's famous misanthropist, Celeste.

Throughout the play, Duncan, a voice for the press, understands the workings of politics and tries to temper Malkin's idealism with arguments of practical realities. His formative influences, like Malkin's (and unlike Colin's) have been "Mill and Hegel, Marx and Tawney, Wells and Shaw and so on," whereas "Colin's spiritual fathers are Dostoevsky, Kierkegaard, Henry Miller, Kafka, Camus,

Sartre, men who think hope breeds falsehood" (28). His publisher, Duncan tells Malkin, has "no party loyalties. It doesn't matter to him if the Government finds itself in a spot. He often criticizes it violently himself. . . . He never stops proclaiming his total political independence" (92). However, in his view community interests would not be served if "this government were jeopardised, as it might be if a well-respected ex-Cabinet Minister continued to smear it" (93). Duncan, although sympathetic to Malkin, warns Liza that to a moralist like herself "every business deal is a form of blackmail. To the rest of us life is as it is and business is business" (95). In the end he fails to change the uncompromising position of Malkin and Liza.

Levy's highly lauded talent for dialogue is in evidence throughout the play in the service of both exposition and debate of ideas, as seen in Malkin's questioning of Colin about the phoney charges of his arrest at Trafalgar Square:

Malkin: What happened to him, the man who seems to have started it.

Colin: He ducked out during the melee and disappeared in the crowd.

Malkin: He'd been arguing against you?

Colin: Yes, but he also argued with the police. He said we had every right to talk balderdash if we wanted to.

Malkin: And somehow the man who started it wasn't arrested. Do you think he could have been a police agent?

Colin: I suppose he could. Never thought of it.

Malkin: So. Then you were carted off to the police station and charged with obstructing the police in the course of their duties.

Colin: That's right.

Malkin: Which you described in court as bloody nonsense.

Colin: I said I hadn't obstructed them; they'd obstructed me.

Malkin: What details did they allege?

Colin: The police?

Malkin: Yes.

Colin: Very elaborate details—read out of a notebook and quite unrelated to anything that happened.

Malkin: Such as?

Colin: I'd started the trouble by abusing them with obscene language, then I pushed one of them off balance and tried to snatch his helmet, then I incited my friends to 'give it 'em.'

Malkin: Couldn't you produce witnesses?

Colin: A couple. Which made three of us swearing one thing and three coppers swearing another. (24)

In other exchanges, dialogue creates climactic moments, as when Liza suggests the possibility of looking for another job. Their conversation shifts to men and women, and Malkin offers his view that "the moments of copulation—not always but when we're lucky—are moments of communion, deep communion—the rare moments when we human beings are not alone—maybe it's the one common language" (59). Liza accuses him of using women as things and then suddenly veers to: "Communion. Was the moment with Gillie a moment of communion?" Stunned and silent, Malkin at last asks, "How did you know about—?"

Liza: I asked you a question.
Malkin: (after a moment) Yes, it was: very much so. At least it seemed to be.
Liza: Seemed? If it seemed to be, then it was.
Malkin: I asked you a question too. How do you know about this?
Liza: Mrs. Craig told me ten minutes ago. It appears that, before going to bed—on the night that Molly died—she came up here to see if you wanted anything. You didn't. You'd got it.
Malkin: You mean—
Liza: I mean she opened the door and found you at—holy communion. . . . Ignorant woman that she is, she thought you were merely having a roll in the hay.

It is in scenes like this one "where the best writing comes," writes the *Times* reviewer, when "Mr. Levy drops the political theme altogether for a sparring match between Malkin and his torch-bearing secretary, (played with great spirit by Constance Cummings)—a duel of equal strength full of the sense of middle-aged desolation."[10]

Joe's downhill fortunes, beginning early in the play, when Duncan informs him that the latter's speech at Grimsby in favor of a full open inquiry of the scandal "surely was his point of no return," move rapidly after this exchange between Liza and Malkin. Now he knows that the confidential is well on its way to becoming public. Startled by her knowledge of events, he is both embarrassed by and more keenly aware of his affection for Liza.

Produced three years after the outbreak of the Profumo scandal, *Public and Confidential* bears just enough similarities to the more wildly melodramatic events of the real-life story to have recalled for audiences a most embarrassing bit of national politics. The scandal involved John Profumo, Secretary of State for War from

1960 to 1963. Profumo had conducted an affair with Christine Keeler until rumors ran amok and became more than the ruling Conservative administration of Harold Macmillan could handle. Thus, an
investigation was conducted.

The ripples of the affair were more sensational than the affair
itself, for these involved a prominent osteopath and accomplished
portrait photographer, Stephen Ward, whose lavish lifestyle included a friend, Christine Keeler—a showgirl and model who vigorously maintained she was not a prostitute. Also among his
friends was a Russian naval attaché by the name of Captain Ivanov,
who, according to Lord Denning's final report that blanketed the
newspapers for days, was a spy intent on getting information from
Christine Keeler, with whom Profumo was involved. Through Lord
Astor, his patient, Ward had access to a cottage on the Astor estate,
Clivedon, where he administered treatments to Lord Astor. Ward
himself was tried, charged with earning a living wholly or partly
by procurement of prostitutes and by inciting Keeler to procure
an underage prostitute for a client. It was at Wimpole Mews, a
residence of Ward, that Keeler met Profumo. In the end, Ward was
found guilty, Keeler was not tried, and Profumo was declared not
to have breached national security.

The ripples were felt on the other side of the Atlantic in charges
that Ivanov was interested in acquiring information about the dates
of President Kennedy's Cuban forays in the early 1960s. The scandal acquired a life of its own in Parliamentary debates, in letters
to the press, in charges of unfairness and coverups, in a race by
French and American publishers to pirate editions of Lord Denning's final report of the investigation, and in a highly sympathetic
film about Stephen Ward, the leading role played by John Hurt.

The furor attendant on the events was fed by the Burgess-
McLean-Philby spy ring revelations whose completion would not
occur until more than a decade later when the fourth member
of the ring proved to be Blunt, curator of the Queen's private
art collection.

As late as 1981, in what appeared to be delightful type-casting,
Marilyn (Mandy) Rice-Davies appeared in a revival of Tom Stoppard's *Dirty Linen* (1976) as Maddie, a secretary who hilariously
works her sexual way through an investigative committee of the
House of Commons. At eighteen, Rice-Davies, a friend of Ward's
and Keeler's, had testified at Ward's trial as a lesser player in the
whirlwind of events that prompted her to attempt a series of es-

capes from the events by running off to Spain, only to be dragged back by Scotland Yard. On her opening night Stoppard presented her with flowers. To reporters she denied that she was Maddie.

Levy's play, coming as it did only three years after the revelations of the Profumo affair, seemed mild. It was politely dismissed as another belated treatment of the debate about private and public morality. The use of the young left-wing idealist—his ferreting out of corruption in the government, his imprisonment, and his turning against the politician for personal reasons even though his political cause and Malkin's were identical—lacked the sometimes-farcical melodrama of real life events. In addition, it appeared at a time when the style of the Ibsenite well-made problem play was at a low ebb. *Public and Confidential,* thus, was seen by the *Times* reviewer as a replay of *The Right Honorable Gentleman.*

Since 1966, the issues of the play have been hauntingly repeated in the many charges and counter-charges of scandals in which exposés of private lives have affected public affairs. Public corruption—such as Watergate, Irangate, and Iraqgate—and private affairs of political figures—such as John Kennedy, Gary Hart, William Clinton (in the United States) and Paddy Ashdown (in England)—have become public. The result among the young has been the creation of cynical attitudes like those of Colin and among older idealists a sense of isolation like that of Liza and Joe.

Its association with events of its time notwithstanding, *Public and Confidential* can be seen as part of a long-standing tradition of British plays dealing with public and private morality, as evidenced in recent revivals of Harley Granville-Barker's *Waste* at the National Theater and in 1993 of Oscar Wilde's *An Ideal Husband* in the West End.

The political issues—the influence of the press, the use of national security as license to violate civil liberties, and the broader and even more vague matter of national interest—take on a universality that keeps Levy's drama from being primarily a period piece. More essentially, however, the play is yet another of Levy's dramatic studies of the divided self, a man torn between expediency and conscience. In a political setting, the continual battle between body and soul is one between private need and public loyalties. As Joe's jealous god, Liza taunts Joe into a conscience-driven decision.

In this, his last stage play, Levy has not veered from the ideas of his earlier serious plays. The conflicting demands on man made by the opposing realities of life—the mind and the body, conscience and experience, and, in their broadest form, good and evil—have their price that is paid mostly by the women characters such as Mrs. Moonlight, Mrs. Bottle, Paul Robinson, Kate Settle, and Martha Cotton, but, also, in the few plays in which the leading character, such as John Tennison and Joe Malkin, is a male.

Two years earlier (1964), John Osborne's *Inadmissible Evidence* dealt with the psychological disintegration of a lawyer, and nearly three decades later, in a similar drama by Simon Gray, *Holy Terror* (a reworking of his play, *Melon*) traces a similar deterioration of a publisher. Theirs, however, are stories told in flashbacks. Levy's is a realistic problem play, forward moving in the present and concluding with Joe's spirit intact. In its sharp focus on one man's career disintegration, *Public and Confidential* joins what has become, in its modern form, a genre unto itself.

7

A Miscellany

Some of Levy's remaining plays—a highly successful musical extravaganza, a central European adaptation, an unsuccessful fantasy/farce, a trilogy of television plays, and a radio drama—are interesting for their ideas that he addressed more fully or more successfully in the plays just discussed.

Ever Green (1930)

The most successful of these is *Ever Green,* a musical for which Levy wrote the book and Richard Rodgers and Lorenz Hart wrote the music and lyrics. Described in the *Times* as "really a revue with something like a narrative linking the different episodes together,"[1] the musical ran for 254 performances, its spectacular quality the work of the impresario of English spectacles, Charles B. Cochran. "Superb entertainment,"[2] "gigantic new C. B. Cochran production,"[3] "a piece . . . written by Benn W. Levy with delicious impudence"[4]—these were the standard critical responses to a musical that established Jessie Matthews in her long career as a musical actress.

The impudence lies in the concept that "the lively young woman presented by Miss Jesse Matthews is really an old woman of sixty and that the middle-aged woman to whom Miss Jean Cadell gives a sublime tactlessness is her daughter."[5] The story idea is one that Levy two years earlier had used as the centerpiece of *Mrs. Moonlight,* his romantic/grotesque fantasy play about a woman who to her death retained her youthful beauty and who, at one point, assumed the identity of a young relative to be able to revisit the family she deserted many years ago. *Mrs. Moonlight,* also one of Levy's most popular plays, outdistanced *Ever Green*'s 254 performances with its own 294.

The pattern of critical response to *Ever Green* was similar to that about other Levy plays. Crediting Cochran with being his own most formidable rival, the *Times* critic refused to claim that this revue was better than ever, but acceded that it was at least as good as ever. Of the huge number of spectacles, the most memorable was a "fair in full swing at night," using a revolving stage. From provincial fair to a scene "in spangled halls and a parade of the Young Ladies apparelled in various costly fantasies," then to a Spanish scene in which villagers dance a "Caledonian measure" and "the grotesques of tradition are touring the streets"[6]—these are only a few of the "gorgeous" spectacles on which the audience feasted.

Based on the career of Fannie Ward, America's perennial flapper, the idea for the musical supposedly was suggested by Rodgers and Hart. The idea of a woman of sixty still in her youth served as a justifiable excuse for scenic splendor, lavish spectacle, "the dancing of Miss Joyce Barbour, the astonishing acrobatics of Carlos and Chita, the beautifully regimented dancing of Mr. Cochran's Young Ladies and the Tiller Girls,"[7] and, course, the entertaining Jessie Matthews, Jean Cadell, Sonnie Hale, and Leon Morton. Story, plot, characterization, and ideas exist for the sake of the spectacle.

The fanciful youth-age dilemma and the "what if" question, a subject that Barrie so successfully explored in his plays, is one that lingers in some of Levy's plays. In an interesting instance of life imitating art, Jessie Matthews, who enjoyed the greatest of her many musical successes in *Ever Green,* starred at the age of seventy-two, in a one-woman, award-winning concert in Los Angeles.

Levy's only spectacular, *Ever Green* belongs to those plays, like *A Man with Red Hair* and *Young Madame Conti, Springtime for Henry, Clutterbuck,* and *Public and Confidential,* in which the purity of their respective genres is maintained throughout. Thus *Ever Green,* whose youth-age idea serves well as a pretext for gigantic spectacles, consistently maintains its quality as superb entertainment.

The Church Mouse (1931)

Another of Levy's adaptations from central European authors (Siegfried Geyer and Ladislaus Fodor), *The Church Mouse,* produced in London six months before the opening of *Springtime for Henry* in New York, seems, at least in its plot, a rehearsal for the latter. In Susie Sachs, the maid who forces her way into a bank and makes the manager accept her as her secretary, there is a vague suggestion of Nella in *Young Madame Conti.*

Instead of the automobile industrialist Dewlip, the male lead, a Baron, is a rakish bank president. Like Dewlip, the Baron has difficulty separating business from pleasure where his secretaries are concerned. Dismissed by reviewers as a piece with marionettes for characters, the play seemed "tediously empty" and "an exercise in a particular convention of humor."[8] But the question of what that humor is remained a question to Charles Morgan of the *New York Times.* To the *Times* reviewer, "the play is a play of fragments" even though entertaining with "adroit and amusing inventions [which] are scene spinning and little more."[9] The plot, after a promising first act, degenerates into "incidental humorous decorations, evidently part of the mysterious Viennese formula."[10]

As with so many other productions of Levy's plays, the acting received accolades, particularly that of Sir Gerald du Maurier, who was "firm, discreet, unerring in his choice of emphasis and his avoidance of the cheap finery which his part invites" and who "holds together the fragments in his own person."[11] Also, a Viennese actress, Leonora Bonda, brought to London for the role of the maid, realized a "satisfying glitter . . . from parts of her performance."[12]

Again, attention is called to Levy's dialogue, which "flows easily" and contains passages with "admirable sparkle."[13] At least in part, the criticism of plot as merely adroit scenes and characters as marionettes seems to stem from the critics' unfamiliarity with the original play or from their "missing something which a Viennese audience would perceive and enjoy."[14]

Whatever the criticism of *The Church Mouse,* its story, when transformed into a conventional farce about two rakish industrialists in *Springtime for Henry,* was revitalized into an American success. This success directly depends on the amoral purity of Levy's use of standard farce techniques that wittily combine themes of sex, corporate buyouts, and middle-class mores.

If I Were You (1938)

A farce based on an idea from a Thorne Smith novel, *If I Were You* was cowritten with Paul Hervey Fox, produced by Fox, and directed by Levy. This play, Levy's last one that deals with identity changes, is about an energetic wife, Nellie Blunt, and her husband, whose bodies are exchanged by the magic of a pixie servant girl. In a series of improvisationally styled scenes, husband and wife have difficulty remembering who she/he is and attempt to regain their real identities. But such scenes, lacking a driving authorial idea, tend only to belabor the basic concept. Smith's "broad fantas-tification"[15] is thus turned into rowdy slapstick with no invention by the authors to give direction to the scenes. To Brooks Atkinson, in the "hearty roistering" that follows the change, there is one inspired moment of theater in the "furious brawl behind a sofa and a fleeting glimpse of the pixie in long flannels."[16]

With previews at the McCarter Theater in Princeton, New Jer-sey, before its opening at the Mansfield Theater in New York, the play closed after only eight performances, one critic admitting to some people in the audience thinking it funny: "They roared at it, they did."[17] Atkinson's verdict on the play was to describe it as an "exercise in japery."[18]

As with some of Levy's less successful plays, *If I Were You* has promise in the first act, but fails to deliver on that promise.

A Television Trilogy (BBC, 1952)

The Great Healer

Three short plays—*The Great Healer, The Island of Cipango,* and *The Truth about the Truth*—reflect the concerns of Levy's full-length stage plays, the first a conventional comedy, the second a Chekhovian-Rattiganesque piece, and the third a Pirandellian com-edy about a playwright, an actress, and a maid.

With its mixture of naturalism and fantasy, *The Great Healer* is the story of two vaudeville actresses whose early friendship is resumed on the occasion of the fiftieth wedding anniversary cele-bration of one of them. She is Kitty, the actress who, by conniving, stole her upper-class husband from her friend, Rosie, to whom he was engaged at the time. Unfulfilled in her marriage, she reverts to her lower-class nature, when her former friend makes an unex-pected appearance to congratulate her on her anniversary. After a few glasses of champagne, they relive old times. Defying the hus-band who fussily awaits confirmation of rumors of royal honors, they noisily leave the stuffy party and make their way to the local pub. In a twist of fate, the butler of the obviously dysfunctional family turns out to be the illegitimate son of the betrayed actress, a case of identity reminiscent of the butler in Levy's earlier play, *The Devil.*

The sentimentality of the play is undercut by the ironic realism of their situations: one trapped in a loveless marriage and the other, alive with vitality, just as unfortunate in her personal life.

The Island of Cipango

The exotic title of this second play in Levy's trilogy is a sharp contrast with the unromantic and unfulfilled lives of the three main characters.

The setting is a dismal office in the home of an editress who runs a woman's magazine. The assistant editor, Brocket, is intelligent and alcoholic. He drinks from self-loathing as a writer of letters to the lovelorn, expressing his self-contempt by referring to his boss as "Medusa" and addressing romantic aspirants as "Dulcineas" and Gerald as "husband." His assistant/secretary is Dorothy, a woman in a comfortable but unromantic marriage with Gerald, a clerk in the same office. Gerald knows that his wife is in love with Brocket, and he bears that knowledge with the understanding patience of a Chekhovian husband; for example, Masha's schoolteacher husband in *The Three Sisters.*

Within this triangular situation, one of Brocket's correspondents, Opal, takes his advice seriously, makes an appearance, and asks to meet her nonexistent pen pal who has promised to take her to Cipango. Brocket's self-loathing is only intensified by his face-to-face encounter with a pathetic lonely heart. At the end he leaves with her, vowing to see her to Cipango no matter how he may have to get the money to do so.

In a superbly ironic O. Henrylike twist, Gerald presents his wife with a turquoise brooch that he says Brocket had asked him to give her if he (Brocket) should leave. Dorothy's ironic response is that she wished Gerald, rather than Brocket, had bought the brooch for her:

Gerald: Nice of you to say so, Dot.
Dorothy: Say so? I *would,* rather.

*Gerald: (unconvinced)*Would you? Well, there you are. Just shows how
  little I know.
Dorothy: I think you know a great deal.
Gerald: Oh well . . . This bun's on the stale side.
Dorothy: I know. They're yesterday's, I expect.
Gerald: Yes.[19]

The real irony lies in Gerald's having bought the brooch and then
lied about the donor, in deference to Dorothy's romantic feeling for
Brocket. Levy's characters suggest those of Chekhov, whose lives
of quiet resignation are touched momentarily by fantasy and by a
world that cannot be. All three accept the truths of their lives with
a clear understanding of them. For Dorothy it is the denial of her
longings for romance, for Gerald the knowledge of Dorothy's romantic interest in Brocket, and for Brocket a guilt for his wasted
life and his betrayal of Opal.

Like Rattigan's schoolmaster in *The Browning Version,* they
have faced their respective realities and emerged, however harshly
life has treated them, with their dignity intact. Rattigan's Chekhovian schoolmaster who, after the most disappointing day of his
life, returns to the routines of life, addressing his unfaithful wife
with the final comment in the play: "Come along, my dear. We
mustn't let our dinner get cold." Levy's play ends on a similar note,
as Gerald and Dorothy share the one bun left for tea. For now, the
mundane remark about the stale bun makes possible a veneer of
dignity to get them through the moment of intense disappointment.

The Truth about the Truth

In this Pirandellian experiment involving the relationship between art and life, Levy intermingles two plots, one from real life
and the other from the play of an unsuccessful playwright. Life
imitates art in the life of an actress, Diana, and her maid, Violet,
in their dealings with a would-be playwright, Dodson who is, also,
a not very successful printer from the provinces. In a turnabout of
male-female roles, he becomes a farcical victim of the two women.

Levy describes Violet as a maid whose eccentricity would be
welcomed in aristocratic circles, but who is wildly bizarre to the
conventional middle class. For example, before announcing Dodson's arrival to Diana, Violet introduces herself to him as a witch
and then impudently proceeds to engage him in a debate about his

play, accusing him of being one of those playwrights who write predictably and do not tell the truth. Then, responding to his challenge to support her accusation, she irritates him with an accurate outline of the plot of his play—titled, as is Levy's play, *The Truth about the Truth*. The Pirandellian play-within-a-play confusion is deliberate, the Italian dramatist's name even mentioned at one point in the dialogue. In their debate about contrasting truths, Violet rapidly gains the edge, keeping up her side of the argument with a surprising knowledge of dramatic jargon. Driven to exasperation when she finally utters the word he had been expecting, "escapism," Dodson resorts to name-calling, reminding her that her profession is witchcraft and his, stagecraft.

In their views on the relationship of art to life, they represent distinct contrasts. To Violet, truth is literal life, and it is the dramatist's responsibility to find some fresh way to present it. To Dodson, truth is larger than life and thus involves exaggeration. Perhaps reflecting Levy's own personal conflict between politics and art at a time that he had decided not to "stand" ("run" in American parlance) for a second term in Parliament, Dodson argues that the artist is one whose exaggerations are true and the politician is one whose exaggerations are false.

Their debate about art (in particular, Violet's uncanny prediction of Dodson's plot) serves as the framework for the real-life plot, which in turn simulates that of Dodson's play. Diana reveals that, after graduating from the Royal Academy of Dramatic Arts (RADA), she had acted in a failed play, *Marching Orders,* and had been fascinated with the idea of meeting a live playwright (Dodson) for the first time. Her recounting of the experience turns out to be the plot of Dodson's play. Now a successful actress who has had a surfeit of Ritz, sables, Cartier, and caviar, she longs for tripe and onions, so she has arranged the meeting with Dodson, rather than receiving his script by mail. She aggravates Dodson's growing discomfort by acting out his predictable plot, even entering, at one point, in a gown exactly like the one described in his script, which is about an actress, a playwright, and an impudent maid. Both Diana's conversations with Violet and Dodson and her telephone calls to male friends are duplicates of the dialogue Dodson had written into his play.

Finally, the phone having broken down and Diana delaying the reading of the play (since the reading would only be interrupted by the repairmen), Dodson leaves, scowling and scarlet at having been used. He has been given his "marching orders." His departure for his "Midland cell" in Burton-on-Trent leaves Diana and Violet to proclaim, respectively, "What an extraordinary young man!" and "What an exit!" (20).

Of the three television plays, *The Truth about the Truth* is the wittiest, both in dialogue and in the ingenious interweaving of art and life. Levy's stagecraft consists of a continuous turning in on themselves of four levels of reality: Diana's bored existence (Levy's play, titled *The Truth about the Truth*), the play by Dodson (similarly titled), Violet's prediction of Dodson's plot, and, finally, Diana's acting out of that prediction. Thirty years later, Tom Stoppard employed a similar device in *The Real Thing* (1982), a play about actors and a dramatist named Henry, whose play is being rehearsed as act 1 of Stoppard's play and then played out in their personal lives.

In all three of Levy's television plays, realism triumphs over romance. Out of failures in marriage, career, art, and, indeed, life, like those of Chekhov, O. Henry, and Rattigan (an unlikely trio), he has created poignantly comic and ironic cameos of people whose success consists of living with the truths about themselves. All three deal with life as a game of truths, a subject that courses its way through all of Levy's plays.

Anniversary or The Rebirth of Venus (1941, BBC radio)

Yet another play about a search for love by a woman, *Anniversary* deceptively begins as a mystery, changes in midcourse into a debate on the mating game, and ends as a parable of modern life between the sexes. On a train from Boulogne to Paris, a woman, after fending off some would-be sharers of her compartment, is finally outmaneuvered by a persistent economics professor. Wearing a veil and carrying a box with a gun, she intends to kill herself when the train nears Amiens. There a year earlier she had met her former lover, an engineer whose work eventually took her place as mistress in his life. Her plans to shoot herself on the anniversary and at the place of their meeting turn into a new romantic entanglement with the Boulogne University economics professor who insists on co-occupying her compartment.

In another O. Henrylike ironic ending, Levy deftly handles an undercutting of the potential sentimentality by having Clara leave the box with the gun for the next occupant, a girl who is joined by a man recognized by Clara as her engineer. She responds to the girl's reminder of the forgotten parcel: "No, I didn't forget it. I left it. For you. Good afternoon."[20] The engineer who has joined the girl in the compartment has, as well, recognized Clara's voice as she wills her box to the girl.

Clara is among Levy's characters such as Nella in *Young Madame Conti,* Madame Tantpis in *Springtime for Henry,* and Susie Sachs in *The Church Mouse*—women who demonstrate Levy's affinity with the continental treatment of romance rather than that of Barrie, to whom he has often been compared. In each case sentimentality is undercut by a naturalistic survival instinct. Like the characters in a Schnitzler play (e.g., *La Ronde*), Clara takes on added dimension as a parable of a continuing human experience, whose only change consists of a different set of characters.

The story of *Anniversary* is a slight one. Its technique, however, is not slight—the suspense-creating dialogue in which for more than half the play Clara deflects the questions of the Don. Dispelled when she admits her guise as widow, the mystery turns to romance, only to veer from romance to parabolic irony in the final scene. All three—mystery, romance, and parable—are successfully realized by the flow of dialogue that maneuvers the turns cleverly.

As the Don's curiosity is aroused, the widow responds to his assurance that he is not up on the ritual of picking up strange women on a train:

> *The Widow:* Listen! Why do you think I am wearing this ridiculous veil?
> *The Don:* I've no idea. I thought it was part of widowhood.
> *The Widow:* So it was, in Queen Victoria's time: not since.
> *The Don:* Ah, that was my period. I'm a little shaky on the twentieth century.
> *The Widow:* I am not a widow.
> *The Don:* You're not.
> *The Widow:* Figuratively perhaps! Literally no.
> *The Don:* You wouldn't by any chance be a . . . No. *(He shakes his head.)*
> *The Widow:* A spy?
> *The Don:* Yes.
> *The Widow:* No. I'm afraid not. I'm sorry. (5–6)

The mystery is created solely in the dialogue of the play, a technique appropriate for the medium of radio. The suspense is built by the stichomythic question-answer technique. At one point, the path of questioning is curved by the Don's confession of his doubt that the academician "can tell a beautiful woman from her description but I doubt if we could tell one by sight." The Widow ironically accommodates him with a description of herself—"high cheek bones, red-gold hair, light eyes set rather deep and far apart, a pale skin and a full large mouth that I paint scarlet."

> The Don: No! But Madam, you are ravishing!
> The Widow: Exactly. That's what I told you.
> The Don: Don't think me fulsome but you—you're the loveliest creature I've ever met.
> The Widow: I haven't told you about my teeth.
> The Don: (dashed) Ah, I knew it. Here's the flaw. How are your teeth?
> The Widow: Perfect.
> The Don: It is too much.
> The Widow: So now perhaps you understand why I am wearing this veil.
> The Don: Forgive me, no. I must seem very dense.
> The Widow: (after a moment) Ah! I understand. And with your appearance, people . . . I see! (7)

This apparently diversionary exchange of lines at the same time leads to her explanation of the real reason for the veil and dispels that very reason. Taking its place is a verbal sexual seduction, in which the two hurriedly complete arrangements to spend time together in Paris. Double entendres take over:

> The Widow: It's settled! I come with you to your conference tomorrow morning and you come with me to my Bel Tabarin tomorrow night! How old are you? Sixty?
> The Don: No, no. Forty-six.
> The Widow: Better and better.
> The Don: We—er—we mature early.
> The Widow: You've matured beautifully. You're exactly ripe. Oh, this hateful train! I wish we were out of it. I wish we'd arrived! (22)

The urgency of the moment drives them to get out of the train at the next station, Clercy, and travel the rest of the distance to Paris in a hired open car. As they do so, The Man (the lover who had jilted her) and The Girl, a new potential conquest, occupy the train compartment vacated by The Woman and The Don. On this note, the play ends with its suggestion that the Widow's action may be a game she has played before, and, as well, that The Man and The Girl will act out yet another reprise of that game. The bathos of a possible shooting is cleverly averted, and a sharply ironic tone takes over. Is The Don, too, playing The Widow's game? Or is he a victim of his own intellectual puffery? Only after they have arranged their rendezvous in Paris do his earlier comments return hauntingly as an explanation of her failed love affair with the engineer:

> The war you have been waging, though you didn't know it, was against the Royal Institute of Engineers. You won the first round that week in Paris. But the Royal Institute scored the final knock-out. He was merely the battle-ground and the prize. And if you'd won the prize, you would have destroyed it in the process. If you'd read as many books as I have, you'd have known that you were outmatched from the start. (19)

The patronizing superiority of the Don is still another in the many variations of the arguments posed by Levy's male protagonists. From the first through the last of his stage plays, the arguments have constituted the debates in his comedies, farces, morality plays, and realistic dramas. The aural nature of radio drama allows Levy to exercise maximum use of his forte as a dramatist—dialogue. He is able even to divert the play's mode from mystery to romance and, finally, to ironic parable, blending three genres in which he worked throughout his career.

As a pastiche of moods, *Anniversary* succeeds where his full-length pastiches for the stage sometimes falter or fail when the promise of the first act is not fulfilled in the remaining acts. His short pieces for radio and television, his first acts, and parts of some plays such as the prologue to *The Jealous God* are not marred by the plot spinning or the repetition to which his longer plays sometimes fall victim. In their compactness, they effectively dramatize a theme that pervades his stage dramas—the irreconcilable division of body and mind, the real and the ideal, or, as reflected in one of Levy's titles, *Cupid and Psyche*.

8

Conclusions: Mirror to an Age

With all but seven of his twenty-two staged plays produced in the 1920s and 1930s, Levy belongs, in John Elsom's view, to a "host of lesser writers"[1] who, like Ibsen, Shaw, Maugham, and Coward, sought a compromise between naturalism and the well-made play. Elsom's chosen criteria for his definition of the well-made play consist of three Aristotelian principles—hero, crisis and the unities of time, place, and action. Heroes, although superior to others in breeding or nobility of mind, are like others in their possession of a character flaw. The crisis is that point in the play of highest plot complication, a point at which the fortunes of the hero take a turn for the better or the worse. The three unities consist of time, place, and action: a twenty-four hour span within which the action occurs, one locale, and one main action without distracting subplots.

Among others, these criteria have generally been the basis for the older comedy of manners and the more recent drawing-room comedy made famous as the well-made play or French boulevard play—the *pièce bien faite*. Applied in its mechanical sense, the term had become strongly pejorative on the English stage by the middle of the twentieth century.

Until the 1950s, when Brechtian epic theater and the Beckettian absurdist theater broke through the strictures of the well-made play, British dramatists of the first half of the twentieth century had attempted to break or bend the rules by various means. Shaw adapted from Ibsen the latter's compromise with naturalism, adding a dependence on the liveliness and wit of the dialogue. T. S. Eliot and Christopher Fry attempted to bend the rules by means of poetic language. In the matter of the formulaic crisis, Rattigan's rejection of it is illustrated in *The Deep Blue Sea* in Hester's attempt at suicide at the beginning rather than at the end of the play and in her consequent choice to "struggle on alone, walking towards a sunset of flowery wallpaper and tattered furniture."[2] J. B. Priestley used an O. Henry–like unexpected twist at the end, as in *The Inspector Calls.* Noel Coward and N. C. Hunter followed the Chekhovian design of using a "plausible naturalistic incident,"[3] enclosing that incident in accurately observed social/historical texture.

Levy's plays reflect affinities with all of the above. His own definition of the well-made play avoids the detailed particulars such as the three suggested by Elsom or those of the even more highly prescribed formula in Stephen Stanton's introduction to *Camille and Other Plays.* Instead, Levy's comments on his style are expansive. He criticizes "the kind of play that is benumbed and devitalized by its author's technical savoir faire, the play without an independent life of its own, the play fettered and earthbound by the playwright's cerebrations; for what we rightly look for is not a well-drilled carriage-hack but Pegasus. And winged horses are not the product of scientific calculation. . . . Then, if he [the artist] is blessed beyond his deserts, one morning in his stable, lo and behold, is Pegasus. . . ."[4]

In the interest of naturalism, Levy loosely observes, sometimes ignores, the unities of time and action, but it is the artificial crisis and, thereby, the plot with which Levy experiments. With rare exceptions—for example, the use of a cup and saucer at the end of one act and the smashing of a vase at the end of another in *Art and Mrs. Bottle*—Levy de-emphasizes the artificial teeter-totter action that creates suspense and that leads to an equally artificial climax.

In *Mud and Treacle,* the wordless Prologue depicts the ending of the play, thereby demystifying the plot action of its potential tension. Instead, the emphasis shifts from the action to its cause, as characters engage in debates on the nature of love, sex, social theories, and so on. What Levy has described, in a dedicatory note to his daughter, Jemima, as his "own slow-footed, aberrant rationality,"[5] replaces the requisite emotional/psychological progression of suspense. The resulting loss of focus and impetus in the serious plays sometimes creates a sense of repetition rather than movement, especially when the debate remains unresolved.

His inconclusive endings derive partly from Levy's sense of the repetitive nature of most conflicts as they recur in successive generations, taking on the fashions and forms of the time. In the interest of naturalism, he thus rejects both contrived conclusions and the artificial crisis inherent in those conclusions. In a dedicatory note to his son, Jonathan, he writes that the

> clothes, slang and theatrical convention [of *Cupid and Psyche*] will have shifted their shapes just perceptibly. But Miss Thompson's brand of feminism will continue to contradict itself; Mildred, still earnestly endeavoring, will continue to caricature her betters; Mac will still fear a mechanical universe that reduces him to insignificant impotence, and Thompson, conversely, will continue to fear the responsibilities of free will; while Deptford with his instinctive power of adaptation will continue to love life and Gabriel with his resentment of pain will still hate it.[6]

Levy continues with the advice that although he (Jonathan) will resolve neither these conflicts nor most others, he should take sides, for "I like a partisan. It is not easy to fight your enemies and to love them. But it has been done. So why not you?"

Levy's love of debate is the source of success in his comedies but of mixed success in the serious plays where the intellect gets in the way of dramatic values, resulting in a deliberate dispersal of focus in both plot and theme. In his way, he has bent the well-made play conventions to his own style and thematic purposes.

Although each of Levy's plays rests on its own merits, the first four are significant as introductions to his subsequent work. There is hardly a subject, theme, or stylistic characteristic in the later plays that is not at least suggested in *This Woman Business, A Man with Red Hair, Mud and Treacle,* and *Mrs. Moonlight.*

This Woman Business, in particular, contains the seeds of situations and characters to be found in much of his subsequent writing. Overriding all other themes are (1) the battle of the sexes and (2) the feminist themes emerging from that subject. These concerns in most plays are dramatized within the narrower framework of marriage or situations in which marriage is contemplated. Societal roles of women, as in the plays of Barrie, Maugham, Rattigan and, earlier, Pinero, create domestic and moral problems whose solutions seem non-existent. Levy, however, goes beyond his contemporaries in the way in which his women take their problems into their own hands in naturalistic fashion. In *This Woman Business,* Crawford begins the succession of women characters who do so.

A thief-turned-life force, Crawford reminds the misogynists that she has been mothering them all since she arrived, having reconciled Brown to both his wife and to Crofts, successfully fending off Honey's amorous attempts, and unresentfully agreeing with Judge Bingham that she is an adventuress, since every woman who is worth her salt is an adventuress. Her final bit of Shavian proclamation is addressed to Hodges, who, despite his protestations to the contrary, is attracted to her:

> You think Woman's inferior to Man because she can't waste time on his morality and art and laws and the rest of his toys. It's quite true, she can't. She'll smash them to pieces when they interfere with her own ends; but her own ends are the human race! There, you can put that in your essay . . . . There's the whole truth about myself . . . .[7]

The truth to which Crawford refers takes on broader significance in Levy's remaining plays, beyond the subject of the battle of the sexes to the discovery of truths about themselves. For example, the variety of middle-class artists in *The Devil* undergo self-examinations, their fantasies and realities colliding, with moral lessons for all. Crawford's truth, with happy consequences in Levy's comedies and farces, takes its toll in the moralities of characters such as Kate Settle in *The Jealous God,* Martha Cotton in *Return to Tyassi,* and Liza Cotton in *Public and Confidential.*

Levy's second play, his adaptation of *A Man with Red Hair,* deals with the darker side of human experience, at its best cynicism, at its worst human cruelty, seen in the gothic dimensions of Crispin's evil, which takes intellectual/psychological cruelty to its ultimate end in the form of the complete control of one human by another. Societal evil becomes his concern in later plays, as in the impersonality of a central European court and the cruelty or corruption in the guise of small town morality. Weaned on the writing of mystery scripts for films in the 1920s, Levy invests some of his dramas with a sense of mystery and horror. The darker ironies of individual and societal injustices begin in *A Man with Red Hair* and continue in his morality plays, especially in his adaptations of continental plays by Bruno Frank, Marcel Pagnol, Gaston Baty-Flaubert, Siegfried Geyer, and Ladislaus Fodor.

In his third play, *Mud and Treacle,* the character Crispin is revisited in Solomon, a psychologically realistic version of his predecessor. Solomon's mind-body struggle externalizes itself as a psychosis that results in insanity and murder. Levy works out of conflicts that develop into a modern version of the medieval morality play, the mode for a series of serious dramas to follow, such as *The Devil, The Jealous God,* and *Public and Confidential.* As a writer of modern moralities, Levy is concerned not so much with the medieval reward of good and punishment of evil as he is with good as the pursuit of truth and evil as the refusal to question, debate, and protest. His is an ongoing Faustian quest that never says to the moment, "Stay, thou art fair." To end the play and yet keep the debate going may remain an unresolved structural problem in some of Levy's serious plays, but it is effectively realized within the confines of a comedy such as *The Rape of the Belt.*

Levy, who intended his fourth stage play, *Mrs. Moonlight,* as a satire on the sentimentality and fantasy of a James Barrie drama, was surprised at the critics' serious response and the public's embrace of it as a moving drama in the tradition of Barrie. Even in its success as a "sentimental" drama, however, the romantic element has a built-in naturalism that foreshadows the Ibsen-like realism of Kate Settle in *The Jealous God* and Liza Foote in *Public and Confidential.*

In the first four plays, then, Levy's dual world is established, variously identified as male and female, mind and body, intellect and instinct, society and the individual, fantasy and reality.

One may see, as well, especially in *This Woman Business,* characters who will be revisited in later plays. Serious variations of Crawford appear in Kate of *The Jealous God* and Liza of *Public and Confidential.* Her darkest manifestations are Nella in *Young Madame Conti* and Emma in *Madame Bovary.* She is reinvented in the women of the comedies and farces: the two wives in *Clutterbuck,* Miss Smith (Madame Tantpis) in *Springtime for Henry,* and Hippolyte and Antiope in *The Rape of the Belt.* Crawford's feminist theories are forcefully and modishly trumpeted in the words of the Pankhurst-like Miss Thompson of *Cupid and Psyche.*

The male characters of later plays are there as well in his first play. The poet Honey reappears in *The Poet's Heart,* a pre-Brechtian expressionistic play in which Tennison moves in and out of the realistic and dream worlds, his dilemma resolved only in old age as his Don Juan–like character acquires a contemplative persona. Judge Bingham, as a public figure representing the expectations of the socio-moral code, undergoes a variation as the politician Joe Malkin in *Public and Confidential.* Addleshaw, the businessman-rake, takes center stage in *Springtime for Henry* in the two roués, Henry Dewlip and John Jelliwell. Croft, the anthropologist who has his strongly held theories on the place of women in ancient and modern societies, is given a new identity in *Return to Tyassi,* in the dead ex-husband (and his brother) of Martha Cotton, and, in a much fuller treatment of theories about women, in the biologist Thompson in *Cupid and Psyche.*

Stylistic patterns, as well, begin in the four early plays, continuing and deepening in later dramas. There is, first and foremost, Levy's ear for dialogue to which all critics have called attention, dialogue that is at times Shavian, at times Wodehousian, and still other times, as one critic put it, simply witty backchat. Always his dialogue carries the sharp edge of Levy's own debating skills. Even in those plays that garnered mixed reviews, it is his talent for dialogue that compensates for faults such as loss of focus in theme or plot.

A second important characteristic, the debate, is introduced in his early plays, even if that debate seems at times one-sided in *This Woman Business* and *A Man with Red Hair.* In the first it is conducted in a series of disquisitions by each of the males on the subject of women, only to be vigorously and delightfully challenged by two unexpected intruders in the persons of Crawford and Addleshaw. In *A Man with Red Hair* the debate is totally one-sided, taking the form of Crispin's masochistic sermons on the human need to suffer pain. The debate in later plays is conducted more or less on a level of equality among the participants, realized especially successfully in the arguments and counterarguments of Nella Conti and the court members in *Young Madame Conti* and in the sophisticated bantering of Antiope and Hippolyte versus Theseus and Heracles in *The Rape of the Belt.* To Levy, an effective parliamentary debater and a public speaker, the debating style came naturally.

Very much a dramatist whose personal participation in his time took the form of military service in two world wars and later in political and cultural wars as a Member of Parliament, Levy reflects his era in his plays, even as he questions it. The influences of his time are seen in the many similarities of his plays to those of his contemporaries. The drawing room play—comedy or drama— reigned supreme, with Shaw towering over the lesser dramatists with his thesis play or comedy of ideas. At the time of Shaw's death in 1950, the dramatic era which he had begun was in what has been identified by critics as its twilight. Coward and Rattigan enjoyed the lion's share of popularity with their polite middle-class plays, mostly adhering to the established values of the culture, even as they occasionally condemned the abuses of those values in their miniature portraits of individuals and families. *Hay Fever* and *This Happy Breed* by Coward and *The Winslow Boy* and *The Browning Version* by Rattigan are only a few examples of these portraits. Other popular dramatists such as Barrie, Maugham, Priestley, and Lonsdale settled for comfortable middle-class comedies or problem plays that dealt with romance, marital conflicts, and social problems, while others such as Eliot and Fry wrote for elite audiences. It remained for the angry young men and the continental influences of Beckett and Brecht to effect the first major changes on the English stage since Shaw did so in the 1890s.

As one of the many playwrights writing in the dramatic currency that existed between the advents of Shaw and Beckett, Levy made minor adaptations, particularly in his morality plays. Although the greater number of his plays mixed comedy and drama, his longest-running plays are the comedies, his fantasy play, *Mrs. Moonlight,* and his music-and-dance spectacular, *Ever Green.*

Most obviously, his major affinities are to Shaw, in plays such as *This Woman Business, Mud and Treacle, The Poet's Heart, Cupid and Psyche,* and *The Rape of the Belt.* All have something in them of Shaw's thesis play. He has great fun at the expense of middle-class respectability. In his battles of the sexes, the female life force contends with male rationality. Levy's Crawford is the young upstart, as is Shaw's Vivie in *Mrs. Warren's Profession.* Levy's Doggie, the class-hating Labourite in *Mud and Treacle,* is in the tradition of Snobby Price in *Major Barbara.* Levy's young Tennison in *The Poet's Heart* bears resemblance to John Tanner in *Man and Superman.* Miss Thompson, the new woman in *Cupid and Psyche,* strides with vigor through a medley of fashionably modern ideas. And the defeat of the two Amazon queens, Hippolyte and Antiope, in *The Rape of the Belt,* resembles the sadness accompanying Shaw's bleak view of contemporary civilization in *Heartbreak House.* Characterized by socio-moral arguments, rather than philosophical ones, Levy's plays, however, remain close to their naturalistic roots and in this respect have much in common with Shaw's early Ibsen-like plays such as *Mrs. Warren's Profession.*

The second of his contemporaries to whom Levy bears most resemblance is Coward, particularly in *Clutterbuck* whose source of laughter consists, as does Coward's *Private Lives,* of the symmetrical construction of the sympathies and the hostilities that the two wives and the two husbands share. The release of tensions and the disruption of marital boredom is only temporary, with the accepted social order as the normal order of things, an order that is temporarily upset but restored in the end. The same is true of *This Woman Business* and *Cupid and Psyche,* which, like Coward's early *Hay Fever* or Rattigan's *French Without Tears,* follow the order-chaos-order sequence of comedy. Importantly, Levy's dialogue also resembles more the informal, sometimes chatty, quality of Coward and Rattigan than the poetry and intellectual wit of Shaw.

Contrasting with both Shavian and Cowardian traditions, however, *Springtime for Henry* belongs to an older genre of English comedy—the Restoration-style farce in which the reigning order is the amoral world of the roué. The two rakes deviate from the prevailing social order, so that when that morality temporarily reforms one of them and disrupts their lives, a revolt inevitably occurs. In their ideal world of natural instincts, the two rakes freely dance their way through their complications like bacchantes with vine leaves in their hair. Their amoral world, interrupted by an aberrationally moral impulse, is not too different from that in the highly organized anarchy in the plays of Joe Orton, a later contemporary of Levy's and a devasting critic of societal attitudes. In Levy's canon, *Springtime for Henry* stands apart from the other comedies in this respect.

Levy does not extend the boundaries of existing drama in any major way, except for his realistic depiction of women who do take matters into their own hands in more realistic and more rational ways, perhaps, than do those of his contemporaries. In so doing, they de-victimize themselves, and, as with Shaw's women, do realize a status of equality or superiority in the battle of the sexes and in defiance of societal restrictions. Levy, as political activist, is very much a part of the vortex of his times and, as dramatist, is a mirror to his age, reflecting both its dramatic styles and thematic concerns.

His dramas and comedies, however, like those of his traditional contemporaries, suddenly seemed old-fashioned in the context of the changes which Beckett and Brecht brought to the stage. In England, there was 1956 with its angry young man, Jimmy Porter, in Osborne's play, *Look Back in Anger,* produced a year before

Levy's *The Rape of the Belt* and ten years before Levy's last play, *Public and Confidential.* It remained for Harold Pinter's comedies of menace, Alan Ayckbourn's comedies of embarrassment and his dizzying use of physical stage space, Tom Stoppard's linguistic dazzle, and Joe Orton's deliciously organized anarchy to give a new face to traditional comic forms. Pinter's minimalism and Stoppard's parodic exoticism provided a strong share of what seemed wholly new comedy.

In farce, although Ayckbourn and Orton worked within the traditional form, they extended the boundaries of Shaw, Coward and Levy. Ayckbourn at first experimented with the use of stage space and with plot chronology, allowing actors or directors to rearrange his plot chronology in a given performance. Orton's extension consists of a total rejection of prevailing social morality, using conventional techniques of farce to parody themselves and conventional attitudes, behavior, and language to parody themselves—the result a carefully structured chaos that becomes the new social order.

As a corrective, comedy has traditionally functioned as a means of releasing tensions created by order and authority on both the private and social levels. Disorder temporarily becomes the order of the day, but eventually order resumes its place. Its circular pattern was challenged by Shaw's linear movement toward a philosophically higher order of life, with an occasional exception in a play such as *Heartbreak House.* Whether circular or linear, however, the pattern postulates an optimism, whatever problems lurk beneath it. Ayckbourn's, on the other hand, is an increasingly dark vision of society and life, opposed in an ironic way by Orton's joyous celebration of anarchy. Levy's comedies and dramas serve as correctives and, as well, the linearly dramatized optimism of Shaw (e.g., *Cupid and Psyche* and *The Rape of the Belt*). His morality dramas, however, share with Ayckbourn and Orton their darker view of life.

Although best known for his comedies, he is a mirror to his age in the wide variety of genres represented by his plays—gothic horror, melodrama, fantasy, Ibsenite problem play, morality play, mythical burlesque, musical extravaganza, and his adaptations of other writers' work. His writing spans the middle half of the twentieth century—the old and the new dramatic eras. He embraced the high priests of both: Shaw, a clear influence on his plays, and Beckett, whose plays he admired. He echoed the concerns and styles of a large group of popular dramatists between Shaw and Beckett, most notably Coward, Rattigan, and Barrie, and, as well, the continental dramatists whose influence on the English stage was very much a part of the times—Ibsen, Chekhov, and Pirandello.

Appendix 1: Anatomy of the Theatre

BENN LEVY

For these four papers that I am to read to you, I have chosen a general title that I hope will not be misleading. It is not my intention to dissect the components of the theater with a view to demonstrating how plays should be written, acted or produced. That lesson is not to be had for the asking. Indeed, it will be part of my contention that the only thing connected with the theatre which is worth teaching cannot in fact be taught. It is indeed only on secondary matters that anybody discussing the drama is worth listening to, and beware of him who claims more.

These secondary matters, however, are not negligible. It is well to clear our heads, for example, about the proper or the best functions of the theatre and, having done so, to decide how they may be stimulated; to decide how the theatre should organise itself or be organised; to decide whether we favour a popular theatre or an aristocratic theatre; a didactic theatre or a tired businessman's theatre; an actors' theatre or a producer's theatre or a dramatist's theatre, or a combination of all these things; and, if we decide on this last, which on the face of it, is the most attractive proposition, to decide whether indeed it is feasible or Utopian. Once we have decided what kind or kinds of a theatre we would like, it is also worth examining how far the State can or should help it on its way.

Now it is open to anybody to assert without fear of demonstrable refutation that the function of the theatre is to elevate the soul or to divert the weary or to enrich the mind or to titillate the passions or to excite the prejudices or to ease the digestion: all these points of view are arguable and each has its partisans. Who is in the right of it cannot be demonstrated. Pick your dogma, and no one can gainsay you. It is as though you were choosing a hat. You may choose it to keep your head warm, to decorate yourself, to keep the sun off or the rain out, to keep your hair in place or to conceal your baldness. What no one can prove is the absolute, the right, the proper function of a hat.

All I can hope to do, therefore, is to explain why I, for my part, favour

---

"Anatomy of the Theatre" is one of four Shute Lectures delivered by Benn Levy at the University of Liverpool. All appendices in this volume have been provided by Constance Cummings Levy.

the hat that I propose to model for you this evening, and, by discussing the reason for my choice, try to sell it to you.

First let me take you back to the past; not because the functions of the earliest theatre must necessarily be accepted for our times, but because we can at least accept that an institution must continuously evolve and cannot maintain vitality if all connections with its own roots be severed. The history of the theatre is well-trodden ground and in any case cannot be usefully condensed into a few perfunctory paragraphs. The pre-history of the theatre, however, is less familiar. We know, that is to say, that the theatre derives from ceremonial but what does ceremonial derive from? Anthropologists differ. Many tend to assume that the ceremonial and legend of early peoples represent an attempt to answer symbolically those questions which excite the curiosity of science in its maturity; that they are early attempts, in short, to rationalise the universe. The view that I, for my part, find more persuasive and of which Professor Radcliffe Brown is the protagonist, regards scientific curiosity as belonging to a later stage of civilisation and supposes ceremonial to be a means of stabilising, transmitting, and reinforcing social values and social coherence, of embodying and inculcating social morality. Natural law, a later concept, is the province of science. When an Andaman Islander constructs a bow in a certain way, it is not because he has calculated that, owing to the laws of nature, that is the most efficient way of doing it, but because, in the words of Radcliffe Brown, "any other way is wrong, is contrary to custom and law. Law, for the Andaman Islander, means that there is an order of the universe, characterised by absolute uniformity; this order was established once for all in the time of the ancestors, and is not to be interefered with, the results of any such interference being evil, ranging from merely minor ills such as disappointment or discomfort to great calamities. The law of compensation is absolute. Any deviation from law or custom will inevitably bring its results, and inversely any evil that befalls must be the result of some lack of observance. The legends reveal to our analysis a conception of the universe as a moral order."

We cannot help noting, though its author does not, how well this hypothesis corresponds to what we know of the early ceremonial and theatre of ancient Greece. Three comments immediately suggest themselves. If social morality be the prime concern of ceremonial and legend, it is not surprising that the origins of theater and church are inextricable and that in the rudimentary forms of theater the distinction between priest and poet is hard to make. But a less familiar consequence of this hypothesis is the clarifying light it throws on ancient Greek culture. There is so much in early Greek drama and poetry that is hard for us to accept and that we would have thought to have been wholly inacceptable to the enquiring scientific Greek mind that concerned itself so eagerly and so potently with problems of natural law and absolute truth. Not for them, one would have said, the unquestionable rule of custom or religious dogma. As this was a period of transition, however, when the newborn scientific mind was applying itself not only to natural phenomena but to hitherto accepted moral concepts, without, however, having yet wholly displaced the old order, the coexistence of these contrary attitudes is no more than we should expect.

But there is a third point also to which Radcliffe Brown's hypothesis leads us, and one which seems to favor the protagonists of a propagandist theatre.

Dance, song, legend, and ceremonial in early civilizations are frankly didactic. Their purpose is social and propagandist, and literally conservative. The notion of a song or ceremonial, whose tendency ran counter to accepted custom, is as unthinkable as in contemporary Russia. The social danger of allowing art to have its head is rationally obvious, and instinctively accepted by primitive societies. Plato, no less than the Kremlin and the Andaman Islanders, was alert to the danger. "Let me write a nation's song and I care not who makes its laws," is a familiar and profound quotation. Freedom for singers, therefore, can well be construed as an abdication of government. Whether this abdication should or should not be made really depends on whether you believe that the present and the past are better than the future. If you believe that the future holds no addition to human wisdom, but only subtractions from it; if you believe that the standards and the little store of knowledge that you and your contemporaries and partisans have achieved is the apex of potential human achievement, then it would be not only folly but immoral not to throw up defenses against the restless questioning artist. Every device of propaganda and of censorship becomes a duty. On this one point communist, fascist and Catholic are agreed. Tolerance can only belong either to the agnostic philosopher, certain of nothing save that he may be wrong, or to the mystic convinced that God is in His Heaven and that somehow truth will out. The latter, in his confidence, need not bolt the door against the future, while the agnostic, with his lack of confidence, must not. It is to these two philosophies that the doctrine of freedom belongs.

Where that doctrine is absent, didactic art, didactic drama, is inevitable. How far has either a place in liberal civilisation?

The first and simplest answer is that it can claim a place just as rightfully as in an authoritarian society. The key difference is that it would be heterogeneous rather than uniform—or at least, uniform only by an inconceivable accident. Liberal doctrine is maintained by a free multiplicity of opinion, emerging either in works of art or elsewhere. It does not require a self-denying ordinance on the part of artists, committing themselves to a kind of opinionless nihilism as though they were the B.B.C. In fact, where the social order is freely attacked and freely defended both sides of the continuing conflict will be and should be reflected in its art. It does not follow that when art is not exploited to cement the social fabric, it must therefore dissociate itself from social issues. The choice is with the artist. There will be no compulsion and no pruning.

If, however, the artist has the choice, what choice should he make? In fact the choice is, I think, largely illusory; for the simple reason that all great art is didactic willy-nilly. Life is its raw material. If art reflects life, it does so, however pure the intention, through a distorting mirror. That distortion constitutes a commentary whether we will or no. It is the conscious or unconscious consequence of the artist's personal values. An artist is not a dictaphone or a camera. He is at once more truthful and less accurate than they. Commentary is ineradicable.

But even if this were not so and if the theoretical aspirations of the "pure" artist were indeed attainable, art would still be basically didactic; for the illumination of life even without commentary, if such a separation were conceivable, is itself didactic. It extends knowledge; it expands the human consciousness. It teaches.

If the artist is thus destined to teach, whether he wishes to do so or not, should he not then accept his fate, select a creed, and frankly embrace a propagandist purpose? If he does not, will he not automatically dwindle into a confectioner, a decorator, a toymaker? If he does, will he dwindle into a sociologist, a missionary, or a topical commentator? Are these indeed the alternatives? Must a dramatist be either a mere entertainer or a mere pamphleteer?

From what I have said above, it is clear that provided he has the root of the matter in him, he will be primarily neither one nor the other, though secondarily he may be both. His conscious objective, however, is not wholly irrelevant. He may consciously aim to entertain, and thus to fill his purse; or to instruct, and thus to appease his social conscience; or to manufacture beauty and thus to satisfy an aesthetic theory. But let him not be enslaved by such purposes, for they can dislocate irreparably his own artistic mechanism. All he can do is to write, paint, sing, act, dance, or compose as wholeheartedly as he knows how and pray for the best. "It is just as bad," wrote Granville Barker, "to be thinking," while you write or produce a play, either of all the social evils you mean to expose, or the rest of the social service your theatre is doing, as it is to be calculating the money it will earn." I would add, it is just as bad to be thinking about the artistry that you are engaged upon. All these things, social effect, personal profit, and even beauty, are not the purpose but the by-products of creation, of the unthinking hot blind act of creation. What parents concentrate their minds upon their child at the moment of its begetting? Still less do they concentrate in that moment upon the money the child may bring them, or upon its social mission in life.

The quality of an engine is irrespective of its destination. The Kemble Express is no better an engine when it is bound for London, with all its complex social problems, than when it is bound for the lyrical harmony of the Cotswolds. It may think it's a better engine but it isn't. Similarly an artist cannot raise his own artistic status by the simple expedient of setting out to grind a social axe. Indeed he may, though not inevitably, lower it. An artist injures himself if he allows these conscious objectives, of which it is hard indeed to divest himself completely, to dominate his performance. He may head for the Cotswolds or for London. But if he fails to arrive there, he must not be perturbed, even though he be surprised. Least of all must he bind himself to his self-ordained schedule. He must not force his direction. He may arrive at his destination or he may not, but the decision must be allowed to lite in the lap of the gods. The gods are not only his indispensable collaborators but his senior partners.

This is the explanation of the comparative failure of propagandist art. It explains why *Widowers Houses* is a lesser play than *Heartbreak House* or *Major Barbara,* why *A Doll's House* or *Ghosts* are lesser works than *The Wild Duck.* It is not denied of course that even these lesser works are substantial achievements, but that is because a great artist can not easily destroy, though he can constrict, the divinity that is within him.

All this explains also why artists make bad politicians. The propagandist or politician must be consistently true to his political purpose. The artist must be true to something incalculably fluid, namely, himself. He knows by temperament no other loyalty. He cannot be loyal even to his yesterday's self, or to his tomorrow's, let alone to leaders or colleagues. He may be a doughty and a powerful warrior, but he is an unreliable one, just as likely to set about his friends as his foes. Of such material trusty propagandists are not made.

And yet this is not to say of course that he should isolate himself from the conflicts of his time. If he is above the battle, it must not be through indifference, nor must he be timorously fugitive from it. Unless he himself has fought, on one side or on many, he will be the lesser man, and therefore the lesser artist. "The man who writes plays for you," wrote Shaw to Ellen Terry, "must be more than a mere playwright." It was in reply to a letter of hers criticising him for wasting his time and talents as a vestryman in St. Pancras local politics. The rejoinder was a way of saying that while mere playwrights may be bred in ivory towers, great playwrights must be bred in the great world. Good swimmers are not trained on the river bank.

And yet, needless to say, experience is not enough. Even the man who is susceptible to experience (and not everybody is), even such a man, having had it in full measure has not necessarily the full equipment of an artist. He still lacks not merely craftsmanship, but that indefinable quality which distinguishes his work from that of the accomplished craftsman and which I am reduced to defining algebraically as X. Experience, craftsmanship, purpose, and subject matter are the tributaries and accessories of art. In the last analysis, only X counts, the unknown quantity, or rather the unknown quality which distinguishes the artist from the nonartist, but defies definition. A high-minded propagandist purpose is no substitute for it. A self-conscious purity will not capture it. Good taste, technical dexterity, aesthetic theory, nor grandiose subject can no more than temporarily disguise its absence. They may conceal the quintessential vacuum: they cannot fill it. Picasso, painting Guernica in more or less flat geometrical design, or a mother and child in orthodox academic idiom, emerges an unmistakable great artist, his stature founded not upon his purpose but upon what cannot be learned or taught.

Writers are frequently asked how they do their job, to describe the process. "The art of writing," said Sinclair Lewis, in reply to such a question, "is the power of applying the seat of the pants to a chair." In conformity with this answer Mr. Somerset Maugham is said to allot certain hours of the day to his desk, during which he sits, writing on a piece of paper incessantly the words W. Somerset Maugham, W. Somerset Maugham, W. Somerset Maugham. He sits there until such time as his pen can find more varied things to write. Books abound on how to do it; authors, sometimes of distinction, have purported to explain how they have done it. But the answers, short or long, usually amount in effect, to an evasion. They may describe the working habits of the writer, they may offer retrospective analyses of craftsmanship, or they may adumbrate a theory of the aesthetic. But the heart of the matter, the sine qua non, the secret of how the trick is turned and why not everyone can turn it, remains incommunicable. "I write my plays," said Mr. Shaw, "as my aunt used to write planchette," In other words, he can not tell us. Artists are secretaries. Moses did not compose the Ten Commandments. He "took them down." Useless, therefore, to have asked him to explain the mystery of composition.

If it is true, therefore, that the mystery is intelligible only to those who have experienced it, no one should be surprised that I have sought to express myself in negative terms. In any case, to talk around a subject may sometimes illuminate it, so I should like, before leaving it altogether, to discuss very briefly the nature of artistic experience and the process of transmutation.

Drama is a commentary on life. Only when the currency of drama is debased, is it a commentary on commentary, or rather a stale reflection of commentary. Childish make-believe is a child's apprehension of the component parts and characters of the world about it. By inventing and playing parts, he directly notes, as it were, the stern father, the persuasive mother, the functions and characteristics of the doctor, or the greengrocer, or the soldier. He extends his repertory of notations to the animal world. Indeed very early on, even when he is not ostensibly engaged in games of make-believe, he is creating characterizations for himself to play in daily life. Sometimes he amuses, and sometimes he shocks his elders by these simulations, according as whether his elders have appraised them as fantasies or as insincerities. Nor do these fantasies or insincerities cease with childhood. It could indeed perhaps be argued that one educative or social value of drama is to divert fantastications from life to the theater, that the child or the man can achieve genuineness by getting it out of his system. I don't know what the psychologists would have to say to this theory. I offer it as a notion for them to play with, if they've not already done so. They would, however, agree that the impulse to make-believe or to fantasticate would persist whether there were a theater or not, and it is certainly to the good that these congenital, personal falsities should be transmuted into artistic truths.

This transmutation is a common enough paradox. All art tells the truth by telling lies. It is after all a form of mendacity to select facts which suit your purpose and even then to distort them. But that is what the artist does. The physical inaccuracies of El Greco tell the truth about saintly asceticism. The improbable bulbousness of Rubens tells us a great deal of essential truth about womanishness. The frankly undisguised mendacities of the postimpressionists at first completely concealed from most of their contemporaries the truths that we now perceive them to have been telling. So it is with fiction, dramatic or otherwise. The false oversimplification, the singleness of contour, the unreal magnification that we see in Malvolio and Pecksniff, in Richard the Third and Emma Bovary have enlarged our common vision of the truth. Dickens in particular is transparent in his methods. He will offer you the picture of a human being from which he has deliberately eliminated all characteristics but one. The sole remaining ingredient that is left, for example to Uriah Heep, is a spurious humility. And yet, as the result of this falsehood, we have learnt more truly about mankind.

Do not make the mistake of supposing that Checkhov and his school provide any exception. They are playing the same game, though they are less easily caught out at it. They are pruning this, highlighting that, suppressing the other, elongating something else, but, because it is their chosen idiom, they are at more pains to cover up their tracks. That is neither a virtue nor a vice. Let it not be thought, however, that Checkhov for all his naturalism could have achieved his truths by wandering among the originals of his portraiture with a shorthand notebook. Literal transcription reveals less than it conceals. Were it not so, the artistic function could be dispensed with. Reporters would suffice.

How do we recognise this truth that emerges from a welter of falsification? Indeed, through the direct instrumentality of falsification, when we see it? How particularly do we recognise it for true when the artist ex hypothesi is telling us much that we do not know already? When shall we believe him and when not? For all that it may be blindingly new, we recognise it by experience, by a combination of direct experience, and imaginative experience. What we have experienced directly enables us to achieve experience imaginatively. Watch the child at his game or make-believe. He has met the doctor, he has seen him at work, he has heard his patter, he has unconsciously pigeonholed him, indeed even analysed and summarized him. From this starting point he is able to invent doctors, or a generic doctor, or if you like, a plausible individual doctor, operating in imagined circumstances. Where the truth is concerned, therefore, discovery and invention are synonymous terms. A child can make up the truth about the doctor just as well as, or better than, he can observe and retail the truth about the doctor. Indeed the process of retailing in so far as it is unselective, in so far as it fails to eliminate the inessentials that clutter up the concept of doctorishness is liable to be less penetratingly true.

This interchangeability of direct and imaginative experience and the normal human capacity for both, explain why it is sometimes said that every man to a greater or lesser degree is an artist. That is merely another way of saying that every man is subject to experience and to a greater or lesser degree can absorb it and strain it through the sieve of the pattern-making, anthropomorpic mind which is all that God has given us. This is halfway to the achievement of imaginative experience; and that is to be an artist.

The halfway house is inhabited by the critic. It is a large house. It has to be, for we are all critics. Of that more presently.

Now if direct experience is the condition of and the stepping-stone to imaginative experience, the converse is also the case. Our capacity for imaginative experience enlarges our capacity for direct experience. Life washes comparatively meaninglessly over the shoulders of the unimaginative man.

Experience consists of what a man can remember of what he has seen, heard and felt, and his individual classification of it. At worst, he can remember something, even though he can classify or distill nothing. He is part of the universe though at worst he sees it hardly at all. I say hardly at all advisedly, for no human being sees nothing of it. His capacity to see the universe is indeed the delta which divides him, man, from the animal. Experience may be first- or secondhand. Firsthand experience derives not only from observation of the external world, its objects and its animata, but of course from internal observation no less. When a child perceives or builds his notion of a doctor (I use the two terms indifferently) he is dredging from himself no less than from doctors. If he discerns and crystallizes characteristically doctorish attitudes, it is not merely because the doctors he has seen sometimes assume an attitude of owlish concentration and earnestness. Has he himself not furrowed his small brow and pursed his lips over the problem of seven times eight? His portrait may include a medical geniality, the false bonhomie of the bedside manner. It could less easily do so, however, if he himself had never insincerely responded in kind to avuncular heartiness. This relating of internal to external experience may mean that the man of observation, the man of imagination, is also the man with the most fluid and multifarious ego. You cannot, in short, see many sides to the world unless there are many sides to yourself. The well-named single-track mind may be quick to its objective, but it arrives, as it left, a pauper.

The other source of experience is secondhand. I use the word without derogation. I mean merely that it has been predigested and made available by the professional artist. But it, also, cannot be assimilated with equal facility by all men. It yields most richly to those who have not only a natural capacity but a practised perception. In this it does not differ from direct experience. To him that hath, shall be given. That is why it is of course sentimental twaddle to pretend that we needs must love the highest when we see it. That is the doctrine of original virtue. It is a mere flattering of democracy.

If the artist in pursuit of his truth is flagrantly selective in his facts, so also are the journalist, the barrister, and the priest. Are they not therefore all equally artists? The points of difference, although fairly obvious, are perhaps worth noting. It is the purpose and principle of selection that are different. The barrister's purpose is persuasion, not revelation. It is not his job to illuminate the truth as he sees it, but to highlight that aspect of the truth that he wishes the judge and jury to fasten upon. It is even regarded as an ethical obligation to convince a jury of what he himself may know to be false, in protection of his client, namely, his client's innocence. At best he is concerned with only one-half of the truth: the other half is the responsibility of his legal opponent, the theory of the courts being that two half-truths may disclose the truth.

The journalist sometimes has something of the same attitude. He presents his facts in a manner calculated to advance his cause. This may be either his personal cause, or his political cause, or the political or personal cause of his newspaper-proprietor. Circulation, if the pun will be forgiven, is the lifeblood of newspapers. The journalist's personal cause is therefore best served by seeking popularity, by tickling his public on the one hand and tickling his proprietor on the other. If by these methods he has secured eminence himself, he is then in a position to indulge a third objective, namely, the ventilation of his own personal predilections. He may even have reached a status of such security that he can allow himself the luxury of writing as well as he can—if he has not by then forgotten.

It is sometimes asserted, especially by journalists, that a good gruelling apprenticeship in Fleet Street is an excellent training for the literary artist. The discipline of deadlines; the need for clarity, the competitiveness, the heterogeneity of subject matter, the editorial hackings and slashings, all these, it is argued, are calculated to knock the nonsense out of the aspiring artist. They may. They may also knock the art out of him. I certainly would not deny that Fleet Street must provide salutary correctives to the affectations, the laziness, the self-importance and the self-indulgence to which artists are prone; but the price may be too high. Indeed it does appear in fact that the fence between Grub Street and Parnassus is seldom vaulted except by those lucky journalists who, born with sufficient arrogance or independent income, can resist the editorial or proprietorial exigencies and find themselves a free corner, perhaps as a reviewer, authorised to say their own say in their own way, though the heavens fall. It is not many journalists, however, who have enjoyed this happy state.

The fact is, and the explanation is, that self-indulgence and self-importance are not wholly to be deprecated in an artist. It may be self-indulgent to bid Lord Beaverbrook or Lord Kemsley to jump into the nearest lake and to seek their literary hacks elsewhere. It may be self-indulgent to have thus rejected a good income while your wife can barely make ends meet, and to sit staring idly hour after hour at a blank sheet of paper on your desk. It may be self-indulgent—I suppose it always is—to decide to do what you prefer doing, however painful your preference may be. But what that self-indulgent decision really means is that you have rejected, not necessarily with self-righteousness, but instinctively, the journalist's or the advocate's functions of dealing in half-truths, simply because you are more at home with a different kind of falsehood; namely, the artistic falsehoods which express your fleeting vision of the truth. This is partly why self-importance or conceit in an author is not necessarily a defect, and why he is not necessarily the better artist if editorial blue pencils have knocked the pride out of him. It is very easy for an artist, seeking to tell the truth as he sees it, to be oppressed and discouraged not merely by the nighttime bogey of his own capacity—that doubt is never very far away—but also by the misgiving that he may in fact have nothing to say, nothing to tell us, and that he may as well therefore tell us nothing profitably as a leader-writer on a newspaper as impoverish himself by knocking out a succession of unpublished or unproduced or unprofitable manuscripts.

As for the propagandists, political or priestly, though they too practise unnatural selection, they are easily distinguishable from the artist. For they are forever protecting their faith, not forever testing it. In this essential habit of mind lies the difference. On this issue, science and art are ranged antithetically against politics and religion. It is no accident that state and church have so often eyed their scientists and artists with a nervousness that evinces itself in censorship or even cruder persecution.

Appendix 2: The Position Stated

BENN LEVY

If you are a private citizen, you may say or write whatever you please, subject only to the laws of libel, obscenity, blasphemy, and sedition. Should you be accused of any of these offenses, the law will protect you if you are innocent. In court you will have the right to defend yourself and, if the verdict goes against you, to appeal and then to appeal again. Your accusers must defend their position and in public. These are the elementary rights of free speech on which what we now call our way of life is founded.

If you are a journalist or a novelist or an essayist or a poet or a historian or a public orator in Hyde Park or a lecturer, these rights are still preserved to you. You may say and write what you please and if anyone accuses you of overstepping the mark according to the agreed law of the land, then your accusers must justify themselves in a court of law where you will be given full rights of legal representation, the right to call witnesses, and the right of appeal.

If, however, you happen to be one particular sort of writer, namely a writer of plays, then all these elementary rights are withheld from you. You may not write as you please even within the allowable limits of the law. You may write only what a fellow citizen permits, a fellow citizen installed in the Lord Chamberlain's Office at St. James's Palace.

If this fellow citizen happens to disagree with what you have to say, he is empowered to inflict penalties upon you unknown to the law. He may mutilate or even destroy a year's work or more and deprive you of all compensation. He may deprive you, in short, of a potential livelihood. Moreover, you have no right to defend yourself in court and you have no right of appeal. You cannot even ascertain in advance what rules, if any, will govern his judgment, which remains personal, variable, and therefore capricious. His power over you is quite literally despotic; it is final and absolute. It even overrides the sovereignty of Parliament, which is forbidden to protect you.

"The Position Stated" is one of four Reith Lectures (on stage censorship) delivered by Benn Levy on BBC Radio.

This is the constitutional anomaly, which, rooted in a quirk of history, persists to plague us. It is the simplest and most straightforward issue of civil liberty that could exist. And, by their reaction to it, you may judge conclusively which of your friends really care about constitutional freedoms and to which the phrase is merely a slogan useful for brandishing at Communists, Fascists and McCarthyites—if and when it is convenient to do so. Here is an acid test for bona fide liberalism.

It is irrelevant to point out that the unfortunate gentlemen who, just now, are expected to pontificate upon contemporary dramatic literature do their job as gently and generously and conscientiously as it can be done. It is equally irrelevant to quote the innumerable and inevitable blunders in the record of censorship: what should we expect? It is irrelevant to argue that dramatists are only a small minority of the population and it is no great matter whether they be bereft of normal civil rights. That is an argument that we can all rebut when Fascists use it. It is irrelevant to argue that certain incidents (e.g., rape), though relatively innocuous on the printed page, would be obscene upon the stage; irrelevant because, if playwright and public were allowed the protection of law, the difference is one that the law would not fail to observe.

In the two-hundred-year-old controversy that has continued on this issue only one valid argument (and that a purely empirical one) has been advanced; namely, the convenience of managers.

You may say that the convenience of managers cannot weigh very heavily against the basic civil rights of playwrights and public, their right to speak and hear whatever the law allows. But in fact there is no need to strike any such balance sheet of rival claims since there is no difficulty whatever in providing managers with the necessary protection.

What they fear, quite sensibly, is that, without the insurance of a Lord Chamberlain's certificate in their pocket, they would be subjected to frivolous prosecutions by high-minded and low-minded irresponsibles and to harassment by a rash of self-appointed censors varying from town to town and calculated therefore to bedevil any schedule of touring dates. In fact, no such chaos exists in all the other countries unblest by a Lord Chamberlain, but the occasional instance can be quoted from "abroad" (which is a large place) where a town has cancelled a booking or taken hostile action and the thing could happen here. Moreover, it is true that licensing authorities, by threatening to withhold or withdraw theatre-licenses, could weight the scales far too heavily on the side of propriety. But both these points can be taken care of very simply on the lines of a bill that was proposed in the House of Commons in 1949 and passed on Second Reading by a two-to-one majority. It contained, very properly I think, two provisions to meet the managers' case.

In the first place it provided that licensees of theaters should have the *right* to a licence provided they abided by the normal regulations (e.g., fire regulations) for the protection of the public and that no licence could be withdrawn or withheld simply because the licensing authorities happened to disagree with the theatre manager's taste in plays.

Secondly, it protected managers against frivolous prosecution in the same way that newpapers were protected in 1888; that is to say, by laying down that no prosecution could be launched without the approval of a Judge-in-Chambers who would be required to satisfy himself that there was at least a solid prima facie case. If it be argued that book publishers have no such safeguard, I think it is fair to remember that theatre managers have a somewhat larger investment at stake and should not be an open target for the irresponsible crank.

In this way, it seems to me, the interest of managers, dramatists, and audiences can be served without one being sacrificed to the other and without the outrage of a censorship ensconced above Parliament and beyond the law.

Appendix 3: The Censorship

BENN LEVY

When a play is banned for public production, it is expected of the author that he should not only feel but also air a grievance. And it has been pointed out to me that although this indignity has fallen upon me I have signally failed to make the conventional protest. Now I sincerely hope that I am no more fair-minded than the next man, but notwithstanding I find it impossible to feel grieved at this particular act of censorship, for all that I am convinced that there is nothing to be said for the censor as an institution.

Given a censor acting upon certain principles, he could not, I imagine, have done otherwise in this instance. He is set up to guard the public against attacks upon its virtue and modesty made by such a diabolical, unprincipled and mischievous persons as dramatists are well known to be. As a rather shy and old-fashioned person I find this picture of myself delightfully flattering, and the idea of there being nothing save a thin defence of censorship between my unbridled savagery and the public, virtue, a welcomed buttress to my self-esteem.

But the point to emphasize is that such a defence or indeed any other artificial defence is wholly inadequate. Let us agree that the public might usefully be safeguarded against plays that are definitely inflammatory and aphrodisiac (to my mind the only grounds upon which a play should be banned even theoretically); it is literally impossible for these or any other principles to be put consistently into practice. One has only to remember some of the egregious blunders that the censor in England has made, *Ghosts* was banned, so was *Mrs. Warren's Profession,* so was *The Showing Up of Blanco Posnet* and *Mona Vanna*. On the other hand, *Our Betters, Spring Cleaning,* and *Fata Morgana* were admitted, three plays which, whatever their merits, might at least have been regarded as no less exceptionable by whomsoever might be disposed to take exception. The last of these plays very well illustrates one of the difficulties that

---

"The Censorship" is another of Benn Levy's many oral and written pieces on a subject to which he devoted much time in and out of Parliament.

makes a censor's duties impracticable; for even if the manuscript were harmless, the acting could and did alter that.

And again, even if it were possible to agree upon the proper principles that should decide an authority to ban a play (which it is not), it is no less impossible to agree as to where they are or are not involved. Why should Mr A's judgment be of more value than the next man, simply because he finds himself in the censor's office? Who in his senses would adjudge Mr B as a properer guardian of public morals than that high-minded old moralist Ibsen or that indefatigable, lifelong preacher Mr Bernard Shaw?

So much for serious plays. What about the whole question of nudity on the stage? Here again it is impossible to agree principles. At present in most parts of the world any kind of suggestive garment is permissible providing there is a garment. And yet it is widely recognized that complete nakedness is far less aphrodisiac. I am convinced for my part that Malthusians, Stopesians, and other people who are concerned to put a brake on the increase of population could do no better than advocate a wholesale extension of those horrible and indiscriminate displays of raw meat which in London are called butcher shops and in Paris, revues.

Conceivably I am in a minority as to this but the point helps to demonstrate how censorship, which is contraversial in theory, is hopelessly impracticable in facts.

Notes

Preface

1. *Slough Observer,* 14 December 1973.
2. Ibid.
3. Michael Foot, *Tribune,* 14 December 1973.
4. *Slough Observer,* 14 December 1973.
5. Michael Foot, *Tribune,* 14 December 1973.
6. C. H. Rolph, *New Statesman,* 14 December 1973.
7. Michael Foot, *Tribune,* 14 December 1973.
8. Ibid.
9. Ibid.
10. Alan Strachan, *Contemporary Dramatists* (New York: St. Martin's Press, 1973), 477–78.

Chapter 1. Introduction: Chronicler of an Age

1. Alan Strachan, *Contemporary Dramatists,* ed. James Vinson (New York: St. Martin's Press, 1973), 478.
2. John Johnston, *The Lord Chamberlain's Blue Pencil* (London: Hodder and Stoughton, 1990), 234.
3. Benn Levy, "A Programme Note," typescript, *A Tap on the Door.*
4. Review, The *Times,* 9 November 1932.
5. Kenneth Tynan, review, *Observer,* 5 December 1957.
6. Review, The *Times,* 16 April 1925.
7. Benn Levy, "A Programme Note."
8. Benn Levy, "Prefatory Note," *The Member for Gaza* (London: Evans Plays, 1968).
9. Ibid.
10. Benn Levy, *New Statesman,* 25 March 1950.
11. Ibid.
12. Ibid.
13. Ibid.
14. Ibid.
15. Hubert Griffith, review, *Evening Standard,* 28 February 1928.
16. The *Times,* 15 August 1946.

Chapter 2. 1925–1928: Contemporary Attitudes

1. Review, The *Times,* 16 April 1925.
2. Benn Levy, *This Woman Business* (New York: Samuel French, 1925), 12. Page numbers of subsequent quotations from the play occur in the text.

3. Brooks Atkinson, review, *New York Times,* 8 December 1926.

4. Ibid.

5. *Morning Advertiser,* 16 April 1926.

6. Review, *Punch,* 28 April 1926.

7. *Observer,* 25 October 1925.

8. Benn Levy, *A Man with Red Hair* (London: Macmillan, 1928), 23. Page numbers of subsequent quotations from the play occur in the text.

9. Review, *The Times,* 28 February 1928.

10. Ibid.

11. Review, *New York Times,* 9 November 1928.

12. Benn Levy, *The Devil* (London: Martin Secker, 1930), 52.

13. John Osborne, *Look Back in Anger* (New York: Bantam, 1957), 119.

14. Benn Levy, *Mud and Treacle* (London: Victor Gollancz, 1928), 75. Pages of subsequent quotations from the play occur in the text.

15. Review, The *Times,* 10 May 1928.

16. Ibid.

17. Charles Morgan, review, *New York Times,* 23 December 1928.

18. Review, The *Times,* 6 December 1928.

19. Ibid.

20. Benn Levy, *Mrs. Moonlight* (London and New York: Samuel French, 1930), 149. Pages of subsequent quotations from the play occur in the text.

21. Review, The *Times,* 6 December 1928.

22. The *Graphic,* 22 December 1928.

Chapter 3. 1930–1931: Games of Truth

1. Benn Levy, *Art and Mrs. Bottle* (London and New York: Samuel French, 1934), 35. Pages of subsequent quotations from the play occur in the text.

2. Review, The *Times,* 13 November 1929.

3. Benn Levy, *The Devil* (London: Martin Secker, 1930), 18. Pages of subsequent quotations from the play occur in the text.

4. Charles Morgan, review, *New York Times,* 20 February 1930, sec. 8.

5. Review, The *Times,* 3 January 1930.

6. Ibid.

7. Morgan, *New York Times,* 20 February 1930.

8. Ivor Brown, *Theatre,* n.d., n.p.

9. James Agate, review, Sunday *Times,* 19 January 1930.

10. John Mason Brown, review, *Saturday Evening Post,* 5 January 1932, n.p.

11. Benn Levy, Typescript (adaptation of *Topaze* by Marcel Pagnol), 1. Pages of subsequent quotations from the play appear in the text.

12. C. E. J. Caldicott, *Marcel Pagnol* (Boston: Twayne Publishers, 1977), 64.

13. Review, *New York Times,* 13 February 1930.

14. Caldicott, 66.

15. Ibid.

16. Ibid., 64.

17. Review, The *Times,* 9 October 1930.

18. A. V. Cookman, review, *New York Times,* 8 November 1931, sec. 4.

19. Benn Levy, *Hollywood Holiday* (London: Martin Secker, 1931), 27–28. Pages of subsequent quotations from the play appear in the text.

20. Cookman, sec. 4.

21. Ibid.

22. Ibid.

23. Brooks Atkinson, review, *New York Times,* 15 March 1951.

24. ———, review, *New York Times,* 10 January 1932, sec. 8.

25. Ibid.

26. Ibid.

27. Ibid.

28. Benn Levy, *Springtime for Henry* (New York: Samuel French, 1931), 26. Pages of subsequent quotations from the play appear in the text.

29. Brooks Atkinson, review, *New York Times,* 10 January 1932, sec. 8.

30. The *Times,* review, 9 November 1932.

31. Brooks Atkinson, review, *New York Times,* 15 March 1951.

Chapter 4. 1936–1940: Women and the Social Structure

1. Benn Levy, *Young Madame Conti* (London and New York: Samuel French, 1938), 12. Page references of subsequent quotations from the play appear in the text.

2. Charles Morgan, review, *New York Times,* 6 December 1936, sec. 12.

3. Review, The *Times,* 20 November 1936.

4. Brooks Atkinson, review, *New York Times,* 1 April, 1937, sec. 13.

5. Ibid.

6. Ibid.

7. The *Times,* 20 November 1936.

8. Benn Levy, *Madame Bovary,* typescript, 1. Pages of subsequent quotations from the play appear in the text.

9. Brooks Atkinson, review, *New York Times,* 17 November 1937.

10. Ibid.

11. Ibid.

12. Review, *New York Times,* 6 October, 1937.

13. Ibid.

14. Vincent Canby, review, *New York Times,* 25 December 1991.

15. Benn Levy, *The Poet's Heart,* typescript, X–6. Pages of subsequent quotations from the play appear in the text.

16. Benn Levy, *The Jealous God* (London: Martin Secker, 1939), 115. Pages of subsequent quotations from the play appear in the text.

17. Review, The *Times,* 2 March 1939, 12.

18. Ibid.

Chapter 5. 1946–1966: Playful Philosophical Debates

1. Benn Levy, *Clutterbuck* (London: Heinemann, 1947), 13. Pages of subsequent quotations from the play appear in the text.

2. Brooks Atkinson, review, *New York Times,* 5 December 1949.

3. The *Times,* 14 August 1946.

4. Benn Levy, *Cupid and Psyche* (London: Victor Gollancz, 1952), 31. Pages of subsequent quotations from the play appear in the text.

5. Ibid., 102.

6. Ibid.

7. Benn Levy, *The Rape of the Belt* (London and New York: Samuel French, 1957), 4. Pages of subsequent quotations from the play appear in the text.

8. Review, The *Times,* 13 December 1957.

9. Kenneth Tynan, review, *Observer,* 15 December 1957.

10. T. C. Worsley, The *New Statesman,* 28 December 1957.

Chapter 6. 1946–1966: Tribalism and Myth

1. Benn Levy, *Return to Tyassi* (London: Victor Gollancz, 1951), 43. Pages of subsequent quotations appear in the text.

2. Review, The *Guardian,* 1 December 1950.

3. Review, The *Times,* 30 November 1950.

4. Benn Levy, *The Tumbler,* typescript, 1:1. Pages of subsequent quotations from the play appear in the text.

5. Walter Kerr, review, *Herald Tribune,* 25 February 1960.

6. Brooks Atkinson, review, *New York Times,* 25 February 1960.

7. Frank Aston, review, *New York World Telegram,* 25 February 1960.

8. John McClain, review, *Journal American,* 25 February 1960.

9. Benn Levy, *The Member for Gaza* (London: Evans Plays, 1968), 103.

10. Review, The *Times,* 8 August 1966.

Chapter 7. A Miscellany

1. Review, The *Times,* 4 December 1930.

2. Review, *Evening Standard,* 4 December 1930.

3. Ibid.

4. The *Times,* 4 December 1930.

5. Ibid.

6. Ibid.

7. Ibid.

8. Charles Morgan, review, *New York Times,* 3 May 1931, sec. 8.

9. The *Times,* 17 April 1931.

10. Ibid.

11. Ibid.

12. Ibid.

13. Charles Morgan, review, *New York Times,* 3 May 1931, sec. 8.

14. Ibid.

15. Brooks Atkinson, review, *New York Times,* 25 January 1938.

16. Ibid.

17. Ibid.

18. Ibid.

19. Benn Levy, *The Island of Cipango* (London: Samuel French, 1954), 38.

20. Benn Levy, *Anniversary,* typescript. Pages of subsequent quotations appear in text.

Chapter 8. Conclusions: Mirror to an Age

1. John Elsom, *Post-War British Theatre* (London: Routledge and Kegan Paul, 1979), 41.

2. Ibid., 45.

3. Ibid., 46.

4. Benn Levy, "Prefatory Note," *The Member for Gaza* (London: Evans, 1968).

5. Ibid.

6. Benn Levy, *Cupid and Psyche* (London: Victor Gollancz, 1952).

7. Benn Levy, *This Woman Business* (New York: Samuel French, 1925), 116.

Bibliography

Primary Sources

Art and Mrs. Bottle, or The Return of the Puritan. London: Secker, 1929; New York: French, 1931.

Clutterbuck: An Artificial Comedy. London: Heinemann, 1947; New York: Dramatists Play Service, 1950.

Cupid and Psyche. London: Gollancz, 1952.

The Devil: A Religious Comedy. London: Secker, 1930. republished as *The Devil Passes*, New York: French, 1932.

The Great Healer (a television play). London: French, 1954.

Hollywood Holiday (with John Van Druten). London: Secker, 1931.

The Island of Cipango (a television play). London: French, 1954.

The Jealous God. London: Secker & Warburg, 1939.

A Man with Red Hair (adapted from Hugh Walpole's novel). London: Macmillan, 1928.

The Member for Gaza. London: Evans, 1968.

Mud and Treacle, or The Course of True Love. London: Gollancz, 1928.

Mrs. Moonlight: A Piece of Pastiche. London: Gollancz, 1929.

The Poet's Heart: A Life of Don Juan. London: Cresset Press, 1937.

The Rape of the Belt. London: MacGibbon & Kee, 1957.

Return to Tyassi. London: Gollancz, 1951.

Springtime for Henry. New York and London: French 1932; London: Secker, 1932.

This Woman Business. London: Benn, 1925; New York: French, 1925.

Young Madame Conti: A Melodrama (adapted with Hubert Griffith from Bruno Frank's play). London: French, 1938.

Produced but Unpublished Plays (Typescript)

Anniversary or The Rebirth of Venus (A radio play aired on BBC).

The Church Mouse (adapted from play by Siegfried and Ladislaus Fodor).

Ever Green, an extravaganza with book by Levy, music and lyrics by Richard Rodgers and Lorenz Hart.

If I Were You (with Paul Hervey Fox).

Topaze (adapted from play by Marcel Pagnol).
The Tumbler.

Unproduced and Unpublished Plays (Typescript)

The Auction, based on the novel by Francois Billetdoux.
The Brave Augusta.
The Curtains Are Blowing.
How to Be Nobody or the Evolution of Miss Jones.
The Marriage.
A Seat by the Fire, based on the novel by Elizabeth Montagu.
Safari.
A Tap on the Door, a trilogy of short plays: *Shan't Be Long, Meet to Be Loved,* and *A Part of Death.*

Other Publications

Britain and the Bomb: The Fallacy of Nuclear Defense. London: Campaign for Nuclear Disarmament, 1959.
"Cause Without a Rebel." *Encore* (London), June 1957, 13–35.
"Shaw." *Tribune,* 17 November 1950.
"The Gulf Between." *Tribune,* 23 January 1963.
"The Mirage of the Floating Voter." *Tribune,* 15 October 1951.
"The Play of Ideas." *New Statesman,* 25 March 1950, 338.
"Some Lessons for the New Year." *Tribune,* 26 December 1952.

Secondary Sources

Caldicott, C. E. J. *Marcel Pagnol.* Boston: Twayne, 1977.

Elsom, John. *Post-War British Theatre,* Rev. ed. London: Routledge and Kegan Paul, 1979.

Johnston, John. *The Lord Chamberlain's Blue Pencil.* London: Hodder and Stoughton, 1990.

"Obituary." *New York Times,* 8 December 1973.

"Levy, Benn W." In *Encyclopedia of World Drama.* Edited by Barrett Clark and Goerge Freedley, 46. New York: McGraw-Hill, 1972.

"Levy, Benn W." in *Modern British Literature.* Edited by Ruth Temple and Martin Tucker. New York: Frederick Ungar, 1966.

"Obituary." *Times,* 8 December 1973.

Rusinko, Susan. "Benn Wolfe Levy." In *Dictionary of Literary Biography.* Edited by Stanley Weintraub. 1982, Vol. 13, Pt. 1, 291–98. Detroit: Bruccoli Clark/ Gale Research.

Strachan, Alan. "Benn Wolfe Levy." In *Contemporary Dramatists*. Edited by James Vinson, 475–78. New York: St. Martin's Press, 1973.

Reviews

"*Art and Mrs. Bottle.*" *Times* (London), 13 November 1929.

Aston, Frank. "*The Rape of the Belt.*" *New York World-Telegram*, 7 November 1960.

———. "*The Tumbler.*" *New York World-Telegram*, 25 February 1960.

Atkinson, Brooks. "*Clutterbuck.*" *New York Times*, 5 December 1949.

———. "*The Devil Passes.*" *New York Times*, 10 January 1932.

———. "*If I Were You.*" *New York Times*, 25 January 1938.

———. "*Madame Bovary.*" *New York Times*, 17 November 1937.

———. "*Springtime for Henry.*" *New York Times*, 15 March 1951.

———. "*Springtime for Henry.*" *New York Times*, 10 January 1932.

———. "*Topaze.*" *New York Times*, 29 December 1947.

———. "*The Tumbler.*" *New York Times*, 25 February 1960.

———. "*Young Madame Conti.*" *New York Times*, 1 April 1937.

Chapman, John. "*The Rape of the Belt.*" *Daily News*, 7 November 1960.

———. "*The Tumbler.*" *Daily News*, 25 February 1960.

"*The Church Mouse.*" *Times*, 17 April 1931.

"*Clutterbuck.*" *Times*, 15 August 1946, 8.

Coleman, Robert. "*The Rape of the Belt.*" *New York Mirror*, 7 November 1960.

———. "*The Tumbler.*" *New York Mirror*, 24 February 1960.

Cookman, A. V. "*Hollywood Holiday.*" *New York Times*, 8 November 1931.

———. "*Springtime for Henry.*" *New York Times*, 4 December 1932.

"*The Devil.*" *Times* (London), 13 January 1930.

"*Ever Green.*" *Times* (London), 4 December 1930.

"*Hollywood Holiday.*" *Times* (London), 16 October 1931.

"*The Jealous God.*" *Times* (London), 2 March 1939.

Kerr, Walter. "*The Rape of the Belt.*" *Herald Tribune*, 6 November 1960.

———, "*The Tumbler.*" *Herald Tribune*, 25 February 1960.

"*Madame Bovary.*" *New York Times*, 6 October 1937.

"*A Man with Red Hair.*" *Times*, 28 February 1928.

———. *New York Times*, 9 November 1928.

———. *New York Times*, 17 June 1928.

McClain, John. "*The Rape of the Belt.*" *Journal American*, 7 November 1960.

"*Mrs. Moonlight.*" *Times* (London), 6 December 1928.

———. *New York Times*, 30 September 1930.

Morgan, Charles. "*Art and Mrs. Bottle.*" *New York Times*, 8 December 1929.

———. "*The Church Mouse.*" *New York Times*, 3 May 1931.

———. "*The Jealous God.*" *New York Times*, 26 March 1939.

———. "*A Man with Red Hair.*" *New York Times*, 25 March 1938.

————. *"Mrs. Moonlight." New York Times,* 23 December 1928.

————. *"Young Madame Conti." New York Times,* 6 December 1936.

"Mud and Treacle." Times (London), 10 May 1928.

"Public and Confidential." Times (London), 8 August 1966.

"The Rape of the Belt." Times (London), 13 December 1957.

"Return to Tyassi." Times (London), 30 November 1950.

"Springtime for Henry." Times (London), 9 November 1932.

Taubman, Howard. *"The Rape of the Belt." New York Times,* 7 November 1960.

"Topaze." Times, 9 October 1930.

————. *New York Times,* 13 February 1930.

Watts, Richard. *"The Rape of the Belt." New York Post,* 7 November 1960.

————. *"The Tumbler." New York Post,* 25 February 1960.

Worsley, T. C. *"The Rape of the Belt." New Statesman,* 28 December 1957.

"This Woman Business." Times (London), 16 April 1925.

————. *New York Times,* 8 December 1926.

"Young Madame Conti." Times (London), 20 November 1936.

Index